Also by Timothy S. Hall

Surgical Systems: Structure and Function

Surgical Systems: Quality Management

Surgical Systems: General Surgery Resident Curriculum

Cover Design by Elizabeth H. Nussbaum

LEAN Healthcare Innovation: Out of Struggle

Timothy S. Hall MD

Surgical Systems

Two Golden Rules Publishing

http://twogoldenrules.wix.com/inf

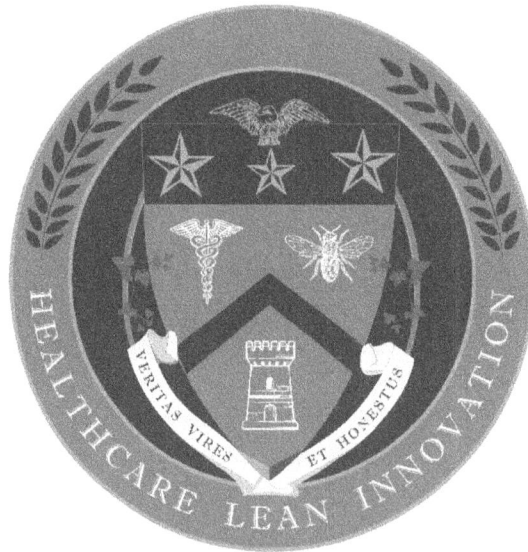

Published by Two Golden Rules Publishing, Connecticut
Reproduction, transmission, or archiving of this material is not allowed without authorization.

Send requests for permission to reproduce, reimage or represent this material to tshall737.com,
twogoldenrules.wix.com/info
ISBN   978-0-9885542-8-3

TABLE OF CONTENTS

Acknowledgements   ix

Preface   xi

1. Introduction: The Crisis   1

Why Now?   1

Why LEAN Healthcare Innovation? 5

Principles of LEAN   8

LEAN Healthcare Innovation: A System Approach 11

The LEAN Implementation Attributes that fit Healthcare; The Change "Necessity"   14

Why a LEAN Transformation? Part of LEAN Healthcare Innovation   15

Synergy; An Added Benefit from Transformation   17

Why a LEAN Healthcare Innovation Requires Personal Development?   18

Personal Development and Change   20

Personal Development for Physicians as Organizational Members 21

Innovation versus Improvements; Why a LEAN Transformation Incorporates Innovation 23

Summary   24

5 Whys- Failures in LEAN Transformation 28

References   31

2.   Literature Review   35

Healthcare organizations and Fundamental Business Management Practices   35

Fundamental Business Practices   36

Improvement and Change Management in Healthcare   38

Healthcare Staff Characteristics and Change Success   40

Examples of LEAN Implementation Success   41

General Reviews of Lean Transformations 42

Historical Success of Quality Improvement in Healthcare 46

Conclusions 48

Summary of Problems Cited in the Literature About LEAN Applications 48

References   51

3.   Leadership in LEAN Healthcare Innovation   55

Leadership Theory and Style 55

Leadership of Knowledge Workers   56

Leadership in Systems Management and Change; Complicated and Complex Systems   57

"Emergent Change" In Complex Healthcare 57

Leadership System Management in Healthcare   58

Leadership Activities in LEAN Implementations, Leadership Standard Work:

     Current State   61

Leaders versus Managers   62

Leadership and Management Complementary Behaviors   64

Leadership Failure in LEAN Implementation, Planning and Assessment   65

Management of Resources and Priorities: Leadership Failures   66

Formula for Change; A Planning Assessment Tool   69

Visioning in Healthcare for Change   71

The Chief Executive Officer   71

Leadership Balance and Competencies in Change   73

LEAN Leadership Attributes 74

Leadership in a LEAN Transformation   76

Leadership in the Phases of Transformation 80

Leadership Management in Business Basics as They Affect Change   82

Leadership Personal Development in Change   84

Leadership in LEAN Healthcare Innovation; Innovation Laboratories   88

Leadership Roles and Behaviors in LEAN Healthcare Innovation

An Example of LEAN Leadership Innovation: A New Definition of Waste,

     Political Conflict   90

Summary   90

Pugh Decision Analysis of Leadership Styles for a LEAN Transformation 92

References   96

4.   **Managers in a LEAN Healthcare Innovation**   **101**

Plan, Organize, Coordinate, Control 102

Manager's Roles in LEAN Healthcare Innovation   103

Failure Modes for Managers in LEAN   106

Managers in LEAN Transformations   109

The Manager's Influence on Business Practices   110

Personal Development for Managers in LEAN Healthcare Innovation   112

Management Innovation in a LEAN Healthcare Innovation   114

Manager Activity in a LEAN Healthcare Innovation   116

Summary   117

Analysis of a Manager's Activity; Pareto Chart Predication of Necessary Changes in   119

References   121

5. **Organizational change in a LEAN Healthcare Innovation**   **123**

General Considerations; Chronic Organizational Problems   124

Resistance to Change   126

The Patient Centered Health Improvement Approach: A New Definition of Successful Patient

Outcomes   127

Staff Engagement, Issue #1   127

An Engaged Workforce for Excellence in Practice   131

Lean Staff Education and Staff Modeling Failure: The LEAN Rollout   132

Timing; It Can Be Everything, Especially if it's Bad Timing   133

Evidenced Based Medicine and the Scientific Method   134

"The Wall", The Failure to Address Poor Performers   136

Modeling for Organizational Change and Transformation   137

The Unity Organizational Model for Change   138

Foundational Support for a Cultural Change Model 141

A Team Approach and a "Questioning Culture"   141

Business Management Practices and Staff Incorporation   142

Business Models in Healthcare and Organizational Culture Change   143

Personal Development of Staff and the Organization in LEAN   144

Reflection, Deliberation, Open Mindedness and Engagement   145

Personal Norms, Social Norms and Social Principles in Change   147

Using Behavioral Models and Theories of Change   147

Behavior Theories in Decision Making   148

Conclusions   149

Execution of Cultural Change and Habit Change   150

Personal Development, Changing Habits and "Schelling Points"   152

Commitment Devices 152

Sustain: Social Norms, Group Identity and Social Principles   153

, Changing Social Norms: Hand Washing   154

Enhancing Self Efficacy Linking to Changing Group Norms; the Agency Exercise   155

Addressing Social Principles as Part of Cultural Change   156

Foundations for Organizational Change: Employee Rights and a Safe Environment for
Change   157

Physician Engagement; Accountability, Physician Leadership   158

Organizational and Staff Innovations in LEAN   161

Theoretical Foundation for Service Innovation and Innovation Education   162

Excellence Through Innovation; Initiation and the Inversion Exercise   163

An Innovation in LEAN; A New Definition of Waste "NonFlow" and
the "Flow" exercise   164

Summary   167

Force Field Diagram for Staff Acceptance of a LEAN Transformation   169

References   170

6.   Epilogue; Making the Decision to Start a LEAN Healthcare Innovation   175

Reasons to Institute a Significant Organizational Change; Do You Smell Smoke   176

Avoiding the Mistake of Omission   179

Learning from CEO Failures 180

Confirming a Decision to Change: Insights and Action Steps   181

An Option to Address the Coming Crisis; LEAN Healthcare Innovation   183

Conclusions   184

A Tool for Determining the Method for Consensus Organizational Decision Making 186

References   187

Appendix   189

Final thoughts   195

Figure Legends   199

Index   203

Exer (Exercise)

Rec (Recommendation)

Acknowledgements

To my wife and daughters for all their support and tolerance for me and my life in medicine.

Preface

"Life is essentially a cheat and its conditions are those of defeat; the redeeming things are not happiness and pleasure but the deeper satisfactions that come out of struggle."

F. Scott Fitzgerald

This book is about survival; the survival of the US healthcare system. In the past, healthcare improvement efforts focused on patient benefit, error prevention and gaining a competitive edge. The failure of most improvement efforts was not as concerning as it might have been because patients were generally satisfied, most systems generated positive margins and poor outcomes were uncommon. The first chapter of this book details how the healthcare environment has changed and how the impact of these changes is creating a crisis for healthcare organizations and for those who practice medicine.

"The aim of the book is transformation of the style of American management"
W. Edwards Deming. Out of Crisis

Just as Deming felt that American business needed management transformation in the 1980s, American medicine is in need of a transformation now. US medicine is in need of a "sea change" to improve efficiency, quality and system management if patient freedom of choice without rationing is to survive. As will become clear, I believe that the answer is an adaptation of the Toyota Production System, LEAN systems. Unfortunately, it is an objective statement to say that the majority of LEAN applications in healthcare have had limited success and true LEAN transformations have not occurred. I believe the explanation for the problems related to LEAN implementations is that the LEAN application must be adapted differently to work in healthcare. This adaptation must account for the significant differences in practice and process in medicine and the extensiveness of the independent judgment required of physicians and nurses. The adaptation must also be adjusted for the organizational fragmentation that is present in healthcare; fragmentation that separates business and administrative staff from healthcare providers. A new adaptation that differs from the old approach to "just improve or do better", but requires innovation that challenges antidotal concepts and applies experimentation in clinical venues to healthcare processes previously neglected. This is a variant of LEAN that we have called, LEAN Healthcare Innovation. The presentation of this approach is intended to be, as much as possible, a scientific presentation of a supportive argument using data and study information along with actual practice related experiences.

The first chapter provides the argument that existing circumstances demand that we make radical changes in healthcare or many institutions will not survive; that we are in crisis. This argument is centered on the concept that the sweeping change will require a very different new approach, LEAN Healthcare Innovation. The explanation of this approach is that this is not just another application of the Toyota Production System, but a modification explicitly designed for healthcare that includes a cultural transformation, system management, enhancement in business practices, the personal development of staff and a dedication to innovation.

The second chapter is a selective review of studies of improvement efforts, change initiatives and LEAN applications in healthcare. There are two reasons for providing this review. First to provide an objective appraisal about the success of LEAN in healthcare and second to provide recommendations that may enhance future improvement efforts. Following the literature review, the next 3 chapters focus on the impact of different employee groups on change efforts such as LEAN; Leadership, Managers and the Organizational staff. Because it is expected that the primary audience for this material will be in healthcare, each chapter contains background information and business concepts pertinent to these organizational roles. Specifics about these business concepts are interpreted to emphasize their importance in a change effort like LEAN, combined with LEAN concepts that support success. Since study data documenting LEAN efforts is limited, studies from the related areas of organizational change or improvement are mixed in with examples of common LEAN implementation failures and successes. Recommendations and exercises aimed at avoiding these disappointments are provided. Because the success of any change effort, particularly a LEAN "struggle", requires a full commitment that effects every aspect of a healthcare organization, each chapter includes a comprehensive approach to; business practices, LEAN implementation and transformation, staff individual personal development and the embracing of innovation. An application of a LEAN technique related to the subject material follows each chapter.

The epilogue is meant to be the concluding argument to make the decision to start LEAN Healthcare Innovation by; providing an assessment of the current state of the healthcare environment, including recommendations from prominent past CEOs to avoid their mistakes and in providing a decision support algorithm for making a radical change.

"Would my very words, so little attuned to the fashionable vocabulary of today betray me?"

Avedis Donabedian, An Introduction to Quality Assurance in Health Care

I hope this book will give healthcare organizations an option for survival. My apology for my approach; to making the argument as scientifically as possible with a writing style that is not as entertaining as is seen elsewhere. In a field that is dominated by anecdotal evidence and inference, I felt that it was important to provide as much study related data as was feasible, despite the dry content. I hope my lack of *"a fashionable vocabulary"* will not deter you from seeing the value that LEAN Healthcare Innovation may have for your organization.

Timothy S. Hall, MD

Chapter 1

Introduction: The Crisis

$\mathbf{W}$hy Now?

We are at an unprecedented time for healthcare in America. The Accountable Care Act has been implemented; the most significant intrusion into US healthcare since the Medicare program was instituted in 1965. The predicted changes in reimbursement casts a bleak picture for healthcare providers. According to modeling from Dr. Steven Parente, the Chair of Health Finance in the Carlson School of Management and the Director of the Medical Industry Leadership Institute at the University of Minnesota, the impact of the Accountable care act includes:

1. Significant premium increases.
2. The majority of exempted insurance plans will no longer be accepted after 2017.
3. Limited patient options for physicians and hospital networks.
4. A forced exodus from insurance programs and decreasing customer options.
5. A "focus to achieve maximum efficiency for the average patient "as defined by the federal government".
6. Reduced access to specialized facilities and physicians.

Additionally, significant changes are expected in the payer mix and reimbursements for most medical institutions. The Congressional Budget Office predicts a dramatic reduction in employer sponsored coverage by 2020 and an estimated 10 to 15% increase in Medicaid enrollment by 2019. The predicted impact is an increase in patients that are uninsured, poorly insured or enrolled in Medicaid. The negative impact of these changes will create an untenable financial profile for most healthcare organization's payer mix and subsequent revenues. (CBO 2010, CBO 2104, Parente and Ramlet 2009). These predictions, that reductions in patient volumes with good insurance and overall lower reimbursements will subsequently reduce revenues by 20 to 40% for most healthcare providers, is also the projection by Shideh Sedgh Bina a founding partner of Insigniam and Editor in Chief of Insigniam Quarterly (Shideh Sedgh Bina 2014).

If these predictions are not dismal enough, this is just the beginning of the impact of the Affordable Care Act. In 2014 2,225 hospitals faced readmission penalties and 1,451 hospitals faced "quality" penalties. As of June in 2014, as reported by Kaiser Health news, HSS released an analysis predicting the financial impact of the Hospital Acquired Condition reduction program (HAC). They estimated that 761 hospitals will face penalties ranging from 1 to 5.4% of their CMS revenues. The predictions indicate that safety-net hospitals, large hospitals and large academic centers will be hit the hardest with these penalties. (HSS, Jordan Rau/Kaiser 2014)

When one considers that in 2013, the median operating margin for the average size hospital was slightly negative -0.7%, it can be assumed that without unprecedented improvements many institutions will not be financially viable. This impending crisis will not be adequately addressed by the traditional efforts to improve. An opinion that has been strengthened by RW Bush when he notes that although health systems are continually innovating in management and clinical practices, significantly greater sustained changes will be necessary for survival (Bush 2007).

How Do We Change?

Unfortunately, these problematic changes are "piling on" to existing difficulties in healthcare. As James Womack has pointed out; an additional challenge for US healthcare, as compared to other industries, is that health care has struggled to identify who the "customer" really is. While it is critically important that value be defined by the primary customer, the patient, the view that there is only one customer in healthcare is too simplistic and does not represent the healthcare environment reality. In addition to patients, the health care system includes additional co-customers such as; independent physicians, community groups, insurers, and government regulators. While the voice of the patient is critical, the co-customers, particularly referring or collaborating physicians are also critical and must be considered for the future survival of most healthcare organizations (Womack JP et al IHI 2005).

William Shoemaker of the American Hospital Directory has provided suggestions for necessary changes. Their data demonstrates that patient satisfaction and high quality care correlate with profitability. *"Companies that are well run tend to have happy customers"*. They propose three conclusions; First, to survive, US healthcare organizations must improve their business practices for efficiency and to reduce costs. Second, healthcare organizations must improve patient care service quality to attain better reimbursements. Third, healthcare organizations cannot just improve, but must improve at faster rates and reach higher performance levels that have rarely been achieved in healthcare (Shoemaker, W 2012).

◉⌗ℭ~:▽:△

What is Necessary?

With these impending problems, can healthcare organizations improve to the magnitude necessary for survival? It will require more than implementation of important quality improvement projects or even revamping the existing "Quality Management Program". To survive will require more than "re-engineered leadership" or upgraded management practices. Improvements will be required throughout the organization in quality, patient satisfaction, cost reduction and partnering; all improving to 30 to 40% levels. For most hospitals the magnitude of their current problems and the required improvements will not be possible without a novel type of effort from the entire organization.

Assuming that healthcare organizations can improve their focus on patients and co-customers, can they get their medical staff enlisted to support the necessary improvements? In general, according to a Harris poll of 23,000 employees, only 37% are clear about organizational goals and only 20% are enthusiastic about those goals or see the linkage to their job (Covey 2004). In general, only17% of organizations foster open communication and only 20% of employees highly trust in their leadership (Sheridan, 2012). If these statistics are disappointing for employees in general, the results are worse for physician partnering with healthcare organizations. The relationship between physicians with their healthcare organization represents a critical difference for healthcare versus other industries; it is a relationship that is more varied, with unusual liaisons and often a history of poor interactions and limited integration. As noted by the Advisory Board, physician engagement is poor for most medical organizations and most physicians don't feel like they have a true relationship with the medical institution to which they send their patients (Advisory Board Physician Engagement, 2016). The importance of this problem is put into context by William Covey;

"Almost all the work of the world is done through relationships with people and in organizations ... a relationship with a purpose, meeting someone's needs, which should be set up to allow all members to inwardly sense his or her innate worth and potential for greatness and contribute his or her unique talents and passion". (Covey 2004)

This explanation of the importance and value of relationships within organizations is not consistent with physician's and healthcare organizations interactions. The term "healthcare organization or facility" is used to identify a healthcare business entity, however in reality, most healthcare organizations are more like amalgamations of minimally integrated providers with diverse interests, varying social norms and conflicting incentives adding up to complex logistical problems. In reality, most healthcare organizations are so disorganized and fragmented it is hard to call them a system. Unfortunately, the physician organizational relationship is the key consideration for implementing successful organizational change.

In the impending healthcare environment; decreasing revenues, poor business practices, poor staff satisfaction, failed business relationships and limited physician engagement portends healthcare organizational failure in the near future. To address this situation will require a completely different approach, not a business solution implemented by external government regulations or consultants but an overall internal organizational change; a different way of thinking about organizational change. When does it need to happen? As noted by Covey "with *people, fast is slow and slow is fast*" which underscores the reality that this type of change requires years, which means that it is critical to implement a program as soon as possible (Covey 2004).

This chapter will present a strongly biased opinion about the best solution to the impending crisis for healthcare; LEAN, the evolved improvement program from the Toyota Production Systems. But as the sections will outline, not just LEAN, but LEAN with; a system approach, cultural approach, a personal development approach and an innovation approach, a different entity, LEAN Healthcare Innovation. A reasonable response to this suggestion will be that many organizations are applying the LEAN approach and have not seen the expected improvement as seen in other industries. The chapters that follow will provide explanations and solutions to support a different outcome.

"We have two options...boldly tackle the challenges ahead, or hold off and hope an asteroid strikes."

Figure 1.1 Denial is rampant in healthcare (see figure legends)

⟡⟡⟡⟡⟡⟡⟡ ⟡⟡ ⟡⟡⟡⟡⟡⟡⟡ ⟡⟡ ⟡⟡⟡⟡⟡⟡⟡⟡⟡⟡

Why LEAN Healthcare Innovation?

If the case for major improvement and change in healthcare is clear, the next question is what approach. LEAN has become the catch phrase for the Toyota Production System which was characterized by James Womack and Dan Jones, in *Lean Thinking.* The authors, the subsequent organizations they have formed, and multiple others have written and commented about the application of this system in the auto industry and multiple other industries over the last 30 years (Womack and Jones, 1996). But, is LEAN the right answer for healthcare? The first step in clarifying the approach is to make a general assessment of US healthcare's current state and its probability for successful change; the Sun Tzu metaphor would be to scrutinize the army's readiness for battle. The following is an assessment of US Healthcare based on the Sun Tzu approach.

1. Culture or Spirit- This is a new era of government oversight, involvement and control. Healthcare organizations and providers are uncertain and confused about the new role of the federal government in healthcare. The only consensus is that the ACA should not have been implemented in its current form, but no one is clear how it should be changed and what the ramifications of that change will be. The current situation is demoralizing; it creates cultural confusion and disorganization. Grade=D

2. Timing- Part of the reason the ACA faces opposition is because of the divided opinions about the need and method for change. The US healthcare system is clearly the costliest, but it is so because there is no rationing of care and it provides the most freedom of choice for the patient in any system. Access to healthcare for certain noncritical conditions have been limited, but it is also true that anyone in the US can remove their identification, claim not to understand English and be admitted to an emergency department and then receive exactly the same quality of care as any other patient. This occurs regardless or even when it is obvious that a patient cannot pay. Despite the fact that the US population has not agreed by consensus that they wish to ration care or give up their healthcare freedom of choice, the ACA was implemented and the infringement on both has occurred. "*If you like your doctor, you can keep your doctor*"? The timing of this transition seems poor. Grade= D

3. Area of influence- The military term VUCA, the volatile, uncertain, complex and ambiguous environment that is healthcare is still being approached with competency based skill appraisals and historical care processes which are proving insufficient. Adding to this problem is that the impact of the ACA and Medicaid/Medicare regulations impact different regions of the country differently. The healthcare environment and regional populations vary widely. The patient population on the southern border of Texas is dramatically different than the one in suburban Connecticut as are the associated necessary services, the approach to maintenance of patient relationships and for appropriate reimbursement. One central approach for all of US healthcare is guaranteed to fail for most if not all, as it has for the National Health Service in the UK or for the Veterans Affairs Health Services in the US. Healthcare organizations in VUCA environments need local approaches to improve. Grade=C

4. Logistics, Situation Report- A patient requires an "admitting" or attending physician that provides the staff with directions or orders. But the hospital personnel are often not employed by the physician and most physicians are not employed by the hospital. The physician usually

carries responsibility for the organization's staff and patient outcomes regardless of the staff's lack of accountability specifically to him or her. Our current approach is disjointed.

The key business unit in healthcare is the provision of service by the healthcare provider, primarily the physician, as dictated by their judgment. Two important facts about improving medical processes include; First that evidenced based medicine applies to only 20% of medical care and second, most medical organizations provide services based on the historical evolution of the processes which have never undergone in-depth scrutiny of those logistics. The possibility that physicians will be able to improve these processes is low. Physicians responding to decreasing reimbursements have increased their clinical hours and their subsequent time commitments; the ramification of their increased workload is that they are unlikely to provide additional time for review and improvement of a medical organization's processes, on a "volunteer" basis. All of these factors, disorganization, independence, variability and time constraints have led to unexamined and antiquated logistics in most healthcare organizations.

Grade =F

5. Leadership- Medical organizations may have leadership, but since many of the physicians practicing at an institution are not financially linked to the organization, they do not consider the hospital or medical organizational administration "their" leadership. This often includes the employed physicians that believe that organizational administrators lack the expertise or experience to properly direct a physician. This schism is reflected in that physicians are usually not part of an organization's visioning processes, mission statements or strategic plans despite their critical role in providing successful services; their separation from these activities is a critical failure.

In essence, there is no real leadership in healthcare because of a lack of trust, lack of empathy, lack of shared expertise and a misunderstanding of the roles between administrators and physicians. The common experience is an "us versus them" mentality. Grade= D (Wing RL, Sun Tzu)

> *"The State that separates its scholars from its warriors will have its thinking done by cowards and its fighting by fools."*
>
> *Thucydides*

Conclusion

The assessment of the readiness of healthcare organizations to undergo the "major battle" necessary for survival is that most organizations are not prepared or capable.

"Failure is not fatal, but failure to change might be"
John Wooden

Principles of LEAN

After assessment, the next step is to consider solutions. So why is a LEAN approach the answer? LEAN is the only system that incorporates all the necessary components to provide success for the particular circumstances that torment healthcare. It is a systematic approach which at its core empowers the direct providers, our key area of focus. It embraces the importance of local circumstances and the tacit knowledge that is so critical for successful clinical and organizational outcomes for healthcare. LEAN methods are focused on logistics as a way to understand and how to improve; a focus that is critically necessary for healthcare's poor logistics. LEAN also requires respectful leadership and management that bridges organizational gaps and stresses visioning and value prioritization; all of which has been missing in healthcare. LEAN provides better communication through metrics and visual content that can bring a disjointed fragmented system like healthcare into synchrony. Additionally, LEAN utilizes a "second loop" educational approach, which is the model that best fits medical personnel. Finally, a LEAN implementation works through shared purposes and relationships, a key factor that addresses healthcare provider engagement, which must improve if change is to be successful.

What are the core LEAN principles and how do they mesh with change management in healthcare? The LEAN principles, as explained by Womack and Jones, seemed to be designed to address the current problems in healthcare.

1. Voice of the Customer- With dramatic change comes reprioritization. In situations of uncertainty it is easy to lose focus on the patient's needs or the concerns of partners or co-customers. Concerns about finances in a "skimpy" margin industry like healthcare can skew an organization away from patient concerns, as can the introduction of new technologies, professional hierarchies or just outdated thinking about what is important in patient care. LEAN starts with values, visioning and mission that includes the entire organization, including physicians and nurses. The current state of healthcare reflects a lack of focus on the

patient. Blood draws are based on the laboratory schedule, radiology services are provided in the radiology department and the physical therapy schedule is based on their departmental staffing. Even the patient's most personal issues; what they wear, when they eat or sleep or wake up is determined by the hospital. Most medical staff don't even knock when entering the patient's room, don't introduce themselves or explain their purpose for the visit. Each of these examples represents opportunities to improve patient satisfaction and clinical recovery by listening to the voice of the patient.

2. The Value Stream Analysis (VSA)-Only a few healthcare organizations have taken a detailed step by step approach to evaluate the processes in care services and fewer still have applied a "VSA approach" to the majority of their efforts. The VSA process also requires a more detailed analysis of each step in the process of care for patient added value. An even greater issue is that few organizations have ever really established what is referred to as "Standard Work" in areas of clinical practice or medical processes. "Standard Work" is the consistent formulized approach to providing care which is thought to be the best, which has been tested for variability, reliability and error prevention. You cannot improve a system if there is no consistent system. You cannot upgrade standards if there are no established standards. Part of the VSA process is the identification of standard work, its formulization, establishment of its success rate, reliability and need for improvement. In addition, an in-depth Value Stream Analysis will help develop the staff's most important skill in LEAN, to identify "waste"; healthcare activity that absorbs resources but creates no value. The VSA gives immediate feedback on waste and clarifies it; in terms of a specific product or service, in terms of performance, for delivery of quality and for cost. It also determines the value equation which specifies how to get from where you are, to where you aspire to be; an equation that healthcare needs.

3. Flow- The concept of flow in medical processes really focuses on efficiency. This may be defined by avoiding delays and redundancies but it also emphasizes an important difference in managing knowledge workers in healthcare. In healthcare, your management approach is not of things, like machines, but of managing people and patients. Efficiency with machines may relate to time or supplies used; with people, efficiency is determined by effectiveness, reaching the desired outcomes which are the successful treatments and patient satisfaction. A patient that feels rushed out of a physician encounter is usually unsatisfied even with good

treatment. In medicine it's not minutes that count, but quality time to meet expectations; providing understanding and relief. In a LEAN implementation, scheduling, processing, and the coordination of services are areas of focus to improve efficiency. In healthcare to assess effectiveness requires oversight and management by experts in medical practice that also understand improvement strategies. Efficiency improvement meshed with effective management is critically needed in most healthcare organizations. Patients should no longer be laying unattended in hallways waiting for a service that may not be necessary or die while awaiting treatment in the "waiting room."

4. Pull- Pull is the concept in LEAN that each step initiates the next when it is needed through coordinated signally. It provides an important concept to improve medical organizations and systems when it is linked to patient progress. Patient length of stay estimates and clinical pathways are standardized based on expectations that neglect triggers for individual patients. For example, "Progress notes" rarely mention where the patient is in relationship to anticipated problems or "expected progress" and the signs or symptoms indicating improvement or decline. Other examples of poor signaling or lack of pull include the common approach to discharge coordination, physician to physician communication and patient transfer between facilities. Outstanding medical care is more than just providing good care. It is evidenced by anticipating the patient's needs prior to problems or distress (the program of Anticipatory Nursing Care), yet pull systems that anticipate bathroom needs, pain reduction or family communications are rare in today's healthcare system.

5. Perfection- The concept of continuous improvement has failed in healthcare. Improvement programs are usually isolated teams that swoop in for problems and as David Marx describes, they play "whack a mole", with organizational difficulties (Marx 2009). The necessary resources and expertise of these teams are usually insufficient. Critical partners, like physicians, are usually excluded or don't participate and the results are rarely sustained. In LEAN the entire organizational mindset changes to incorporate improvement as "the new way". The approach is to look past existing assets and technologies and to rethink a service on a patient centered basis. LEAN perfection requires the conscious reassessment to re-define value in terms of specific services and capabilities that embrace change and improvement on an ongoing basis. It's every day in every way. (Womack and Jones 1996)

As expressed by Womack and Jones, "*A perfect process creates precisely the right value for the customer. In a perfect process, every step is valuable (creates value for the customer), capable* *(produces a good result every time), available (produces the desired output, not just the desired quality, every time), adequate (does not cause delay), flexible, and linked by continuous flow. Failure in any of these dimensions produces some type of wast*e." While a perfect process may be impossible in medicine because of patient individuality and organizational differences, the change in mindset to strive for perfection, to reach for higher goals and to pursue excellence in healthcare is possible and is a critical change medicine needs (Womack et al 2009). As noted by Peterson, to implement this change in healthcare using LEAN processes will require;

1. Just in time provision of service.

2. Reduction of unnecessary inventory or resources.

3. Improvement strategies and the application of improvement approaches.

4. Standardization.

5. Application of the Scientific method and evidence based management.

(Petersen 2009)   ◎✖◖~:▽:▢

The POTUS Exercise

An interesting exercise for any organization to help them understand their current lack of "perfection" is to compare their current level of function to what would change if the President of the United States unexpectedly appeared in the emergency department as a patient with an acute condition. An honest appraisal will reveal dramatic differences in responsiveness, resource allocation, efficiency, oversight and coordination of services, when compared to everyday practice. This exercise can serve to introduce the concept of the preferred "ideal" future state.

✖✖✖◉~:▽:△

> *"Healthcare workplaces are altogether, the most complex human organizations ever devised"*
>
> *Peter Drucker*

LEAN Healthcare Innovation, a System Approach

The term healthcare organization or medical system is often a misnomer, more often than not they are really not systems or organizations but really just disorganized groups; hence any improvement process will have to simultaneously aggregate the participants into a system or organization. Another reason that LEAN is a solution for healthcare is that a LEAN transformation is the ultimate system management approach; it involves every process and every employee in every situation and in all ways. A LEAN implementation should address the lack of relationships, the fragmentation and disorganization as it is institutionalized. In addition, systems' thinking is the discipline of seeing wholes, a framework for seeing interrelationships and for understanding the patterns of change (Senge 1990). System tools include feedback loops and automatic error-sensing negative feedback loops to correct performance; these are all components of the LEAN approach if properly applied. Dahlgaard et al writing about improvement in healthcare systems, notes that the "*soft or intangible factors of management (the system factors) like leadership, people management and partnerships must change, such that the new organizational culture is developed to support and improve the hospital's core processes*" (Dahlgaard et al, 2011). These authors, based on their studies, believe that the biggest potential for healthcare improvements is related to system sub- processes, those functions and departments which address the lack of ownership and limited responsibility for organizational activities; this assumption of ownership and accountability is part of the LEAN transformational change. (Dahlgaard and Dahlgaard-Park 2009).

⊚�knⵒⵒ~:▽:O

> "*One of the great insights of W. Edwards Deming was that over 90 percent of all organizational problems are systemic.*"
>
> *Steven R. Covey*

Healthcare Systems; Complex and Complicated

If we are going to approach healthcare as a system then it would have to be considered "complex and complicated" and as Senge suggests, it follows that there will be multiple levels of explanations for problems. Complicated systems involved multiple clearly defined steps that require expertise to manage, as opposed to complex systems that have variable inputs, blurred boundaries with input from staff with varied levels of expertise. Complicated systems can be addressed through a reductionist approach and have solvable problems, whereas complex systems must be assessed as a whole with consideration of the environment and the problems are often not solvable but must be managed. If we focus on simple explanations such as "who did what", the approach is reactive, limited and is emblematic of what has failed in healthcare. For successful improvement, we will need to consider behavioral patterns for explanations and consider long term trends and responses. An effective system approach to improvement also includes defining structural explanations that lead to the root causes of patterns of behavior; this concept enforces the realization that structure can produce behavior. LEAN addresses this by focusing on underlying structural malformations (Senge 1990).

The President's Counsel of Scientific Advisors Recommendations and Business Practices

The need for better system management in healthcare has recently been emphasized by the President's Counsel of Scientific Advisors (PCAST.) The goal of system management is to; analyze, design, manage and measure a complex system in order to improve its efficiency, reliability, productivity, quality and safety. The assessment of PCAST is that there are unnecessary medical costs that do not provide a better quality of health care.

> *"With expanded access placing greater demands on the healthcare system, strategic measures must be taken not only to increase efficiency, but also to improve the quality and affordability of care"* (PCAST).

The president's counsel recommends that the United States "build" a healthcare workforce that is equipped with essential-systems engineering competencies which will enable system redesign. Their hope is that this approach will reduce medical inefficiencies such as long wait times for access, poor communication between clinicians and patients and the difficulties clinician's face when dealing with complex patient disease. The President's counsel states;

> *"the current stresses on clinicians and clinical workloads prevent improvement initiatives. The clinicians cannot "find time" to participate in additional initiatives. Rather successful and sustainable improvement must involve reconfiguring that workflow and overall environment in which these professionals practice, which can help to reduce the burden of work while improving the performance of the system"* (PCAST).

Consistent with the PCAST assessment, in healthcare there are needs for system adaptations in structure, integration, feedback and educational processes to meet the coming challenges. As will be explained in the later sections, part of the current failings of system management in healthcare is the lack of effective change management integrated with successful business management practices. Healthcare is dominated by complicated complexity; systems that do not change in a planned fashion. For this reason, based on their studies in healthcare change, Higgs and Rowland promote that a significant change effort in healthcare that lacks a systems approach will be more likely to fail. (Higgs and Rowland 2005). For healthcare organizations to be successful in the future they must undergo system development; a change that is analogous to Edison's journey in inventing the light bulb. His great achievement was not specifically the light bulb, but instead developing an engineering research laboratory. Similarly, LEAN is a system approach to improvement by not just achieving a limited set of goals, but by creating a new structure for thinking and believing for an entirely integrated organization.

◉⊱◖ ~: ▽ :◖

"The secret of all victory lies in the organization of the non-obvious."
Marcus Aurelius

The LEAN Implementation Attributes that Fit Healthcare, "The Change Necessity"

A LEAN implementation is the answer for healthcare in that it promotes change management as a necessity. In Peter Drucker's, *Management Challenges for the 21st Century*, he makes the following recommendations for successful change management. (Drucker 1992)

1. Change as a policy and measured outcome- *"In a period of rapid structural change, the only ones who survive are the change leaders."* The <u>organization must make change a policy and make it an organizational metric</u>. This is also a primary principle in LEAN.

2. True continuous improvement -When continuous improvement becomes the "normal" for the entire organization it leads to innovation, incorporation of new standard work and a new situation (current state) that is closer to the desired goals (future state). As will be explained below these are the structural elements in how LEAN supports the process of change.

3. Real situational testing- Drucker states, *"Neither studies nor computer modeling are substitutes for the test of reality."* This is a primary tool in LEAN, meaning that "Rapid Improvement Experiments" are performed in the place of work using the staff's knowledge and experience to make successful innovations and improvements. This takes full advantage of local tacit knowledge and of healthcare providers as knowledge workers, not machines that produce healthcare.

4. A focus on Partnering-As mentioned, LEAN requires a new approach to the different stakeholders in medicine in regards to participation, commitment and respect. It requires better leadership and management than has been acceptable in the past. The refocusing on

values and mission that is part of LEAN is a uniting factor for the organization, its partners and for physician engagement. (Drucker 1992)

⑨✂℄~:▽:☆

"In reality, even successful change efforts are messy and full of surprises"

Why A Lean Transformation? Part of LEAN Healthcare Innovation

There is a difference between implementing LEAN tools and techniques and a LEAN transformation. A LEAN transformation is used to denote the philosophical and cultural changes that occur in the organization in addition to the LEAN activities, consistent with Pollard's definition of culture as the shared beliefs and values of the organization. A transformation entails changes in the social system, behaviors and personal beliefs (Pollard 2010). A LEAN transformation is a change in focus from central control to control in the workplace; it's about all the employees and the way they think about every aspect of the company. A LEAN transformation is a re-ordering of priorities and values communicated through visual performance metrics that asks for everyone to be ready to suppress their individual interests for their colleagues and for the organization. Another description of a LEAN Transformation is provided by John Toussaint and Leonard Berry as;

"an organization's cultural commitment to applying the scientific method to designing, performing, and continuously improving the work delivered by teams of people, leading to measurably better value for patients and other stakeholders." (Toussaint and Berry 2013)

In general, studies have demonstrated that cultural change is necessary for improvement and that the success of change management approaches is affected by adapting the organizational culture in technology applications (Schein 1985, McDermott and Stock 1999, Stock et al 2006), for quality management (Beer 2003, Buch and Rivers 2001) and for patient safety (Ruchlin et al 2004). As noted by Dahlgaard et al the current thinking on successful quality management efforts, like LEAN, requires a holistic and people –oriented management discipline, which necessitates total employee involvement in teambuilding to succeed (Dahlgaard et al, 2011). Kumar et al notes that healthcare improvements that focus on overall organization culture and collaboration across disciplines have been found to generate better ideas for improvement (Kumar et al 1998).

> *"A cardinal principle of Total Quality escapes too many managers: you cannot continuously improve interdependent systems and processes until you progressively perfect interdependent, interpersonal relationships."*
>
> *Stephen Covey*

In many applications of LEAN systems, LEAN develops into a limited quality improvement program, focusing on tools and sporadic project improvement. While this approach will lead to improvement in some areas, its yield will be 10 fold less than can be achieved with a LEAN Transformation. Unfortunately for most medical organizations, a 5 or 10% improvement will not prove sufficient to survive the near future for US healthcare. Only a LEAN approach for transformational and cultural change has routinely created 40 and 50% organizational improvements in a 1-year period which are then sustained.

What a LEAN transformation is not is the old type of command and control structure that dominates many healthcare organizations. As described by Covey, in authoritarian cultures;

> *"people say yes when they mean no and there is no healthy conflict. This approach pushes resentment, low quality and performance with the end result that such unexpressed feelings never really die, they're buried alive and come forth later in uglier ways"* (Covey 1989).

In authoritarian organizations, rules begin to take the place of human judgment. The culture promotes self-serving behavior and subordinates integrity. This is part of the explanation for why most physicians are not engaged in major medical institutions and unfortunately without their full engagement, a healthcare organization will not improve efficiency and productivity. Physicians and nurses represent the most important part of the culture of any major medical organization. A cultural transformation is aimed at finally solving the problem of physician and healthcare provider engagement with their organization.

The National Health Service in England is a perfect example of the traditional command and control central bureaucracy that does not focus on the practitioners and culture. As the quality of their system has continued to deteriorate, more and more executive and management staff have been hired and quality initiatives instituted (Blendon RJ and Donelan K 1989, Smith R 2010). The NHS today is a massive expensive bureaucracy in which 27% of UK citizens lack the confidence that it will provide good quality of care (Ipsos MORI 2015). The VA system in the US operates in the same fashion as the NHS; a large central bureaucracy overloaded with managers that are out of touch with their healthcare providers. The VA healthcare system has generated such poor quality that their managers and administrators have lied and committed fraud to avoid accountability (Hicks J 2014**).** As noted above, a transformation encompasses a very different culture, one with new values that support improvement, quality and organizational survival.

> *"Quality is the result of a carefully constructed cultural environment. It has to be the fabric of the organization, not part of the fabric."*
>
> *Phil Crosby*

A LEAN Transformation Enhancing Staff Engagement

James Womack makes the point that a full LEAN transformation is necessary for successful improvement, *"without a receptive culture the principles of LEAN will fail"* (Womack et al 2005). A strong culture provides a sense of stability, belonging, and the feeling of serving a higher purpose. The emphasis on transforming culture in LEAN is focused specifically on reaping the benefits of worker engagement. As noted by Bowles and Cooper;

> *"Worker engagement is no simple topic, involving as it does the rich mosaic of contributing factors ... Some of these can be controlled (whom we hire or promote, the culture we create inside our organizations), others we can only work with, react to and mitigate (the economy, national cultures, etc.)* (Bowles and Cooper 2012).

A LEAN transformation is a mechanism to improve culture through staff engagement. Rick Karlgaard, in his book the "Soft Edge: Where great companies find lasting success", studied successful companies in regards to culture and productivity, and notes that; *"dignity, respect, pride ... the sense of trust; those feelings engender and create real world returns and measurable increases in productivity"*. This is the type of culture that is the goal of a LEAN transformation. In addition, this focus on cultural transformation addresses the core problem in healthcare fragmentation and distracted medical personnel (Karlgaard 2014).

> *(A transformation) "It is a journey across uncharted territory to reach unknown goals that could not be more essential to the future of all organizations" (Kao 2002)*

Synergy; An Added Benefit from Transformation

The final reason to pursue a LEAN Transformation as opposed to just implementing LEAN techniques is that a full force effort to institute a LEAN transformation will synergistically make everyone better through consistency of values and empowerment. Leaders will be able to do what they do best, provide vision for the future and inspire their organization. Managers will be able to take on more responsibility, become more empowered and follow through on the course chartered by their leadership. Staff members will realize their innate talents and abilities and take ownership for their work. The end result is a happier more fulfilled staff focused on what makes patients better, a healthcare organization in which patients are the priority. The result is a whole that is greater than the sum of the parts.

©Glasbergen
glasbergen.com

GLASBERGEN

"There is always room for improvement. It's a
small room with no windows or distractions.
We already moved your things."

Reproduced with permission and License from Glasbergen.com

Figure 1.2 Improvement is a punishment. Why? (see figure legends)

⊘⊁⊖⊚ᴊ♡⊗⊁⊗⊬⤬ ⊘⋎ ⅃ ⊟⋂⅄⊖⋎⊗⊁⊗⊬⤬ .⊁⌖⅗⅗ ?

Why LEAN Healthcare Innovation Requires Personal Development

In the New Economics by W. Edwards Deming, he wrote

> *"the first step is transformation of the individual ... it comes from understanding the system of profound knowledge. The individual transformed will perceive new meaning to his life, to events, to numbers, to interactions between people. ...he will apply its principles in every*

kind of relationship with other people. He will have a basis for judgment of his own decisions and for transformation of the organizations he belongs to".

(Deming WE 2000)

This quote emphasizes the individual's critical role in change efforts and when combined with the definition of a transformation, it is clear that this type of change is not accomplished from external pressure on the staff. A transformation entails changing social norms, personal values, the subsequent derived behaviors and a change in personal priorities. Toussaint and Berry describe a LEAN transformation this way;

"it is not a set of quality improvement tools, it is not a quick fix... LEAN is a cultural transformation that changes how an organization works... it requires new habits, new skills, and often a new attitude throughout the organization from senior management to front-line service providers." (Toussaint and Berry 2013)

For the purposes of discussion, the term "personal development" will be used to mean the character and behavioral changes necessary to embrace transformation. This requires a critical introspective assessment by the employees regarding their own priorities and performance; to decide on changing their approach and breaking prior habits. Also, it means making a personal commitment to the organization. As noted by Connie Moore;

"whenever you make change, the individual is personally concerned ... you will still have resistance and actually incorrect information or incorrect perceptions if you don't get down to the individual level." (Schooff P)

Challenges in the Personal Development of Healthcare Personnel

What are the challenges for personal development or individual growth of the healthcare staff? Medicine is fraught with personalities that are immature, self-focused, competitive and possess a scarcity mindset. Physicians in particular are generally skeptical and untrusting and are usually not successful as organizational members (Belbeze P 2011). To participate in a LEAN Transformation and a cultural change will require many healthcare providers to go through their own personal development to be part of an organization in which the individual is self-sacrificing, socially responsible and trusting. These are changes consistent with a higher level of "emotional intelligence". There are many studies indicating that higher emotional intelligence adds flexibility and understanding of others and it supports alternative thinking (Thompson R 2014) (Hesselbein et al, 2002). For most staff, personal changes are required to be part of a LEAN culture and a LEAN Transformation.

Personal Development and Change

Unfortunately, one area of failure in LEAN implementations is related to underestimating the need for the personal development of the staff. Dahlgaard et al argue, based on their experience with LEAN Healthcare Projects implemented with 5 hospitals and 5 universities, that the first priority should be to "build" quality into people to improve partnerships, processes and products. They believe this effort requires understanding human nature, their needs and psychology. The authors further suggest that the basics for the implementation require an *"understanding of the interrelationships, and interactions between individuals, teams, the organization and the critical contextual factors at each level"* (Dahlgaard et al, 2011). When considering minor changes for improvement, such as isolated practices, limited behaviors or limited protocols, the amount of personal commitment and stress tolerance related to the change can usually be accommodated. But with significant change or improvement (like a LEAN transformation), to adjust to the magnitude of the personal impact, it may first require the staff to consider their personal attributes, beliefs and values to initiate what is an emotionally stressful change. A common failing in change implementations is to not provide the educational tools and mentoring to support personal change. This is emphasized by Steven Covey who asserts that in 90% of organizational activities behavior is understood by understanding human nature. He recommends that to approach improvement successfully, the employee should be measured first as a whole person considering their "paradigms" or principles related to their mind, body, heart and spirit. His point is that workers have a choice in how they respond to change and that they will give back to their work based on how they receive empathy and in the way that they are treated. To not acknowledge the stress and discomfort that the staff experience, on a personal basis, in a big change effort is another explanation for failure and of an organization's lack of improvement (Covey 2004).

> *"Care and Quality are internal and external aspects of the same thing. A person who sees quality and feels it as he works is a person who cares. A person who cares about what he sees and does is a person who's bound to have some characteristic of quality."*
>
> *Robert M. Pirsig,*

Personal Development for Healthcare Providers

A strong argument for focusing on personal development in implementing a LEAN transformation is how it centers on the physicians, nurses and staff providing the care. As noted previously the functional business unit in medicine is between the patient and the care provider. Any system engineering approach should have this as the critical area of attention and as such this entails an approach to improve the composition and characteristics of the care givers as organizational participants. But caregivers such as physicians are not engaged and not ready to take recommendations on how they should improve personally. As noted by the Advisory Board in 2013 in Trends in Physician Leadership Development, 89% of hospital initiatives require physician involvement yet, 67% of the organizations rely on 10% or less of the medical staff (Advisory Board). For non-physician providers, a recent VA healthcare system study demonstrates that the level of engagement of non-physician care givers has a significant impact on patient care quality. The researchers reviewed 907,993 VA patient admissions from 2002-2006 over 4 years, assessing the association of nursing employee demographics with patient admission records for length of stay. They found that a more stable and established nursing staff culture was associated with a reduced length of stay, an indicator of how the direct providers of care and their culture is the key to moving toward improvement in efficiency and quality. (Bartel et al). These surveys and studies speak to the critical role that healthcare providers have on patient outcomes and the need to focus on their personal characteristics to develop into change agents and promoters of a high quality culture.

❂❊❂~:▽:☉

Personal Development of Physicians as Organizational Members

A critical influence on physician organizational behavior is work satisfaction and unfortunately physician work satisfaction is at an all-time low and the current predictions are that it will continue to deteriorate with the ACA (Friedberg MW et al 2013). An approach to address this problem is outlined in a RAND and AMA joint study of 30 physician practices in 6 states, that included 220 interviews and surveys of 447 physicians. They discovered important determinates of physician satisfaction as:

1. Providing high quality care,
2. Having autonomy and greater control over the pace and content of clinical work which can be related to leadership and management roles,

3. Physicians with ownership,

4. Control of factors immediately affecting their day to day clinical work,

5. Values aligned with leaders,

6. Leadership with a balanced approach to practice wide initiatives,

7. Work place collegiality, fairness and respect,

8. Lower staff turnover.

Each of these characteristics is an area of improvement as part of a LEAN transformation approach; the opposite of what to expect from the ACA or an Accountable Care Organization (ACO). The ramifications of the ACA and the proposed ACO approaches are that more physicians will become employed, that there will be more practice consolidation and medical providers will have less practice control. The implications are that there will be an increase in externally implemented rules and regulations; a disregard for the place of work and the providers. This research portends that physician satisfaction will be followed by a commensurate reduction in the quality of care. (Friedberg MW et al 2013).

To compound the problem of declining physician satisfaction, most physicians don't understand the importance of their organizational participation. Physicians may be very clear about the personal issues and the needs of their patients but with few exceptions, most physicians perform poorly with the required communications for coordination of care. To address this integration properly may require re-education of physicians about their personal approach to patient care and the importance of organizational participation. But they already know these issues, they don't participate because of limitations in their core personal values. To support physician personal development will require understanding the root causes embedded in their character for their current performance gaps.

A suggestion to address these issues may be found in treating Physicians as core knowledge workers. Daniel Pink, in his book "Drive" emphasizes that knowledge workers are energized by;

Autonomy- the freedom to direct their lives or work

Mastery- the craving to excel and for purpose

Legacy- to work to serve or be part of something bigger or important. (Pink 2011)

A LEAN transformation approach supports all the determinates of physician satisfaction and the personal energy, as noted by Pink, to energize knowledge workers. LEAN can provide an answer to preventing further deterioration in physician relationships with their organization, but this effort will also require a focus on personal development of physicians to be part of that process.

☉✕℃~:▽:∞

"Just as all politics are local, then it follows that all medicine is personal"

Innovation versus improvement; Why LEAN Healthcare Innovation incorporates Innovation
The need for innovation for business success is commonly agreed upon; in some surveys up to 99% of business leaders agree that innovation is critical, but also agree that a system for innovation is in place in only 2% of businesses (Advisory Board 2016, PWC 2013). In healthcare, improvement has always been an ongoing effort, but considering the imminent crisis, "some" improvement will not be enough for the survival of many organizations, it will require something more. Healthcare needs innovation; it needs Peter Drucker's definition of innovation, *"Innovation: is change that creates a new dimension of performance"*. Can LEAN be that type of innovation? As noted by Margaret Wheatley, innovation taps human creativity and commitment as its greatest resources; this is what healthcare needs and is a LEAN fundamental principle (Wheatley 2002). Gardner in his discussions of how to support innovation indicates that a creative culture is required which is open to trial and error; similar to the LEAN Rapid Improvement Experiments (Gardner and Barberich 2002). Kanter's explanation that innovation requires a good organizational culture and a changing of perspectives to encourage insights is another description of how healthcare will change in a LEAN transformation (Kanters 2002). Unfortunately, some organizational change efforts and even some LEAN implementations often miss the subtle difference between improving or adapting versus innovation. For LEAN to be successful in healthcare it must go beyond adaptations and improvements to real innovation for results that matter; for survival.

❂✇☾~:▽:Ɛ

Leading and Supporting innovation in Healthcare
Individual patient variability is 315 times more important in determining health outcomes than any other factor (Silber and Rosenbaum 1997). Patient variability leads to a greater need for judgment, reassessment and review then in other industries and it means that medical practice is more individualized and personal for a practitioner. In addition, change in medicine is risky and requires more careful decision making. Insights and new information from systematic or global sources must be translated for local application; this requires a new conceptualization for the local approach. All of these factors, patient variability, treatment complexity and translations for local applications are why successful change in healthcare is more like innovation then just improvement; it requires creativity, a supportive culture and a scientific approach similar to experimentation.

Another way to define innovation is the persistent, collaborative aligning of talent, resources and networks. This is another reason why improvement in medicine is more like innovation; to be successful it must address the fragmentation that typifies medical organizations. Jim Collins makes the point that a cultural transformation is in itself an innovation and how that impacts on success;

> *"having a culture that promotes high performance and innovation at all levels is ultimately more essential then any single business plan".* (Collins 2002)

Collins promotes that if dedication to customers and employees is unwavering then innovation, growth and profit follow; a primary principle of LEAN. Unfortunately, many LEAN implementations do not include creating an environment for innovation. In "Adapt or Die: The imperative for a culture of innovation in the United States Army" by Brigadier General David A. Fastabend, Robert Simpson and General Peter Schoomakers, they note;

> *"to succeed we must question everything... development of a culture of innovation will not be advanced by panels, studies, or their papers. Culture change begins with behavior and the leaders who shape it".* (Fastabend et al 2001)

Both Collins and the Generals endorse innovation through culture change as an essential element for successful change; the type of transformation that healthcare needs. The inability of many organizations to execute within these organizational dimensions may explain a number of previous failings of lauded improvement approaches like; process reengineering, continuous quality improvement (CQI), total quality management (TQM) and prior LEAN efforts (Kao 2002). The priorities for the approach to healthcare innovation that is needed for survival are described in Kao's review of improvement efforts in healthcare. His recommendation is an attention to the economies of discovery, not scale. The focus should be on competitive originality and management innovation and this change should shift from command and control to collaboration and enabling. The concentration should not be on cost, but on investment and experimentation, blended with the current way to perform work successfully (Kao 2002). The lack of a focus on innovation as part of a LEAN cultural transformation may be the missing component that has led to failures in LEAN applications.

◉⌘ℭ ~:▽:𝔛

SUMMARY

Assessment

Healthcare preparedness for the conflict related to change and the future changes in healthcare- grade D, essentially unprepared.

LEAN Current State

If we put the current problems in healthcare in the terms of LEAN principles as defined by Jones and Womack, the current state is;

- Voice of the customers- Patients, often forgotten and a complex system of co-customers adding to the lack of focus.

- Value Streams- There are many service lines in medicine and they are more varied and generally undefined.

- Flow- Unlike production industries it is not time that is important in medicine, it is effectiveness with patients, this is poorly assessed in healthcare.

- Pull- While complex, this area of medicine has the greatest similarities to other industries in applicability of pull systems that can increase productivity and efficiency, but are currently underutilized.

- Perfection- This is a variable definition in healthcare, based on the definer. For the healthcare provider it means to do the best possible job in the best possible way as determined for the individual patient needs. The evaluation of reaching this goal requires analysis from experienced providers in the field, with expertise in management, innovation and quality of medical practice with a focus on continuous improvement; this is not a current approach in healthcare. (Womack and Jones 1996)

Conclusions

1. Healthcare differs from other service or manufacturing businesses in that in healthcare the specific provider patient relationship, accounts for 80 to 90% of efficiency, cost, productivity, quality and patient and staff satisfaction.

2. Healthcare organizations and systems are more often disorganized amalgamations that require an effort to aggregate into a culture and a system in addition to efforts to improve.

3. Because of the variability in healthcare organizations there is a greater need for preparation and assessment as a change process originating from outside sources is implemented.

4. Medicine is a VUCA (volatility, uncertainty, complexity, ambiguity) environment and because of the "complicated complex" nature of problems in healthcare, for improvement it requires a system approach.

5. Good organizational business fundamentals are not a given in healthcare and physicians are generally not good business persons. Most organizations will need to improve the organizational business management practices and accountability in addition to the improvement efforts.

6. There is a need for personal development for healthcare staff, particularly for physicians to become an effective part of an organization. This will require improvements in physician and healthcare organizational relationships and alignment.

7. Improvement in healthcare organizations will require a formal, high quality, well-resourced educational program pertaining to change, improvement processes and innovation.

8. To make substantial changes in healthcare, will require more definitive and better resourced data systems that support appropriate metrics.

9. For healthcare the key to significant improvement will be innovation, not just improvement, emphasizing the need for an environment for creative freedom and experimentation which applies the scientific method to system change.

10. Healthcare provider engagement is poor, but it is critical to successful improvement or change. The active participation of all healthcare providers in LEAN is a potential answer to the problem of provider engagement.

"Many times what we perceive as an error or failure is actually a gift. And eventually we find that lessons from the discovery experience to be of great worth."

Richelle Goodrich

Learning from Mistakes

It seems that LEAN has the perfect attributes to be the answer for healthcare survival. One would expect LEAN healthcare applications would result in dramatic successes, but in fact it is just the opposite. While LEAN implementations usually result in limited improvements, the success rate for organizational LEAN implementations is only 10 to 20% and almost nonexistent for true LEAN transformations. This book is focused on why LEAN fails so often in healthcare. What will follow will be sections related to the common areas of failure in LEAN implementations and attempted transformations. We will take an evidenced based approach using study data, and if it is not available, supportive theory. This book will differ from other recommendations for LEAN transformations on several points;

1. In recommending a careful assessment and planning phase,

2. The emphasis of using a system approach,

3. In applying a model for managing change for the organization,

4. In the need to refocus on successful business practices concomitantly,

5. In the need for personal development of the staff,

6. For a greater emphasis on innovation over improvement.

These recommendations are still consistent with those of Womack and Jones. They recommended a focus on; purpose, process and people. Purpose, in the sense of reassessing the organization's strategies on how to provide value to patients and co-customers. Process, in how to determine value and to change organizational structures and execution to generate that value. And people, in terms of how they support, evaluate and embrace LEAN, i.e. the development of a LEAN culture and transformation (Womack and Jones 1996). LEAN is effective at creating improvement, but this conceptualization "LEAN Healthcare Innovation" could be stunning by creating transformational innovation.

"Just as a carpenter needs a vision of what to build in order to get the full benefit of a hammer, Lean Thinkers need a vision before picking up our lean tools"

James Womack

5 Whys-Failures in LEAN Transformations.

The "5 Whys" is a problem solving tool aimed at understanding the root cause for problems using simplicity to initiate a deeper exploratory process.

Why do LEAN transformations fail? Leadership

1.   They fail because the staff does not become fully committed.

2.   They don't fully commit, because the leadership is ineffective at convincing them of the necessity and value of LEAN.

3.   The leadership is ineffective because they don't execute an effective plan to communicate, educate or support the change in the staff.

4.   The leadership does not execute an effective plan because of their lack of understanding and commitment to LEAN.

5.   Leadership does not understand or fully commit to LEAN because they never come to fully believe in LEAN.

Reverse 5 Whys

Why do LEAN transformations succeed?

1.   The staff fully believes and implements LEAN, a transformation occurs.

2.   The staff committed to the transformation because they see the value, understand the process and the necessity.

3.   The staff understood the reasons for the transformation from good communication, education and support for their own personal development.

4.   The communication, education and support were good for the staff because the leadership properly planned and supported the programs, which were considered as necessary.

5.   The leadership plans and support for the LEAN programs demonstrated their belief in the value and necessity of a LEAN Transformation.

Why do LEAN transformations fail? Health care providers

1.   The personal characteristics of the medical staff inhibit their ability to change.

2.   They have these personal characteristics because of a greater focus on education and training but a lack of focus on personal development in other activities.

3. They are not focused on personal development activities like emotional intelligence because it has not been part of organizational requirements.

4. Personal development has not been part of organizational requirements because of a lack of understanding of the personal requirements to embrace change.

5. The lack of motivation to understand their personal requirements to change is related to a lack of integration and engagement with their organization.

5 Whys

Why do LEAN transformations fail? Business practices

1. Business management approaches central to LEAN transformations fail because the business management practices in healthcare are poorly defined.

2. Business management practices are poorly defined in healthcare because the primary providers of services, physicians and nurses, are not educated or involved in business management practices.

3. Physicians and nurses are not involved in healthcare business practices because of the artificial separation of healthcare administration and providers.

4. This artificial separation exists because of a lack of understanding of the critical need to bring the healthcare providers and administrators together to share control.

5. The lack of understanding about the critical need for shared control reflects a lack of personal development by health administration, physicians and healthcare providers.

Why do LEAN transformations fail? Innovation

1. Lean transformations fail because of a lack of innovation.

2. Innovations are lacking in LEAN transformation because the healthcare environment does not support innovation.

3. Healthcare does not support innovation because of a lack of understanding of the value of innovation and the environment it requires to survive.

4. The lack of understanding about the need for the environment for innovation and its value is related to a lack of education and experience with innovation.

5.   There is a lack of education and experience in innovation in healthcare because of the lack of available resources and the lack of commitment to apply the scientific method to processes in healthcare.

REFERENCES

Advisory Board Physician Engagement 2016; www.advisory.com/topics/physician-issues/physician-engagement.

Advisory Board, Spurring Innovation 2016, www.advisory.com/talent-development/leader-development/members/workshop-resources/strategy/spurring-innovation.

Advisory Board, Trends in Physician Leadership Development 2013 advisory.com.

Bartel AP, Beaulieu ND, Phibbs CS, Stone PW. Human capital and productivity in a team environment: Evidence from the healthcare sector. Am Econ J Appl Econ 2014;6: 231-259.

Beer M. Why total quality management programs do not persist: The role of management quality and implications for leading a TQM transformation. Decision Sciences 2003;34:623-642.

Belbeze P "Physician alignment: the collaborative care disconnects Health leaders Media 2011.

Bina, Shideh Sedgh, 10 disruptive forces in healthcare. Becker's hospital review 5 12 2014.

Blendon RJ and Donelan K. British public opinion on national health service. Health Affairs 1989;8:52-62.

Bowles D and Cooper C. The High Engagement Work culture: Balancing Me and We. Palgrave and Macmillan 2009.

Bush, RW: Reducing waste in US health care systems. *JAMA* 2007, 297:871-874.

Buch K and Rivera D. "TQM: the role of leadership and culture". Leadership and Organization Development Journal 2001;22:365-371.

CBO- The budget and Economic Outlook: An Update (august 2010)www.cbo.gov/publication/21670.

CBO-Labor Market Effects of the Affordable Care Act: Updated Estimates. Appendix C (February 2014) *www.**cbo**.gov/publication/45096.*

Collins J. The Ultimate Creation. In Leading for Innovation. Hesselbein F, Goldsmith M, Somerville I. Ed. Jossey-Bass 2002.

Covey SR. The 7 Habits of Highly Effective People: Restoring the Character Ethic. Simon Schuster, 1989.

Covey SR. The 8th Habit, From Effectiveness to Greatness. Simon and Schuster 2004.

Dahlgaard JJ, Pettersen J, Dahlgaard-Park ESM, Quality and LEAN healthcare: A system for assessing and improving the health of healthcare organizations. Total quality management and business excellence. 2011; 22:673-689.

Dahlgaard JJ and Dahlgaard-Park M. LEAN production, six sigma quality, TQM and company culture. TQM magazine 2006; 18:263-281.

Deming WE. The New Economics for Industry, Government, Education. The MIT Press, 2000.

Drucker, P *Management Challenges for the 21st Century*, Harper Collins 1992.

Fastabend DA, Simpson RH, Schoomaker PJ. "Adapt or Die" The Imperative for a Culture of Innovation in the United States Army. www.au.af.mil/au/awc/awcgate/army/culture_of_innovation.pdf.

Freidberg MW, Chen PG, Busum KR, Aunon FM, Pham C, Caloyeras JP, Mattke S, Pitchforth E, Quigley DD, Brook RH. Crosson FJ, Tutty M. Factors affecting physician professional satisfaction and their implications for patient care, health systems and health policy. RAND Health/AMA 2013 www.rand.org.

Gardner H and Barberich Good Work in Business. In Leading for Innovation. Hesselbein F, Goldsmith M, Somerville I. Ed. Jossey-Bass 2002.

Jordan Rau/Kaiser- New HHS Data Shows Major Strides Made in Patient Safety, Leading to Improved Care and Savings. More than 750 hospitals face Medicare crackdown on patient injuries. Kaiser June 2014.

Hesselbein F, Goldsmith M, Somerville I. Leading for Innovation. Jossey-Bass 2002.

Hicks, J. "Watchdog slams VA for calling bad medical practices "harmless errors". The Washington Post 2014.

Higgs M and Roland D. All changes great and small: Exploring approaches to change and its leadership. Journal of Change Management 2005;5:121-151.

Ipsos MORI 27% Lack confidence in local NHS services this winter. 2015.

Karlgaard, R The "Soft Edge: Where Great Companies Find Lasting Success" Jossey Bass 2014.

Kanters RM. Creating a Culture of Innovation. In Leading for Innovation. Hesselbein F, Goldsmith M, Somerville I. Ed. Jossey-Bass 2002.

Kao J. Reinventing Innovation: A Perspective from the Idea Factory. In Leading for Innovation. Hesselbein F, Goldsmith M, Somerville I. Ed. Jossey-Bass 2002.

Kumar K, Subramanian R, Yauger C. Examining the market orientation-performance: a context-specific study. Journal of Management 1998;24:201-233.

Marx D, Whack-a-Mole: The Price We Pay for Expecting Perfection. By Your Side Studios 2009.

Mc Dermott CM and Stock GN. Organizational culture and advanced manufacturing technology implementation. Journal of Operations Management 1999;17:521-533.

PCAST Report to the President: Better Healthcare and Lower Costs: Accelerating Improvement through systems engineering. 2014, www.whitehouse.gov/ostp/pcast.

PWC Unleashing the Power of Innovation. 2013 www.pwc.com.

Parente S, Ramlet M. National and State Impact Analyses of the ACA on Insurance Prices and Enrollment Beyond 2014, Working Papers Medical Industry Leadership Institute May 2014.

Pettersen J. Defining LEAN production: Some conceptual and practical issues. The TQM Journal. 2009;21:127-142.

Pink DH –Drive, The Surprising Truth About What Motivates Us. Riverhead Books 2011.

Pollard CW. Crafting a cultural character. Leader to Leader 2010 S1:38-42.

Ruchlin HS, Dubbs NL, Callahan MA. The role of leadership in instilling a culture of safety: lessons from the literature. J Healthc Manag 2004;49:47-58.

Schooff P. Managing change in process improvement: Why and how to do the job well Business Process Management (BPM) Best Practices ebisQ. www.ebizq.net/topics/int_sbp/features/13385.html.

Senge, P. The Fifth Discipline: The art and practice of the learning organization. DoubleDay 1990.

Shoemaker, W. The cost of Quality: How VBP scores correlates with hospital costs. Healthc Financ Manage, 2012;66:50-56.

Shein, E Organizational Culture and Leadership. Jossey-Bass Publishers, 1985.

Sheridan, Kevin, Building a Magnetic Culture: How to Attract and Retain Top Talent to Create an Engaged, Productive Workforce. McGraw-Hill 2012.

Silber JH and Rosenbaum PR. A spurious correlation between hospital mortality and complication rates: the importance of severity adjustment. Medical Care 1997;35:os77-92.

Stock GN, McFadden KL, Gowen CR. Organizational culture, critical success factors and the reduction of hospital errors. Int J. Production Economics 2006;106:368-92.

Smith R. Rise in NHS managers outstrips doctors and nurses. Telegraph Media Group 2016.

Thompson R. For a more flexible workforce, hire self-aware people. Harvard Business Review Jan 2014.

Toussaint JS and Perry LL. The promise of LEAN in health care. Mayo Clin Proc 2013;88:74-82.

U.S. Department of Health & Human Services May 7, 2014.

Wheatley MJ. We are all innovators. In Leading for Innovation. Hesselbein F, Goldsmith M, Somerville I. Ed. Jossey-Bass 2002.

Wing RL. The Art of Strategy: A New Translation of Sun Tzu's Classic "The Art of War" DoubleDay 1988.

Womack JP and Jones DT. LEAN Thinking. Free Press 1996.

Womack JP, Byrne, AP, Fiume OJ, Kaplan GS, Toussaint J. Going LEAN in Health Care IHI 2005.

Chapter 2

Literature Review

"Those who cannot remember the past are condemned to repeat it"

George Santayana

Whate do we know about LEAN transformations and change management in healthcare? When

you reach the end of this review it should be clear that our scientific evidence concerning LEAN improvement in healthcare is very limited. Lilford et al has also argued that the studies pertaining to LEAN in healthcare are not well delineated and do not apply the scientific method to the interventions applied (Lilford et al 2003). There are reports of antidotal efforts or isolated process improvements to support LEAN implementations, but the data about LEAN transformations and why they fail is essentially missing. To try to make up for the limited data about LEAN that is available and because the success or failure of LEAN transformations is dependent on multiple other functions of healthcare organizations, this review will include an assessment of other areas of healthcare as well. The areas that will be reviewed will include; the foundational business management practices, the organizational culture, the history of change success and prior quality improvement efforts.

Healthcare organizations and Fundamental Business Management Practices

For a broader perspective about business practices in healthcare, it may be beneficial to consider how healthcare organizations differ from other industries. Outside of medicine, only 13% of companies are profitable at 10 years and in regards to success, only 9% are considered above average, only 1% superior. Surprisingly only 5% of the best companies sustain growth and only 16% survive 30 years

(Collins JC and Porras JI 1994, Bossidy L and Charan R 2002). The recommendations for sustaining successful business performance are that a company must provide quality in product/service and maintain the productive capacity in balance. For leadership and management, the recommendations for success include the need to focus on character, team building, and executing excellent results on key priorities. As for individual employee effectiveness, successful companies focus on increasing knowledge, skills and performance for individuals and teams (Covey 2004).

❂✳℃ ~:◇:▽

For healthcare organizations there are additional considerations. Healthcare organizations function as loco-regional services like police and fire and usually do not experience the same competitive pressures similar to other industries. This may explain why many of the recommendations for successful business practices and good quality business fundamentals are missing in many healthcare organizations. However, with the changing healthcare environment, past approaches may no longer be acceptable for future survival.

Fundamental Business Practices

To further emphasize the importance of fundamental business practices in healthcare and how they influence improvement and change efforts, we will compare successful business management practices in healthcare to other industries; from a physician's perspective. One of the best articles on successful corporate business fundamentals is "What Really Works" by Nitin Nohria, William Joyce, and Bruce Roberson in which they studied the business management practices that correlated with enduring overall success. In this study, the authors examined more than 200 well-established management practices as they were implemented over a ten-year period by 160 companies (Evergreen Project 1986 to 1996). They were surprised to find that most management tools and techniques had no significant relationship to corporate success. The authors did identify four areas in management practices that were correlated to success; strategy, execution, culture, and structure. The areas related to talent, innovation, leadership, and partnering were considered secondary contributors to organizational success as they supplemented the 4 primary practices; the winning combination was a 4+2 formula. They found that the formula was associated with a 90 percent chance of sustaining superior business performance as defined by shareholder returns (top 5% of publicly traded companies over this period). Their research demonstrated that improvement tools and techniques were helpful but none were the key to success.

Let's consider an assessment of these successful business practices, as defined by Nohria, as they are applied in the average healthcare organization.

Strategy-The study authors note that strategy must be sharply defined, clearly communicated, and well understood by employees, customers, and partners. This is rarely the case in healthcare organizations.

Execution-The focus should be reliable, "flawless" execution; outside of direct patient care, this is uncommon in healthcare processes or procedures.

Culture-The authors note that culture inspires all of the staff to do their best and empowers employees and managers to work in a challenging and satisfying environment. This type of culture is rare in healthcare; it is more common that no aligned culture exists.

Structure-The authors note that structure should reduce bureaucracy, simplify work and promote cooperation across the entire organization. In healthcare, the structure usually promotes the opposite.

Talent-Of the secondary practices associated with success, Nohria et al note that talent development, promotion and hiring along with integrated job design can contribute to success. The failure in appropriate hiring practices, in career development and in appropriate promotion in healthcare is the primary reason for the degradation cycle of many prominent healthcare entities.

Innovation-Innovation was considered by the authors to be important to maintain success and for a stable market position. Innovations in treatment approaches in healthcare are common, but conversely it is uncommon to see innovations in logistics, processes or structures within healthcare organizations.

Leadership-The authors stress that Leadership can raise performance significantly, if it's connected to the staff at all levels, a recommendation that is almost always missed in healthcare.

Mergers and Partnerships- The final area they identified as important includes Mergers and Partnerships as a source of new businesses and growth, which is usually an area of poor communication and confusion in healthcare (Nohria et al 2003).

When you review business practices associated with successful companies, it is clear that part of the explanation for failure in improvement efforts, such as LEAN, is related to the poor foundational business practices in healthcare.

Why are these business management practices so poorly applied in healthcare? One explanation may be that when one considers the activities provided by healthcare organizations, the vast majority is under the individualized attention of the hospital staff; the nurses and physicians. Because of the individual discretion required to perform this job optimally, it is inherently inconsistent with approaches that promote a more centralized control through the organization. The current business model (of uncontrolled independent contractors) is unlikely to provide efficient and well-coordinated services and explains the limitations of organizational influence for improvement in successful management approaches. If the healthcare providers are the critical variable to improvement in these business practices, then their relationship with the organization should be properly delineated and valued and their role in controlling the medical care environment supported in any business program. It then follows that healthcare providers must understand and be contributors to formulating these business management practices and any effort at a LEAN transformation must identify the structural limitations of the current business model of collaborative care related to their independent practitioners (the techs, nurses and physicians). This concept is reinforced by Boon et al, when they note that the critical need for provider alignment of incentives and engagement in application of business management practices will be a critical part of any successful LEAN transformation (Boon et al 2004).

◉✖ℂ~:◇:□

Improvement and Change Management in Healthcare

The limited success in prior quality improvement efforts in healthcare may explain some of the problems in achieving organizational change or improvement with current LEAN implementations. As noted by Vest and Gamm efforts like total quality management (TQM) and process reengineering, although pushed by healthcare institutions, have failed to translate into sustainable results (Bigelow and Arndt 2000). A review of TQM applications to hospitals revealed that it frequently faces an adverse culture and managers that incorrectly assumed employees would automatically adhere to the new philosophy (Kanji and Sa 2003). This supports the results of the study by Stock et al that identified the role of an organization's culture as not only important for safe healthcare delivery, but that it also serves as a foundation for improvement (Stock et al 2007). Specifically speaking about culture in healthcare improvement, Kovner and Rundall noted;

> *"...efforts to introduce evidence-based decision making quickly wither and fade away because the organizational culture does not support evidence based management."*

(Kovner and Rundall 2006)

Kanji and Sa found similar results when they evaluated Total Quality Management. They analyzed 200 surveys and found that many organizations have not delivered the promised results from TQM. The reasons for failure included insufficient support from health professionals, lack of leadership commitment and the view that TQM is an isolated program that was not part of core strategy. In regards to structural problems in TQM, the authors found poor management by data, poor performance feedback and that the program was not linked to quality measures. The specific reasons given for system failures in TQM included; an adverse culture, limited managerial options, limits in human resources, lack of performance rewards, poor implementation, leadership naivety about the staff embracing change and staff distrust or disbelief in the initiative. The authors felt this reflected major system problems including; lack of consistency, poor alignment, lack of quality definition and poor system integration. They recommended a focus on a performance measurement system including:

- ❖ Checks on progress toward goals,
- ❖ Accountability mechanisms,
- ❖ Support for future resource allocations,
- ❖ Good communication of goals,
- ❖ Priorities that motivate and drive improvement.

The authors emphasized the importance of the quality efforts being; linked to organizational values and strategy, valid and reliable approaches, easy to use tools and performance linked to rewards. Like many, the authors also noted that leadership is the most important force for quality improvement. (Kanji and Sa 2003).

◎⚡℃~:◇:○

A study of quality improvement program success as a function of organizational culture in healthcare was published by Rad in 2006. The purpose of the paper was to determine the impact of cultural values on the success of the Total Quality Management program (TQM) implementation. Using questionnaires from staff, data was collected on the characteristics of organizational culture and the implementation of the TQM program. The staff impression was that TQM was moderately successful, particularly in the areas of process management, in creating a patient focus and in its implementation by leadership and management. There were fewer benefits with performance, clinical outcomes, strategic planning and resource utilization. Human resource issues, assessing performance and "strategic problems" were the biggest difficulties that prevented TQM success. The authors concluded that success of TQM was associated with stronger organizational cultures and with less bureaucracy ($p<0.05$, Rad 2006).

When we consider the current healthcare culture and the prior quality improvement failures, the track record does not provide a clear pathway for success and has led to a lack of medical staff enthusiasm for such efforts; a background that does not support a LEAN implementation.

Healthcare Staff Characteristics and Change Success

Studies have demonstrated that certain personality traits such as positivity, tolerance for ambiguity and cynicism impact on the tolerance for change (Oreg S et al 2011). In Oreg's review of personal responses to organizational change they defined 5 variables associated with a positive recipient response (Oreg S et al 2011).

> 1. A High level of Participation,
>
> 2. Communication that is specific and supportive,
>
> 3. Processes and decisions that demonstrate fairness and appropriateness,
>
> 4. Resources focused specifically on change,
>
> 5. Competent and effective management.

Studies have shown that change acceptance is associated with the individual's belief that they have control of the change process and of their fate (Fried Y et al 1996, Wanberg CR and Banas JT 2000).

❧

Hage has indicated that the 3 factors positively associated with an individual's acceptance of transformational change are; prior history of innovation, the attitudes of the institutional leadership and the organizational structure (Hage JT 1999). For physician considerations, Schneider and Eisenberg studied strategies and techniques used for aligning current and best medical practices (Schneider and Eisenberg 1998). They cited the six categories of methods commonly used to achieve change: education, feedback, physician participation in change, enforcement of rules, financial incentives, and financial penalties. They noted that the most common approach to change involved a combination of an outreach effort by a trusted opinion leader with an educational program that was interactive and consistent with current practices. Additionally, as noted by Oreg et al, the staff should be assured that there is flexibility and that their recommendations will be incorporated into the new programs (Oreg S et al 2011). It is a reasonable question to ask how often these principles have been applied in change efforts in healthcare; going forward they should be applied to any LEAN implementation.

❧

Another approach to encouraging change for healthcare providers has been the use of Pay for Performance (P4P). Can the P4P approach overcome the healthcare staff's personal problems related to change? In a general review, Peterson et al evaluated 17 studies, from which they concluded that P4P results provided *"low quality evidence for improved patient outcomes"* (Peterson et al 2006). In another review of P4P, Mannion and Davies summarized the central problem in the P4P approach;

"to attribute poor measured performance to poor actual performance it is necessary to make causal inferences from observed data, ... and take into account external circumstances and case mix."

They concluded that there was insufficient evidence to make the causal inferences that P4P works and for understanding the overall consequences of P4P programs aimed at improving healthcare (Mannion and Davies 2008). Until there are better systems for estimating a patient's severity of illness combined with the additional procedural risks associated with practices like surgery, the application of P4P will not be effective at preventing high risk patient avoidance and circumvention of poor medical environments. These limitations of the P4P programs will compromise their potential to improve clinical outcomes and may result in the rationing of care for the most ill or impoverished. These studies are cited to emphasize that P4P programs are unlikely to improve provider acceptance of a LEAN implementation. When one considers the many different factions in healthcare, addressing the providers individually (as noted by Oreg et al) with a focus on their empowerment and engagement, is a challenge and represents one more area that has contributed to the failure in LEAN transformations.

Examples of LEAN Implementation Success

To provide some balance, and avoid too much depression, it is reasonable to note that there are many antidotal examples of success in LEAN implementations for specific processes and services.

"I THINK YOU SHOULD BE MORE EXPLICIT HERE IN STEP TWO."

Reproduced with permission and license from S Harris.

Figure 2.1 It's about execution (see figure legends)

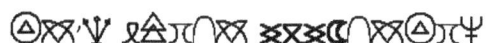

⊿⋈·Ψ ℓ⊿ℸ⊓⋈⋈ ⨯⋈⨯⨴⊓⋈⊿ℸΨ

One example is a study of emergency care that demonstrated improvement in waiting and lead times (19-24%) which was sustained for two years. The authors concluded that the success was related to; creating "*standard work*", working through staff relationships, improved flow, staff empowerment to investigate problems and the development of countermeasures. They noted problems in the LEAN implementation related to a lack of training, poor allocation of job tasks, a negative perception of monitoring and the discomfort with intra-professional collaboration (Mazzocato et al 2012). There have been similar LEAN applications to isolated healthcare processes which were described as valuable but did not result in a true LEAN transformation. For example, some processes that have been improved by LEAN applications include; treatment of community acquired pneumonia (Johnson et al 2013), treatment of femoral neck fractures (McNamara et al 2014), response to postpartum hemorrhage (Crowe and Faulkner 2014), coordination of inpatient phlebotomy (Le et al 2014), treatment of central line infections (Adams et al 2010), outpatient clinic flow (Fischman D 2010), recovery room flow (Kuo et al 2011) and EMR application (Idemoto et al 2016). As a more specific example, Shannon et al used a LEAN approach to reduce central line infections. They were able to reduce their infection rate by 89% and a reduction in death rate by 35% (Shannon et al 2006). Additionally, there have been articles about broader system or hospital successes in trade publications that have credited both Six Sigma (Mantone J 2004, Sherman J 2006) and Lean/Toyota Production Systems (Serrano and Slunecka 2006).

General Reviews of Lean Transformations

As noted above, LEAN applications have improved specific processes and antidotal reports have inferred that a greater success with a LEAN transformation is possible. This section will review the published data about LEAN transformation success.

A study of 77 hospital surveys published by the American Society of Quality in 2009 found that 53% of those surveyed were using LEAN approaches in some form, but only 4% of hospitals reported "full deployment" of LEAN. The explanation for the low acceptance of a full LEAN transformation included; lack of resources 59%, not enough information 41%, and lack of leadership buy in 30% (ASQ 2009). Vest and Gamm also reviewed studies regarding healthcare organizational transformational strategies. The authors examined the peer-reviewed literature from the U.S. for evidence of effectiveness among three current popular transformational strategies: Six Sigma, Lean/Toyota Production System, and Studer's Hardwiring for Excellence. The studies they selected were required to be peer reviewed, not pilots and studies of a specific intervention with quantitative data (i.e. not review articles). Their review found 152 references on Six Sigma, 46 on LEAN and 9 on Studer. After the application of their inclusion criteria, only 9 articles on Six Sigma and 9 articles on LEAN qualified. The Six Sigma studies varied from interventions for quality measures like catheter related blood stream infections to medical processes such as assuring clinic access or operating room through put. None of these were randomized trials and only one contained a control group. The LEAN studies involved clinical care units for telemetry use, ICU services and hospital laboratories. There was one system wide LEAN approach employed by the Virginia Mason Medical Center on patient safety. The authors concluded that LEAN implementations were successful in improving a variety of healthcare processes and outcomes. However, despite these positive features, the vast majority of studies had methodological limitations that weakened the validity of the results. These problems included: weak study designs, inappropriate analyses and failures to rule out alternative hypotheses. Furthermore, documentation of organizational culture change or substantial evidence of sustainment from the LEAN implementation were absent. The authors concluded that despite the current popularity of these strategies, few studies contained definitive information or provided clear evidence of successful implementation of LEAN or Six Sigma as a transformational event (Vest and Gamm 2009).

The one study that seemed to reflect the closest effort at a true LEAN Transformation was the Virginia Mason study. They moved to a LEAN system implementation in 2002 with a focus on the Zero Defect theory (from Shigeo Shingo) which is the concept of stopping mistakes from becoming defects by a reductionist approach to processes; creating small segments that can be easily monitored and identifying mistakes with correction before it becomes a true defect. Their changes included;

- standardization and detail specification of work processes,
- improved mechanisms to spot unexpected or adverse events,
- active processes to find and fix mistakes,
- stopping processes when easy fixes cannot be immediately implemented.

Part of the process was staff empowerment to be able to speak up about mistakes. They used LEAN tools including surveys, walk rounds (Gembas), monthly review of defects and a feedback system for loop closure. They created an "Andon cord" policy to stop a dangerous care process. By generating new resources, they created a better incident reporting system, a hotline and a new communication structure. They refined the incident reporting process incorporating a grading system based on patient harm. In regards to results, 100% of the medical staff indicated that they were aware of the new program and over 6000 events were reviewed. They found that most reports were from nurses and non-clinical personnel and that managers and physicians contributed only 8% of the reports. One of their findings was that a quick response was key to successful improvement. Based on survey results they felt quality had improved, but unfortunately they had no comparable outcome data from controls (Furman and Caplan 2007).

In another general review, Dellifraine et al also evaluated Six Sigma and LEAN implementations from 1999 to 2008. They identified 177 articles that reported on clinical outcomes, processes of care and financial performance related to these implementations. They found that only 34 studies of either approach reported on the impact on patient outcomes and less than 33% of the articles used a statistical assessment to determine the quality of their results. Of the 34 articles they reviewed in depth, only 6 were on LEAN implementations which were primarily dealing with hospital Emergency Department logistics or Operating Room throughput. In general, the results cited in these studies were not rigorous on process, sparse for demonstrating improved quality and only 1 study had a comparison group. They concluded that there was very weak evidence that Six Sigma or LEAN implementations have improved healthcare quality. This review did not document successful results from a LEAN transformation for continuous improvement, innovation or culture at any institution. (DelliFraine et al 2010, DelliFraine et al 2013).

In another review of the literature, Poksinska evaluated LEAN "production" in health care as defined by; determining value from the patient point of view, application of value stream mapping and waste elimination by increasing continuous flow. Initially she identified 200 references, which was reduced to "around 30" based on the required content for analysis. She noted that most of the studies focused on understanding the voice of the customer and that Value Stream Mapping was the most common LEAN activity. The author felt that the LEAN principles of "pull" and "seeking perfection" were not well represented in the articles nor was driving the process of change through employee enabling or empowerment. She concluded from her review that there was no consistent approach to successful LEAN implementation in healthcare. Poksinska found that the common first step in implementation was to convince the staff that LEAN would work. The author noted that positive factors supporting the implementation included; staff commitment, personnel development practices and managerial support. She found that the most common positive result from LEAN applications was improved specific clinical processes and patient access. The studies also noted an improvement in employee identification of waste, improvement in problem solving and a calmer more organized work environment. Conversely, she noted several common problems encountered in LEAN implementations as;

- o Healthcare not being an industrial process,
- o Lack of educators,
- o Customer identification was not straightforward,
- o Retained hierarchical problems and silos,
- o Difficulties to improve an entire system because of fragmentation,
- o Lack of empirical data.

(Poksinska B 2010)

❧❦❧~:◇:∞

A review that focused on LEAN implementations in nursing practice was conducted by Brackett et al entitled "*Do LEAN practices lead to more time at the bedside.*" In this literature review, the authors considered LEAN methods applications specifically for the impact on bedside nursing and the "*Transforming Care at the Bedside*" (TCAB) initiative. This review included articles in which a LEAN tool was used as the primary mechanism for organizational restructuring. Similar to the other summary studies, the LEAN applications were felt to have positive results but with limited evidentiary support. The authors concluded there was limited evidence of a significant positive impact from the application of LEAN methods as it affected bedside nursing care (Brackett et al 2011).

From the NHS, Radnor et al performed a review of the literature and included 4 case studies of LEAN applications. In their review they noted that in most studies the "*impact on performance ... has often been less than anticipated*". The impact of LEAN caused "*enclosed projects that create pockets of best practice*" but not a system impact. In many studies they noted that LEAN implementations were met with resistance because they were considered new ways of managing clinical practice. Their explanation for the shortfalls in outcomes included; deeply institutionalized forces that complicate and constrain reform, competing and contradictory priorities, professional practices and habits resistant to change and organizational complexity as an obstacle to effective management. In their case studies of 4 institutions they noted variable levels of success from the different organizations with several similar areas of improvement including; reduction in waiting times, increased direct patient care, better understanding of care pathways and the cleaning up of the work environment. Overall, there was no significant impact to improve patient care outcomes or to improve as a system of care. The authors felt that part of the explanation for the poor results in their review was; a primary confusion of who was the real customer, the patient or the administrators, a disjointed approach within the organization to implementing LEAN, an over emphasis of tool based approaches and finally "hitting a glass ceiling" meaning not changing habitual behaviors for improvement or changing culture. Their explanation for these problems in the NHS LEAN applications included the structures controlling resources and the focus on waste but not on demand and capacity (Radnor et al 2012).

۞ﺝﭸ~·◇·ﺉ

Using a similar approach Lega et al also reviewed LEAN studies and applied their findings to a case study in an Italian NHS institution. In their literature review they noted how healthcare differed from other industries in which LEAN has been applied. Using multiple studies, they summarized recommendations to increase the probability of a successful implementation of LEAN in healthcare, which included;

> A holistic or system approach,
>
> An education program to develop a "*deep*" understanding of LEAN philosophy,
>
> The use of data for analysis and assessment,
>
> Focused management of the change to LEAN and associated re-design of clinical processes,
>
> The engagement of clinical staff,
>
> Avoidance of isolated LEAN improvement teams,
>
> Active engagement of senior leadership,
>
> Addressing the barriers of change related to misperceptions and the unfamiliar terminology used in LEAN.

Their case study at the Galliea Hospital, an institution considered to have made significant strides toward a LEAN transformation confirmed some of their recommendations. First, a system wide approach was adopted, second physician engagement did occur and third a successful educational program on LEAN principles and the benefits of applying LEAN was undertaken by the clinical staff. Overall they acknowledged that there was very limited evidence of success related to clinical outcomes in implementing LEAN, but they felt the Galliea Hospital was a successful case study (Lega et al 2013).

Historical Success of Quality Improvement in Healthcare

To put these disappointing reviews of the impact of LEAN in healthcare into context, the final study provides a bigger picture view; not specifically about LEAN but about other approaches applied to "save" healthcare over many decades. A study by Bigelow and Arndt reviewed industrial approaches as applied to healthcare. The authors reviewed the solutions to business and logistical challenges in healthcare from the 1960s to 2000, focusing on what was determined to be, at the time, *the only possible response for institutions that plan to survive the latest upheaval*". They noted the problems in each decade being eerily similar as were the criticisms of improvement failures as "not doing it right" and for "leadership failure". The recommendations were to approach improvements by adopting other industries practices. The authors note that these adaptations have all failed and have included; product line management, "Diversification", "re-engineering", "cost accounting", CQI and TQM. By their assessment, none of the hospitals realized any long term benefits for these efforts. The authors noted another pattern as well. The new business practices were advocated without proven merits in any area for efficacy, cost control, increased competitiveness or quality improvement; similar to what is occurring today. The reason for advocating without proven results was always the same, that businesses outside of healthcare "do it better". Similarly, the common solutions to the implementation problems were also the same regardless of the decade in which they were applied or for the approach. The solutions included; better clear communications, demonstration of top management support and increased personnel involvement. A recurring theme was that anecdotal evidence of success was widely promoted, rarely substantiated and results were rarely successful; paralleling our current experiences.

The authors recommend a reconsideration of the concept that business models from other industries are appropriate for hospitals. Additionally, they promote that the focus on using unproven business solutions to healthcare management from other industries may actually diminish a hospital administration's ability to solve the unique problems in healthcare. Their message is clear; the application of a process like LEAN without a major adjustment to healthcare will fail. For any significant system improvement approach for healthcare to be successful, it must recognize the uniqueness of the healthcare environment and it must adapt the approach (Bigelow and Arndt 2000). Additionally, their review, spanning 40 years and considering multiple improvement approaches, documents a consistent pattern of failure, which has persisted even when the reasons for prior failures have been identified. This suggests that there are factors that are accountable for failures in improvement efforts (like LEAN transformations) that have not been considered. Consequently, in the following chapters we will attempt to identify some of those factors that should be addressed to support a successful LEAN approach.

⊙⊰⊄~:◇:⊄

Conclusions

1. At this time, in general, healthcare organizations are not properly prepared for change, based on; morale, timing, the current healthcare environment, existing logistical efficiency or leadership.

2. Identified successful business management practices have had limited application in healthcare or function poorly in most healthcare organizations; particularly for managing demand and capacity.

3. Culture is a critical factor in system improvement and is generally undefined or not supportive of improvement in healthcare.

4. Other quality improvements systems (TQM, CQI) have had limited non-sustained success for specific processes and have provided limited or no sustained system improvement.

5. There is only antidotal evidence of successful process improvements for Healthcare organizations with LEAN and Six Sigma programs.

6. Based on the largest reviews, prior LEAN implementations have failed based on; the lack of being able to identify the customer and value, a disjointed system approach and an excessive focus on LEAN tools but not culture or habitual behaviors.

7. Healthcare organizational improvement programs relying on business practices from other industries have failed to create significant system improvements.

8. Overall, the reviews of LEAN implementations indicate that there is no strong evidence that the promised or expected system improvements have been realized.

9. Recommendations for greater success in LEAN implementations include; taking a system or holistic approach, a focus on education and data analysis as part of the process, a focus on staff engagement, managing misconceptions as part of the change approach and having an engaged and interactive leadership.

10. For successful improvement efforts in healthcare, unidentified reasons for failure should be sought and new approaches considered.

Summary of Problems Cited in the Literature About LEAN Applications

1. Leadership
2. Change management is not a core practice
3. Lack of education
4. Poor identification of the customer
5. Silos and fragmentation
6. Poor Culture (not supportive of improvement)

7. Poor data systems

8. Efforts not clearly linked to Quality

9. Distrust

10. Poor integration

11. Limited rewards systems

12. Limited feedback

13. Healthcare not like the other industries improved by LEAN

14. The need for early victories and the lack there of

15. Lack of Resources

16. Not enough information about LEAN

17. Poor Business Models

18. HR issues

19. Poor assessment of performance

20. Lack of addressing strategic problems

21. The false assumption that employees are comfortable with change

22. An isolated improvement program approach

23. Poor managers in change efforts

24. Poor alignment

25. Lack of employee control

26. Poor communication

27. An "unfair" process in implementation

28. A lack of success at prior innovations

29. Limited enforcement of change directive

"You can't improve until you get better but you can't get better until you improve"

Now what?

The study data on LEAN transformations and why they fail is limited. In an attempt to understand this better, each component of the organization; the leadership, management and the organizational staff will be reviewed for their impact on LEAN transformation failures. The failures will be considered in the context of; basic business concepts, culture, organizational roles, personal response to change and lack of innovation. The healthcare improvement paradox is that you can't significantly improve an area in healthcare unless you simultaneously enhance the entire system's function; this is the conceptualization that all elements in healthcare; business management and structure, personnel and culture are so entangled that no single system element can improve without improvement in the others. A concept reinforcing that healthcare organizations are both complicated and complex systems requiring overall system management. Hence, our approach will be to outline ways to improve in each of these areas to support LEAN. In an effort to avoid generalizations about LEAN transformations, the review will use recommendations from available foundational studies of successful change and transformation with specific examples of LEAN failures as a potential guide to success.

References

ASQ Hospitals see benefits of Lean and Six Sigma. Targeted news service March 2009.

Adams T, Williams, Brown V, Troxler H, Wood S, Tate A, McElroy J, Weber D, Rutala W. Using Lean/Six Sigma quality improvement methodologies to reduce central line-associated bloodstream infections (CLABSI) in a pediatric hospital. American Journal Infection Control 2010;38:e112.

Bigelow B and Arndt M. The more things change, the more they stay the same. Health Care Manage Rev 2000; 25:65-72.

Boon H, Verhoef M, O'Hara D, Findlay B. From parallel practice to integrate health care: a conceptual framework. BMC Health Services Research 2004;4:15-20.

Bossidy L and Charan R, Execution: The discipline of getting things done. 2002 Crown Business.

Brackett T, Comer L, Whichello R. Do Lean practices lead to more time at the bedside? Journal for healthcare Quality 2013;35:7-14.

Collins JC and Porras JI, Built to Last. 1994 Harper Business.

Covey SR. The 8th Habit, From Effectiveness to Greatness. Simon and Schuster 2004.

Crowe SD and Faulkner B. Lean management system application in creation of a postpartum hemorrhage prevention bundle on postpartum units. Obstet Gynecol 2014;S 1:45S.

DelliFraine JL, Langabeer JR, Nembhard IM. Assessing the evidence of Six Sigma and LEAN in the health care industry. Q Manage Health Care 2010;19:211-225.

DelliFraine JL, Wang Z, McCaughey D, Langabeer JR, Erwin CO. The use of Six Sigma in health care management: are we using it to its full potential? Q Manage Health Care 2013;22:210-223.

Fischman D. Applying Lean Six Sigma methodologies to improve efficiency, timeliness of care, and quality of care in an internal medicine residency clinic. Qual Manag Health Care. 2010;19:201-10.

Fried Y, Tiegs RB, Naughton TJ, Ashforth BE. Manager's reactions to a corporate acquisition: A test if an integrated model. Journal of organizational Behavior 1996;17:401-427.

Furman C and Caplan R. Applying the Toyota Production System: using a patient safety alert system to reduce error. Jt Comm J Qual Patient Saf. 2007;33:376-386.

Hage JT. Organizational innovation and organizational change. Ann Rev Sociology 1999;25:597-622.

Idemoto L, Williams B, Blackmore C. Using Lean methodology to improve efficiency of electronic order set maintenance in the hospital. BMJ Qual Improv Report 2016;5:u211725.w4724.

Johnson PM, Patterson CJ, O'Connell MP. Lean methodology: an evidence-based practice approach for healthcare improvement. Nurse Pract 2013;12:1-7.

Kanji G and Sa PM. Sustaining healthcare excellence through performance measurement. Total Quality Management and Business Excellence 2003;14:269-289.

Kovner AR and Rundall TG. Evidence-Based management reconsidered. Frontiers of Health Sciences Management 2006;22:3-22.

Kuo AM, Borycki E, Kushniruk A, Lee TS. A healthcare Lean Six Sigma system for postanesthesia care unit workflow improvement. Qual Manag Health Care. 2011;20:4-14.

Le RD, Melanson SE, Santos KS, Paredes JD, Baum JM, Goonan EM, Torrence-Hill JN, Gustafson ML, Tanasijevic MJ. Using Lean principles to optimize inpatient phlebotomy services. J Clin Pathol 2014;67:724-730.

Lega F, Marsilio M, Villa S. A system-wide approach to implement lean strategies: lesson from a case-study. AIDEA Conference 2013, Lecce 19-21, *www.aidea2013.it/docs/203_aidea2013_economia-aziendale.docx.*

Lilford RJ, Dobbie F, Warren R, Braunholtz D, Boadn R. Top rate business research: Has the emperor go any clothes? Health Services Management Research 2003;16:147-154.

Mannion R and Davies HT. Payment for Performance in healthcare. BMJ 2008;336:306-308.

Mantone J. Successful succession. Modern healthcare 2004;34:28-29.

Mazzocato P, Holden RJ, Brommels M, Aronsson H, Backman U, Elg M, Thor J. How does lean work in the emergency room? A case study of a lean-inspired intervention at the Astrid Lindgren Children's hospital, Stockholm, Sweden. BMC Health Serv Res 2012;12:28.

McNamara R Butler A, Baker C, Mullen J, Lenehan B, Grimes S, O'Donoghue H, Evans P, Liston M, Cummins F, Condon F. Use of Lean principals to improve flow of patients with fractured neck femor- the HOPE study. Ir Med J 2014;107:70-72.

Nohria N, Joyce W, Roberson B. What Really Works. Harvard Business Review 2003;81:2-52.

Oreg S, Vakola M, Armenakis A. Change in recipient's reactions to organizational change. A 60-year review of quantitative studies. J Appl Beh Sci 2011;47:461-524.

Peterson LA, Woodard LD, Urech T, Daw C, Sookanan S. Does pay for performance improve quality of care? Ann Intern Med 2006;145:265-272.

Poksinska B. The current state of Lean implementation in health care: literature review. Quality Management in Health Care 2010;19:319-329.

Rad A. The impact of organizational culture on the successful implementation of total quality management. The TQM Magazine 2006;18:606-614.

Radnor ZJ, Holweg M, Waring J. Lean in healthcare: the unfilled promise? Social Science and Medicine 2012;74:364-371.

Schneider EC and Eisenberg JM. Strategies and methods for aligning current and best medical practices. West J Med 1998;168:311-318.

Serrano L and Slunecka FW. Lean processes improve patient care. Heathcare executive 2006;21:36-38.

Shannon RP, Frnkak D, Grunden N, Lloyd JC, Herbert C, Patel B, Cummins D, Shannon AH, O'Neill PH, Spear SJ. U. Using real time problem solving to eliminate central line infections. Journal on Quality and Patient Safety 2006; 32:479-487.

Sherman J. Achieving REAL results with Six Sigma. Healthcare Executive 2006;21:8-14.

Stock GN, Mcfadden KL, Gowen CR. Organizational culture, critical success factors, and the reduction of hospital errors. International Journal of Production Economics 2007; 106:368-392.

Vest JR and Gamm LD A critical review of the research literature on Six Sigma, Lean and StuderGroup's Hardwiring Excellence in the United States: the need to demonstrate and communicate the effectiveness of transformation strategies in healthcare. Implementation Science 2009, 4:35.

Wanberg CR and Banas JT. Predictors and outcomes of openness to change in a reorganizing workplace. Journal of Applied Psychology 2000;85:132-14.

Chapter 3

Leadership in a LEAN Healthcare Innovation

"I wasn't planning to lead, I was standing in the back and then everyone turned around."

Avery Hiebert

The most common reason given for why LEAN transformations fail in healthcare is leadership

failure. This section focuses on the question of what leadership style and behavior is best to support

LEAN success. To start, since this material is aimed at healthcare personnel, we will briefly review

the current theories and assessment of leadership activities, leadership characteristics and principles.

Since the leadership approach must account for systems management, managing "emergent change"

and the execution of the change event itself, these topics are included in the review.

Leadership Theory and Style

As outlined by Goffee and Jones, leadership concepts originated in antiquity and have evolved over

time. In the 1800s, Weber promoted that leadership was typified by rationality without morality, or

"technical rationality" and was a destructive trait of leaders; conversely he promoted the charismatic

anti-bureaucratic leadership style. In the 1920s, the "trait theory" of leadership was popular, focusing

on successful personal characteristics and concepts, this evolved during the 1940's into "Style

modeled leadership" as exemplified by FDR's open, respectful and democratic personality. In the

1950's the "strong warrior persona" as a description of successful leaders, typical of the Cold War

era mentality was more dominant. The "Contingency theory" for leadership models, in which the

leader constantly adapts to the environment, evolved through the 1960's and 1970's. The 1980's saw

the emergence of the autocratic powerful leader during the era of corporate raiders. Recently, the model of "servant leaders" has emerged coincidently with the change in leadership roles to support the emergence of the knowledge worker. Goffee and Jones, through their studies of leadership material and experience with thousands of executives, have found that successful modern "inspirational" leaders show vulnerability, personal intuition and judgment. They use discipline and "tough empathy" in staff management and they capitalize on their own unique talents. As will be discussed below, a critical leadership requirement in implementing LEAN is to be an inspirational or a transformational leader, demonstrating the more modern leadership characteristics of servant leaders (Goffee and Jones 2015).

ⓞ✖❲~:Ｏ:△

Fundamental Concepts for Healthcare Leadership

Leadership of Knowledge workers

On a fundamental level, many healthcare leaders lead as if it was the industrial age; focusing on things and machines, an approach that demonstrates the lack of understanding that healthcare workers are knowledge workers. In the old world approach, staff are managed by shift work with carrot and stick incentives doled out from a powerful upper authority. The industrial age approach reinforces a position of authority at the top for all decisions and thereby suppresses initiative, independence and creates a vicious cycle of leadership dependence to direct and manage. In most medical organizations, physicians and nurses are listed as an expense, like equipment, not an investment. It's common to hear medical executives discuss their staff as "my docs" or "my nurses" as if they were machines to produce healthcare, forgetting that they are resources that independently use their talents and judgements for organizational success. If knowledge worker productivity is key for survival in the new world of healthcare, leaders can't use an industrial age control model to be successful. To improve knowledge worker productivity, leaders must apply fair treatment, kindness and act with fair principles that allow for creative knowledge workers to find meaning in their jobs; these are the critical roles for leadership in the modern healthcare organization. This leadership conceptualization fits with Peter Drucker's assertion,

> "One does not 'manage' people. The task is to lead people. And the goal is to make productive the specific strengths and knowledge of each individual."

Healthcare leadership must lead, not direct or manage, their organization to the belief that by implementing LEAN, there is a better way to care for patients.

ⓞ✖❲ ~:Ｏ:□

Leadership in Systems Management and Change; Complicated and Complex Systems

System theory and change management is not widely applied or understood in healthcare. It is included in this section because the lack of systems management and conceptualizations in healthcare is another form of leadership failure in efforts like LEAN.

Schein's theories on how to conceptualize organizations as a system and a culture proposes 3 levels of organizational culture; First the surface, which are artefacts of the organization such as the business plan and strategy. The second level is the espoused beliefs and values, standards for behaviors, and a foundation of understanding in the organization. The third level consists of the underlying assumptions that are the basis of the business. Usually, when different members of a "healthcare system" are asked to describe the specifics of the levels as listed above; it is clear, there is no system. This is the first point about systems theory and change, if the organization does not have the shared perceived commonalities as listed above, then the initial efforts at improvement must include creating those perceptions within the organization (Schein 1985).

If there is a system or organizational foundation in place, then the next step is to consider how to manage that system, this requires that it be categorized. Chapman points out that systems can be categorized as hard (complicated), like manufacturing and engineering with components that are relatively fixed as opposed to soft (complex) systems which are more pluralistic and diverse; healthcare is best described as both. In soft or complex systems, a comprehensive approach to change has been found to be more effective, which supports the concept of changing the entire system by LEAN through transformation. The lack of a comprehensive approach may be one explanation for the failure of improvement efforts in healthcare. (Chapman 2002).

⊚⊠℃~:◯:◯

"You won't find what you don't look for"

"Emergent change" in Complex Healthcare Systems

In a change effort like a LEAN transformation, the identification of "emergent change" is an additional level of management. In any significant system change implementation, the impact of change may lead to unanticipated results particularly in complex systems. In healthcare organizations (outside of hospitals), 47% were considered complex systems that experienced emergent change. The emergent nature and process of change in these organizations is described by Senge;

"Your understanding of the system will grow steadily as you calibrate these results and try new endeavors in a way that would not be possible if you were merely following someone's preconceived plan "(Senge 1999).

The emergent properties of systems dictate that the components will interact and cause effects which can only occur because of the change in the entire system; "synergistic effects". Senge conceptualizes this as the disassembly and dynamic complexity of system interactions over time that generates these emergent properties. The emergent system properties create two categories of problems. First, there are complicated problems for which there is agreement about the problem and its solution; these are problems bounded by time and resources. The second type of problems are considered complex, Wicked or "messes", in which uncertainty exists about the problem, the solution and the timeframe for resolution (Chapman 2002). To address this, Senge recommends taking a different system perspective to better understand the change reality; as he describes it *"reality is made up of circles but we see straight lines"*; we miss feedback loops and evolving events. Managing transformational change requires developing deep insight into the dynamic processes in the organization. This is why Senge recommends trying to identify the "feedback loops" in systems and learning from them for improvement (Senge 1990). Schein supports this type of system management and adds that the approach must start by exposing the underlying business assumptions an organization is based on and then to reconsider and reshape them as change emerges. (Schein 1985). To fail to reconsider the system characteristics, to not appreciate how to manage the system as its own entity or to miss the unexpected emergent events, all reflect pathways to failure in a LEAN transformation. The task to create an overall system perspective and to manage from that perspective is a leadership role.

Leadership System Management in Healthcare

Higgs and Rowland studied leadership behaviors in change efforts in different healthcare organizations. The sources for their study included their own 30 years of experience, discussions with colleagues, literature reviews and interviews with 40 subjects about 70 change events. They focused in their evaluation on the critical factors in successful organizational change and the associated leadership competencies. In the classification of system categories, the authors classified healthcare as complicated, rich in detail and complex. Their assessment is that most hospital organizations are complex and undergo emergent types of change throughout the entire system with a low level of control. They concluded that, for most healthcare organizations, change is unpredictable, evolving and requires different approaches for different situations (Higgs and Rowland 2007). Pettigrew and Pendlebury et al support these concepts with the statement:

"Change management is a difficult art… those responsible for it are faced with extremely complex phenomena against which traditional management methods and models are virtually useless" (Pettigrew 1985 and Pendlebury et al 1998).

Various authors and studies promote that change efforts can fail for a lack of understanding the differences in system classifications, complicated verses complex. (Litchenstein 1996). As previously mentioned, while one solves problems in complicated systems, in complex systems, problems are more system dilemmas and are not amenable to a direct solution. They also agreed that successful change cannot be implemented in a complex system with a top down approach. (Wheatley 1993, Wheatley and Kellner-Rogers 1996, Stacey 1996, Shaw 1997). Jaworski and Scharmer proposed that the core practices for success in dealing with complex system change are; First to see reality with new eyes and to identify emerging patterns. Second to envision; to provide a crystalizing vision and intent that is injected into the reality of change. Third, is to provide a focus on execution and to be ready to capitalize on new opportunities (Jaworski and Scharmer 2000).

"You just need to commit to it, and then you will figure out how to make it work"

In summary, these studies found that change events in healthcare occur in complicated and complex systems and that most change was accompanied by emergent events. The process of change was often messy and in a sense unstructured. The characteristics of the successful processes effecting these changes were those with a focus in the workplace and in which the staff frequently developed improvement through novel mixes of shared practices. Additionally, they found lateral or trans-departmental connections helped the improvement process succeed. They found that successful experimentation for improvement was used. During the change events that were successful the staff identified unusual or unexpected connections in processes and then shared knowledge and transferred new behavioral standards, often utilizing informal networks and alliances. As has been seen in other studies, small group activities were critical for success as was working with individuals from outside of the mainstream organization (Sammut-Bonnici and Wensley 2002, Depew and

Weber 1995). Leadership should understand and accommodate all of these findings as part of systems management in change.

Leadership Roles for System Management

To reinforce the concept that leadership must act by system management for a successful LEAN implementation, there are certain specific leadership roles that have been identified for success. For change involving most of the organization, Wheatley promotes that a leadership role should incorporate a transformational "edge" or approach to be successful (Wheatley 1992). Higgs and Rowland concluded that for leadership to be successful in managing a system through change entails the role of "framing" by the leadership and increasing the capability of the staff (Higgs and Rowland 2007). Additionally, they also found a greater success rate in change efforts with;

1. Leadership that recognizes complexity,
2. By high levels of involvement by leaders,
3. A leadership approach of facilitation and enabling (Higgs 2003),
4. Through reframing by leadership (Lichtenstein 1997),
5. By leadership building capacity in others for change (Conner 1992).

They found that less success in change occurred if the leaders believed that change is simple, linear and can be implemented locally, as a "Do it yourself" approach by local managers and staff. A surprising finding was that the personal execution of tasks, persuasion, or influence by leaders to drive change was not related to success.

A supporting study on the role of leadership in healthcare improvement was conducted by the Development Dimensions International company. They surveyed healthcare organizations and correlated perceptions of healthcare leadership roles as they affected quality as measured by HCAHPS (Hospital Consumer Assessment of Healthcare Providers and Systems. The survey found that leadership quality drives performance on patient satisfaction through 2 primary areas; talent management and the development of culture. In addition, they found that top tier hospitals for patient satisfaction were those in which leaders demonstrated that they valued change and innovation (DDI 2013).

The implications of these studies are that leadership's role in system management is critical to improvement efforts like a LEAN transformation. Leaders are more effective if they understand system dynamics, working through others and avoiding a top down approach. These results are also consistent with other study recommendations that leaders should act as "agents" for change throughout the organization and by providing change tools rather than through their own personal efforts. (Pascale 1999, Senge 1997, Buchanan and Boddy 1992). Studies have found that successful change was promoted by leaders in creating capacity, which is defined as building the ability in individuals and the organization to change and adapt. (Conner 1992, Kouzes and Posner 1998, Higgs 2003, Higgs and Rowland 2000, 2001, Goffee and Jones 2000). These findings also support the concept that a transformational leadership role will be the most successful in healthcare improvement. The leadership role in coaching and career development of others are examples of specific activities for successful improvement. (Higgs and Rowland 2000, 2001, Giglio et al 1998). All of these leadership attributes and roles are guiding principles for leadership in a LEAN Transformation; focus on the worksite, staff empowerment, communication, and experimentation.

⊚✸✄~:O:OO

"Leadership is the ability to get individuals to work together for the common good and the best possible results while at the same time letting them know they did it themselves."

"The worst things you can do for others are the things they could and should do for themselves"
paraphrase of John Wooden, A Game Plan for Life

Leadership activities in LEAN implementations
Leadership Standard Work: Current State
This section is about what leaders really do and the required modifications for a LEAN effort. As recounted by Thomas Peters, based on his studies, leaders are often shielded from day to day realities, with too many meetings, and multiple interruptions. Subsequently, leadership decisions are often based on a single presented option because it requires an urgent response. Leadership usually focuses on fighting fires and acute issues and that they are often shielded from bad news or difficult decisions (Peters 2001). To implement LEAN, this approach to leadership activities will result in failure. If there is any doubt what leaders and senior managers are really doing, they should engage in a leadership exercise to assess their activities. They can follow Steven Covey's recommendations on personal time management and create a time management matrix or the organization can undertake the Blue Ocean leadership exercise of creating the "As Is Leadership Canvases" and the "Leadership Grid" analytical tool (Covey 1989, Kim and Mauborgne 2014). The leadership will need to restructure their time for the critical roles of visioning, promotion and staff interaction during the

transition. While firefighting is important, leaders in LEAN implementations will need to delegate more and address critical organizational issues in real-time; not to intervene but to help managers and staff to respond in a rapid fashion. Leaders must lead in a LEAN implementation, not just manage. This is accomplished by leaders aligning people, not organizing them. Management efforts provide the logistics and structure, but leadership aims at making the staff believe that the change is a real process.

For leaders there must be a consistency of words and actions to support the LEAN implementation. This is achieved through the coordinated use of weekly meetings, discussion groups, quarterly department meetings, monthly open forums, newsletters, anonymous questions, and metric charts; leaders use visual communication of values to communicate. The importance of the staff's alignment with the organization's vision and mission is that it creates a sense of security in decisions and actions. The result of leadership providing alignment is energy; by allowing staff to achieve, belong, recognize, have self-esteem, and live up to ideals. In a lean implementation, leaders involve staff in decisions supporting their sense of control during the process. Leaders must then provide coaching, feedback, role modeling, recognition and reward success. The goal of all of these activities is to make the staff feel that they are cared for as individuals.

The ability of leaders to implement change is based on:

1. Their track record
2. The content of their message
3. The integrity of their leadership
4. The trust they have created.

These points are stressed to emphasize that leadership in change must lead as opposed to managing; successful change leaders focus on leadership roles and delegate management activities.

Leaders versus Managers

As reviewed by Abraham Zaleznik in his article "Managers and Leaders" leaders and managers fulfill different roles and in a LEAN implementation, knowing the differences in their focus is critical for a successful application. These activities include:

1.   Influence-Leaders use power to influence thoughts and actions of others. As noted by

Zaleznik "*An organization is a system with a logic of its own, with all the weight of tradition and inertia. The deck is stacked in favor of the tried and proven way of doing things and against taking of risks and striking out in new directions"*. Managers support this process, but it is critical in a LEAN implementation that leaders use their position to propel the staff forward to change. While managers monitor change, leaders continue to influence and adjust the initiative.

2. Personality- In general, managers have different personalities then leaders; they focus on goals, resources, structures, people and problem solving. Managers must operate efficiently and they find enjoyment in that efficiency. Conversely, in change, leadership generates disorder and encourages rule breaking; to see what happens. Leaders must be able to embrace uncertainty and be comfortable with delegation to others. In a LEAN implementation it is critical that leaders, through their interaction with the staff, demonstrate the differences from managers by embracing change and the intrinsic disorder.

3. Shaping Ideas- Leaders approach goals in a very different way than managers. For manager's goals are impersonal necessities, created by others. Leaders actively interact with goals, they shape ideas in a personal way that reflects vision and values and they "mold" culture. This role is critical in a LEAN implementation to support the change process; to live the vision and values, in other words to create a new culture.

4. New approaches. Managers are enablers, planners that focus on getting the job done as described. Leaders go for new approaches and new options, and when necessary, embrace the risk of uncertain results. This is a critical difference for leaders in a LEAN implementation in that they must publicly embrace new approaches while acknowledging the risk of failing. As noted by Zaleznik *"a key difference from managers and leaders is chaos versus order. Leaders tolerate chaos, the lack of structure, but managers seek order and control, as they are addicted to disposing of problems"*. This is a critical difference in that it emphasizes that embracing change is typical of successful leaders but is not typical of successful managers (Zaleznik 2004).

5. Vision-Vision is the hallmark of leadership. By looking for unmet needs, areas to improve, potential in applications, leaders then create new vision. Leaders then provide a compelling and convincing argument of their vision to the staff. In LEAN implementations, successful leadership presents their vision and then gathers the staff's feedback and recommendations to make this an inclusive process.

"I know where we need to go, but I need your help to understand how to get there."

The vision must provide the social identity for the organization's employees and reflect just principles in the creation of that new social identity. The new vision must reflect the critical priorities of the future organization. Managers provide a secondary supportive role in creating this vision.

6. Personnel- Managers usually have a "practical approach" with people, which may lead to a lack of empathy, a focus on compromises and the balancing of different interests to keep things moving. Managers relate to personnel by the role they play. Leaders don't focus on the process or the roles of the staff. Leaders must look at their staff in a LEAN implementation as knowledge workers with tacit knowledge and unleash their talent for improvement. While leaders start this process, it should be continued by managers, which requires a new way of relating to their personnel.

7. Signaling-Managers often signal but don't "message" about decisions. They frequently provide inconclusive information that avoids directness, which can cause employee detachment and the feeling of being manipulated. Leaders must provide clear messaging in a LEAN effort that is properly conveyed through their managers. Leaders use events, symbols and behavior to create a metaphor that further enhances the messages provided.

Leadership and Management Complementary Behaviors

As related by John Kotter in "What Leaders Really do" he promotes that management and leadership should be in complementary roles and this is another critical factor for the success of a LEAN implementation. Managers plan, budget, allocate, organize, communicate, delegate, monitor, and problem solve. Leaders set direction, vision, strategies for change, align people, motivate and inspire. Managers stabilize, but leaders push for change and move both of these contradictory efforts to work together. Leaders prepare organizations for change and push staff forward; managers help them cope with that struggle. If we conceptualize management as coping with complexity and then subsequently bringing forth quality in product or service, then Leadership is about creating change that is necessary for that productivity to continue to be successful in the future. Leaders must overcome problems to change by creating new values and engendering the emotions necessary to drive the process. Leaders set the direction of change which in turn creates vision and strategy. This is a process that requires a deep understanding of business, analysis and intelligent risk taking. Managers adjust behaviors to make these efforts productive (Kotter 2001). This teamwork of leaders and managers working in a coordinated and reciprocal fashion is a critical attribute to bring about change, like LEAN.

⑨✂《~:O:△△

> *"Change cannot be predicted, yet the ability to harness it can be developed"*
>
> *Caroline Conway*

Evolution of Leadership roles in Change

A brief explanation about what seems to be paradoxical in the leadership approach in a LEAN implementation; there is an evolution of leadership behaviors that may seem contradictory, because the leadership approach evolves during the process of change. As will be emphasized in the section regarding CEO behavior, initially, in a change effort, leadership is very directing, promoting and shaping. To properly frame vision and to increase the capabilities of the staff, it requires a definitive top down approach prior to the activation stage of change. However, after the change process has been initiated, all leadership including the CEO, must transition their approach to coaching, enabling and empowering staff. At this stage the monitoring for new emerging unanticipated events and system management becomes an important role for leadership. Leaders change to asking the right questions, teaching and encouraging. The failure of leaders to back off from directly managing the change is another reason that change efforts fail.

⑨✂《~:O:△□

> *"Change- A process, not an event"*
>
> *Ryan Estis*

Leadership failure in LEAN Implementation Planning and Assessment

Because Leadership has accountability for all organizational activities, it is easy to blame Leadership failure for the majority of LEAN implementation failures. This is often the consensus of LEAN consultants about failed LEAN events. Matt Hanrion, a lean expert notes that many LEAN leaders create a poor rollout that is not properly integrated into the organization. Toussaint and Berry note *"for some leaders …interest in LEAN creates fertile ground for rushing something that cannot be rushed, misunderstanding something that is not easily understood, and underinvesting in something that requires ongoing, multifaceted investment.*" They note that a common leadership failure in LEAN rollouts to be in the planning phase, specifically a poor initial assessment of the ability of the organization and personnel to change. Because of this, the leadership then fails to provide the necessary education and training to assure the LEAN program will move forward. The leadership also misses the opportunity to preemptively evaluate obstacles and future problems in the implementation (Hanrion 2013, Toussaint and Berry 2013).

Management of Resources and Priorities. Leadership Failures

1. Failure to make "Change" a priority

Leadership is about decision making and prioritizing. A common error in change management approaches is to not eliminate competitive initiatives which distract staff from change: this is particularly true in medicine. For LEAN to be successful, it must be the priority and considered critical to the mission at the change effort initiation; incorporating this precedence into clinical medicine is the most fundamental challenge.

2. A common leadership failure in resourcing LEAN is to starve it for budget and staff. Healthcare is the poster child for being "*penny wise and pound foolish*". This is particularly true when one considers the planning and resource allocation to start the LEAN implementation. If LEAN is initiated in a piecemeal fashion, which is often the case with limited resources, it will not realize the significant benefits that LEAN should provide and most efforts will fail from the lack of significant visible progress.

> "*Time is the scarcest resource and unless it is managed, nothing else can be managed.*"
>
> *Peter Drucker*

3. LEAN Time

It seems obvious but a critical factor for staff in improvement efforts is to schedule time to participate in and sustain those improvements. If improvement activities are competing with other tasks on the very full plates of the healthcare staff, the implementation will fail. The responsibilities of leading and managing a Lean implementation cannot be an add-on activity, but must replace other obligations. In the planning phase, this must occur through prioritizing, deferring activities or creating efficiencies in current work that creates capacity to assume these new roles. We need to apply Lean principles to individual schedules, management systems and leadership methods if we are to be successful in creating the required time. It is inappropriate to just tell the managers they need to support the Lean activity then complain when it doesn't happen. Early in the implementation, leadership must work with the managers and map the value streams of a manager's activities and priorities looking for waste and non-value added work (Covey or Blue Ocean Waste Exercise). The use of Lean principles to redesign and define their daily, weekly, monthly and annual standard work with metrics and visual management is the introductory exercise to begin to understand LEAN prior to implementation. The creation of time in the schedule for LEAN activities, 10-20% of work time, will be a required change for the entire organization and a stiff challenge for healthcare. But, this is a defining commitment from leadership to LEAN success, organizations unable or unwilling to make this commitment should reconsider embarking on a LEAN effort.

✗✗✗✖~:○:□

✖✗✗~:○:△✖

4. Failure to initiate physician engagement with leadership

A major problem for healthcare leadership is the lack of physician engagement with administration leaders and managers during the change initiative. There are very few organizations in which all the staff physicians had the opportunity to contribute to the organizations visioning process and mission statement. This divide between physicians and administration is further compounded in the implementation of the strategic plans. When you consider that most physicians are unaware of the strategic plan for their organization, it's understandable why the different groups work at cross purposes. The lack of understanding between the physicians and their administrative leadership is a core problem in execution of most healthcare activities, but even more so for improvement or change. This occurs, in part, because of their differences in background and training and also because of the lack of effort to align incentives.

When we consider the problem of physician engagement within medical organizations, Covey outlines an approach for executing plans and approaches to bring groups together. His list of drivers of execution to align groups includes;

1. Empowerment- Address organizational structures such as governance and job redesign to support engagement.

2.   Clarity-Promote common vision and mission for all.

3.   Accountability- Define expectations.

4.   Commitment- Support the staff's ability to embrace the organization as a complete person.

5.   Translation- Translate vision and mission into behaviors and expected results.

6.   Synergy- Aim at "win- win solutions" for the physicians, staff and organization.

Each of these categories represents a common failure in the relationship between physicians and administration for most healthcare organizations and is unfortunately critical for LEAN to succeed (Covey 2004). For any enterprise to be efficient and maximally effective, physician leaders need to fully partner with the organization's administration, share in leadership function and most importantly create a "Guiding Coalition" of physicians, nurses and hospital staff. This is a parallel group to the administrative leadership group. Both groups will then need to be integrated for full representation. This is a different type of engagement at a higher level than is typical of hospital physician staff activities such as the perfunctory medical executive committees with a voluntary chief of staff.

ⓈⓍℂ~:O:ΔⓄⓄ

5. Failure to gage resistance to change

Another area of leadership failure in a Lean implementation is the lack of appreciation of the staff resistance or unresponsiveness to change, particularly at the senior manager and lower leadership levels. In LEAN there is the common misconception that there will be no layoffs with a LEAN implementation. This is often promoted to assure the staff that their improvement efforts will not eliminate their position; they will be assured a position in a re-deployment. The problem is that some leaders misconstrue this to mean that no one will be forced to leave if they do not become a LEAN advocate. Successful LEAN implementations, starting with Taiichi Ono at Toyota and with other companies such as Porsche or Pratt Whitney, found resistant senior leadership that did not embrace LEAN and were terminated (Womack and Jones 1996). Senior leadership must be prepared to push out anyone that will not support LEAN early in the process, failing to do so will kill any LEAN effort. Quint Studer describes that same necessity at the manager and staff level for "low performers" in his approach to organizational improvement (Studer 2003). A critical point about the leadership approach is to start with a very aggressive assessment and planning effort and then a top down promotion of vision, mission and strategy followed directly by implementation. When it then becomes apparent that there is resistance at senior levels, action to correct the problem must be swift.

ᎩᏍᏓ~:Ꭴ:ᎠᎬ

"Empty promises empty the soul of an entire workforce."

Rob Wyse

6. Change Vision Killers

The final areas to address in LEAN implementation failures are the vision killers. When leadership and upper level management demonstrate behaviors that are antithetical to what they are proposing as the organizational values and behaviors for a LEAN transformation, they lose all credibility and destroy LEAN. This failure of appropriate leadership modeling is rampant in healthcare. Examples include administrative staff refusing to provide emergency parking for physicians attending to urgent problems but use the same areas for themselves or the physicians that always park illegally in the emergency department entrance for convenience. Lack of integrity, lack of accountability, bad behavior and lack of respect makes leadership untrustworthy and incapable to realize a LEAN transformation. Leadership cannot be derived from position for successful change movements any more then shadows can function as people; leaders must live their values.

ᎩᏍᏓ~:Ꭴ:ᎠᏇ

Formula for Change: A Planning Assessment Tool

The prior sections have emphasized the importance of assessment and planning to support a successful LEAN implementation. A new modification of the formula for change is provided to help formulize that process. A theory that may help in understanding how organizational change may occur or fail has been offered by David Gleicher's and Beckhard & Harris (Cady et al 2014, Beckhard & Harris 1987). For Leadership, this can be a valuable initial exercise to assess the organization's capability for change and then create an approach that leads to success. Gleicher's modification is the following formula:

$$C = (D \times V) + A > R$$

Change will occur when the current dissatisfaction (D) within the system is coupled with a clear vision (V) of the future and specified in actions (A) that are larger than the resistance to change (R) present in the organization. I suggest a modification that is a better fit for healthcare by providing additional variables to consider;

$$C \approx E \times (D \times V) + A > R \, (DF \, \Delta + \Delta \, S \, /Fi \, \Delta)$$

In this modification of the formula we add an emotional multiplier (E) to the promoters of change. Part of the reason to consider the emotional content of the visioning process and communication is to engage the work force at a personal level. Studies have shown that to break habits is itself an emotional event and it can be supported by an emotional appeal. Since change is a personal matter, even if it is an organizational event, this formula should be applied by leaders and managers for each employee to try to anticipate and manage change. As Kotter proposes, the organization needs a sense of urgency to motivate progress and if this is not provided by an external event, it needs to be created by the leadership. This can be accomplished by using emotional content in the visioning process and communication to further engage the work force; to create urgency (Kotter 1998). On the resistance side of the formula, I have added variables for the resistance to change including the difficulty of the change process (DFΔ) which is the required support for "unfreezing" the habits that constitute the status quo. This is an assessment of the required change in their daily activities which might include new skills, training requirements or new abilities. A common organizational failure is the financial restrictions that limit investing in "up skilling" employees, revamping workplaces, or enhancing other performance support systems, which results in undercutting the ability to change. The percentage of time a new process differs from the prior method can be used to estimate the change difficulty when combined with an estimate of additional procedure complexity or higher skill levels that are required in change. Status change (Δ S) and financial change (Fi Δ), if negative, can be important contributors to resistance independently and merit a review for each employee in the planning phase. This formula application can be created qualitatively and used to adjust resources to those threatened by change. For example, a negative financial impact of change represents an obvious deterrent, regardless of the prioritization of the change value to an employee; this can be a nonstarter.

In summary, once a sense of discomfort is clear to employees about their current situation versus what they want from the aftermath of change, people are more open to adjustment. Using the change formula can represent a good exercise for leadership and management to gage resistance to change in their direct reports when it is combined with asking the right questions such as:

- Do the employees see a loss in change-status, belonging, and finances?
- Is there a lack of trust that the change will be beneficial?
- Is there insufficient knowledge or skill limitations affecting change that will impact the organization?
- Is there fear related to the lack of ability to change, fear of job loss, fear of uncertainty?
- Does the staff feel that they have the time for the LEAN implementation?
- Is the timing to make this change a priority wrong?

- Are the resources insufficient to support the implementation?

Involvement of the staff in providing answers is critical in this exercise to allow for discussion and education about the current situation and the need for change. The steps in this process are for each supervisor, manager and leader to assess their direct reports and report back to leadership on their organization's readiness for change.

᙭᙭ᘔ᙭◉~:○.○

◉᙭℃ ~:○.□℞

Visioning in Healthcare for Change

Visioning provides a clear sense of the overall direction that guides behavior in change. As critical as visioning is, it almost never includes healthcare providers in healthcare organizations. A clear engaging vision must be presented, disseminated to all the staff in a way that is encouraging and inspiring and followed by a request for feedback and possible amendment. From vision we form action steps that represent the specific activities that will fulfill the strategic plan. For leaders the first steps are to engage the staff in the process of change; to help them identify their current reality and then contribute to shaping a new vision. Leadership is about promoting a vision and asking the right questions; "how are we going to do it?" and "What are you going to do?" to diminish resistance. Resistance to change within an organization comes in many forms; the organization "identity", a type of culture, or a restrictive budget. Resistance may stem from poor organizational alignment with the organization's values. It is through a convincing delivery of the vision of the organization's success that Leaders can overcome the many obstacles to change. As was previously mentioned, it is absolutely critical for the physicians, nurses and other healthcare providers to understand and support this vision if they are expected to make it a reality.

"It's like letting go of the child riding the bike just after the training wheels came off"

The Chief Executive Officer

There are several important issues that are specific for the CEO of a healthcare organization in implementing change. The CEO must be fully committed to change, a true believer that must then convince the rest of leadership, and other key management starting with the hospital or organization's board. This parallels Jack Welsh's approach that made his company internalize his vision, identify with him, and think his way (Welsh 2001). In LEAN, this is the only role for *"heavy handed"* leadership, to start the change process and to require the necessary commitment. As the

LEAN implementation begins, it should be clear that those that will not at least try to participate in LEAN or are actively undermining the efforts will be terminated. A recurring regret of leaders in prior LEAN Transformations was failing to terminate the upper leadership resistant to change, early in the process. During the planning sessions for the implementation, the leadership and managers should try to identify the staff that are unlikely to convert to LEAN. As noted by James Womack et al, *"Leaders who wish to change their organizational culture cannot do so by edict. They must intervene and require people to behave differently, allowing them to experience a better set of results. As this process is repeated, a different set of values and beliefs, a new culture will evolve"*. But this process must start with a definitive top down direction from the CEO and Board. This is why Womack also says, *"There will be a need for strong, directive leadership"* (Womack et al 2005). After the initial decision is made to go forward, the CEO should strive for actual cultural authority, a level of authority above position, title or reputation. This is leadership, not of things, but of people based on trust. William Pagonis points out that the critical attributes of leaders in this situation are expertise and empathy; to develop trust and cultural authority from a *"thousand undramatic settings"*. In his article, "Leadership in the Combat Zone" he notes;

"Leadership is only possible where the ground has been prepared in advance, these initial directives are the first steps in ground preparation, to allow empowerment of managers and staff (Pagonis 2001).

Creating cultural authority is an art form; the art of enabling individuals and groups. These leaders focus on developing common meanings and values that truly connect the hearts and minds of the staff. Leaders must leave *"the fumes of personality"* as noted by Iris Murdoch and move to the mindset in which the most important leadership question is *"how can I help"* (Rowe 2006). In this role the CEO is much more akin to a politician trolling for votes and support; campaigning to get the staff on board with the program.

> *"The plans of most chief executives I studied seem to exist only in their heads... as flexible, but often specific, intentions."*
>
> *Henry Mintzberg*

In regards to the CEO's action plans, she/he must plan an employee assessment process, and a new visioning process. The critical first step in implementation is that the CEO must create the most important structural change, to create 10-20% of paid time specifically for LEAN activities for the entire organization. This step is the first and most definitive move for the organization toward transparency, something that is foreign to most healthcare organizations and will be a challenge that only a CEO can take on early in the process. To support LEAN activities, the CEO will need to create 3 support structures.

- A new LEAN Educational Program,
- A LEAN Data Program
- A new LEAN Communication System.

☞☧☞C~:O:□△

Michael Balle in his article, "A LEAN leap of faith", further explains LEAN, not as a religion but as a scientific mindset applied to business. He suggests that for success the CEO must take the leap of faith and make LEAN the strategy. This is the only way to involve every employee all the time in problem solving. Every day each employee should strive to improve safety, quality, flexibility and productivity and apply the scientific method to test if the current practice is really the best way. This is the most important attribute for the CEO, to make LEAN the focus, the priority and the mission. Without this commitment, most LEAN efforts fail (Balle 2013).

Leadership Balance and Competencies in Change

In his book, "*Leading for Change*", Ralph Jacobson discusses the 5 challenges faced by every leader in change events:

1. To Reframe the future
2. To Develop Commitment
3. To Teach and Learn
4. Community Building
5. To Balance Paradox

This list is another reminder of how successful change works; coincidentally, these are all LEAN ideologies and approaches. The final issue on balancing paradox emphasizes a problematic role for healthcare leadership in change. Jacobson describes paradox as a decision point with 2 extreme different options, neither obviously correct or without consequences. He makes the point that if a paradox is treated as a problem it will most likely make things worse. To balance the paradox requires maximizing the good aspects of both alternatives while minimizing their negatives. A leader must know what influences the balance between the two options, how to identify imbalance and how to restore equilibrium. Balancing the different attitudes and perspectives of diverse factions of the organization, is a leadership's critical role during change (Jacobson 2011). A LEAN implementation requires good leadership judgment as to when or on what to intervene. A key concept is that paradoxes must be confronted and unlike problems, they will not be solved, but can be balanced through ongoing efforts. This reinforces the concept that LEAN leadership must use a system approach to identify problems and paradoxes and then solve one and balance the other. Physician engagement is a good example of both a problem and a paradox to which Jacobson's 5 principles should be applied. Most physicians are skeptics (it is part of medical training) who's identities originates from their specialized profession and individual practice. These characteristics contribute to why physicians are generally poor organizational members. In a LEAN implementation, physician leaders cannot be controlled by their ego, to not interpret all interactions on a personal basis, and to recognize the value of non-physician managers and leaders. Healthcare administrators should also acknowledge the importance of physician executives and not require that they pay their salaries with clinical work. We would never ask administrators to supplement their positions with additional office duties, so should it be true for physician leaders. Physician leadership positions are fulltime jobs in a transformation. Both administrators and physicians need to work together through engagement to lead their constituency through the challenge of change and to attain balance.

⊕✳℄~:○:□□

LEAN Leadership Attributes

John Gallagher of Simpler Consulting in his article "The Three Must-Have attributes of leadership in LEAN" stresses accountability, respect and the need for improvement. Gallagher points out that, in his experience transformations require strong leadership and notes the necessary leadership skills are uncommon in healthcare. This is where training in "leadership standard work" is critical for a LEAN transformation (Gallagher 2016). Part of this training is <u>learning to achieve results through others</u>. Engaged LEAN Leaders promote accountability and engagement as essential elements in successful transformations along with respect for people and continuous improvement. George Koenigsaecker's makes a more eloquent statement about what leadership attributes a required for LEAN success; drive, drive, drive; drive for learning, mentoring, continuous improvement and execution. The origins of these recommendations come from the characteristics of historical Toyota leaders;

- o A desire to lead,
- o A desire to work hard,

    o   A desire to get results through others,

    o   A desire and ability to mentor,

    o   A desire to pursue perfection.

At Toyota they referred to their LEAN leaders as a "Warrior Class"; fearless about pushing ahead, committed to improve, to go the extra mile, and committed to a sense of mission.

For a LEAN implementation, Koenigsaecker lists the Lean attributes and behaviors that leaders must represent or demonstrate for success.

1.   To serve the customer,

2.   To pursue the right way, demonstrate integrity, practice active honesty,

3.   Decide carefully, implement quickly,

4.   Practice brutal honesty and humility,

5.   Use "Hansei (self-reflection)" deep reflection on personal improvement,

6.   Speak honestly and with respect,

7.   Learn "Genchi Gembutsu (go and see),"

8.   Deliver, meet the challenges,

9.   Mentor and role model-use 360 reviews and monitor progress.

Assessing these attributes is an important educational and assessment exercise in the planning phase of a LEAN implementation. The exercise constitutes a real time survey of leadership attributes as demonstrated in behaviors as assessed by their colleagues and staff, similar to the Blue Ocean exercise for leadership activities. This is followed by a discussion of the importance of these attributes for success.

Another point made by Koenigsaecker that applies to leadership attributes is in how they govern. He recommends that the leadership consider their approach in 3 areas; the way the organization evaluates work, how the work is organized or conducted and how value is identified and rewarded. In his opinion governance is the biggest reason for failure in LEAN. This is another leadership attribute that deserves assessment in the planning phase of LEAN (Koenigsaecker 2013).

"I used to lead by example but it was too much work."

Figure 3.1 The energy to move the organization (See figure legends)

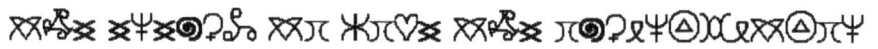

⟫⟪⚡⟫ ⟫⟨⟫⊛⟫⟫ ⟫⟫⟨ ⟫⟨⟪⟫ ⟫⟪⚡⟫ ⟨⊛⟫⟪⟫⊙⟫⟪⟫⊙⟨⟫

Leadership in a LEAN Transformation

John Kotter in his article "Leading Change: Why transformation efforts fail" has provided an outline about leadership failures as they apply to a step by step process for transformational change. He notes "*Leaders who successfully transform business do eight things right, and they do them in the right order*". Based on his experience with over 100 companies, he provides the following recommendations:

1.   Create a sense of urgency.

This is to convince the organization about the need for change. He notes that 50% of companies fail at this first step alone. The reasons include:

- Underestimating the difficulty in driving people out of their comfort zone (change assessment).

- Overestimating the success of their messaging on urgency (change communication)

- A lack of patience (leadership standard work)

- Paralysis regarding risks and bad outcomes (Leadership commitment)

Kotter notes that it often takes a change in leadership to begin transformations. He is also clear that successful transformations require delivering the "Talk". The "Talk" is a frank, brutally honest presentation of the dire current circumstances. As described by one executive, "to make the status quo seem more dangerous than launching into the unknown". The goal is to be sure that 75% of the organization is convinced to change at the outset. For LEAN, this is a requirement and it emphasizes the need for the CEO and leadership to work with their care givers to convince them of the need for change. Physicians, in particular, are difficult to get on board and require additional time and effort.

2. Create a coalition.

This step is required; to ensure support from top leadership and those in power or in prominent positions. First create a group committed to 2 principles, the love of their organization and the belief of "excellent performance through renewal". This assemblage should cut through hierarchy and requires developing a new process for shared assessment of the current organizational problems with recommendations for new directions. The goal is for this group, through special meetings or retreats, to form an identity and bond of commitment to lead change. Kotter notes this effort can fail if a company does not value teamwork. For this to occur, leaders need strategic foresight, a shrewd sense of timing and political acumen to build stable, workable coalitions. For LEAN transformations in healthcare, this is a primary stumbling block, because in healthcare, you need 2 coalitions. The administration must have their guiding coalition, but another must exist for the healthcare providers. Very few healthcare organizations have enough healthcare providers in their administrations to be considered inclusive of physicians and nurses. Prominent physicians and nurses must have their own guiding coalition to create a successful transformation, that then interacts and integrates with the administration coalition. Without this second coalition, despite the administration's efforts, the transformation will not succeed.

ⓢ✖C~:○:☐☆

3. Develop vision and strategy

There are four components to this process. First, while vision may begin with a board member or the CEO, it must be developed further by the guiding coalitions. Second, the vision must be translated to an appealing, embracing message about the future direction of the organization. Third, the message should be developed into a direct, clear, easily repeated communication of 5 minutes or less in length. Fourth, the vision should obviously lead to plans that leverage change in road maps and metrics. In LEAN transformations in healthcare, visioning and strategic planning rarely involve the healthcare providers and they rarely have the opportunity to provide feedback to the leadership for amendment, to successfully address the components above. This type of concise messaging is rare in healthcare.

⦿⨳⦅ ~:⦿:⬜⦿

4.   Communicate vision

Kotter notes that another reason for failure in transformations is the underutilization of all forms of communication. His point is that large groups in the organization must be convinced to help and even sacrifice for transformational success. They must believe that "useful change" is possible. The leadership and their guiding coalition must approach this as if it was a political campaign, to win "*hearts and minds*". They must be the sales staff of change following the most important rule "*ABC- always be closing*" for support. Every messaging and event should be used to promote the transformation. Finally, leadership must "*walk the talk*" they must realize they are symbols of the transformation and their behaviors must demonstrate that they are true believers, they must live the values. For LEAN transformations in healthcare, this is particularly problematic; many physician offices refuse to accept communications from their affiliated hospital; office managers routinely throw out communications to their physicians unopened. Special efforts by the physician leaders are critical in addressing this problem. It is only when the staff voluntarily embraces the movement, metaphorically cast their vote for change, that the transformation will then be successful. For this to occur communication is critical.

5.   Empower action

The removal of barriers for team success is critical to move forward with change. Leaders and managers that are not on board must change or leave. Structural impediments to change must be identified and removed and the compensation system and performance review process must match the intended efforts to change. Early skepticism is reasonable but if it is not resolved through education, communication and discussion, those healthcare providers cannot be a significant part of the organization. As previously mentioned, the most important structural change that every healthcare organization will need to make is to create time for

LEAN. Healthcare providers are asked to change for efforts like the electronic health record or implementation of Meaningful Use, but are rarely given paid time specifically to do so. These prior approaches will not work for a LEAN transformation; healthcare providers are too busy with routine activities to do more. Not providing time for the transformation also sends the message that it is really not important. The performance appraisal and compensation plan should be changed early to reward performing LEAN related activities.

6.   Get quick wins

Kotter notes that transformation efforts take years, and as with most things, momentum will slow if the organization does not see early wins. For LEAN this is also key; because healthcare providers have seen so many new *"improvement"* programs that have often demonstrated limited results and no long term benefit. To overcome this history of failure, short term wins should be planned and exceptionally celebrated and integrated into a LEAN long term commitment.

7.   Leverage wins and drive change

Kotter notes that another failure mode is to declare victory too soon. It's as if everyone will be happier if this *"transformation program"* concludes and they can go back to their normal work. It is critical to make sure the staff understands that the transformation is the *"new way"* and going back is not an option. To reinforce this, each victory should be coupled with a new, more impressive change in sync with the transformation, particularly if it is related to growth. For LEAN it is key to reinforce at all events both positive and negative, that the new way is the only way. During this phase, the promotion and hiring of staff should only be for those that embrace the LEAN principles of transformation.

8.   Embed in culture

As noted by Selznick, a critical factor in LEAN transformations is that the leadership must be expert on promotion and protection of values. They must promote a *"psychological transformation"* in which the staff is attached to the bottom line, the agonies and the ecstasies of organizational success or failure, in other words, the organization must be incorporated into their lives (Selznick 2011). Tom Peters notes; *"Top management is at the apex of the symbolic signaling system… daily efforts…   must focus on sending the effective and appropriate signals to promote this attachment (Peters 2001)."* According to Kotter, the final failure mode is to neglect to "*anchor*" the changes into the organization's culture. There must be a "*religious*" effort to demonstrate how the change created by the transformation have made improvements and that leadership are true believers of the approach. For LEAN, this means an ongoing initiation and incorporation of any new member of the organization as a separate and important event. Just as the white coat ceremonies at the beginning of medical school symbolize a transition into medicine for medical students, so too should the organization have a plan and approach to symbolically introduce new staff into their LEAN commitment as part of their orientation.

Kotter notes LEAN transformations require Leaders to lead and to not manage. He believes that transformations can be paralyzed by too many managers and not enough leaders. Another interesting commonality noted by Kotter and LEAN experts is the recognition of the failure of short cut solutions in transformations. They both note that skipping steps results in "*never producing a satisfying result.*" Both indicate that organizational transformation is a process and must proceed in its own unique and sometimes painfully slow fashion.

"Like a piece of Ice melting on a hot stove, a project must ride on its own melting"

adapted Robert Frost

Leadership in the Phases of Transformation

A LEAN Transformation is a gradual process that requires patience and persistence. As outlined by George Koenigsaecker the phases include:

1- The first phase is generally slow, financials lag, and frequently there are 2 steps forward and then 1 step back. Often this causes poor follow up on progress, limited sustaining of momentum, staff confusion and dismay. At this point, usually 20% of the organization is involved

2- The second phase includes major resistance to the program and 30-40% of the organization is still not sure about LEAN.

3-	The third phase is the beginning of Consolidation; in general, there is more progress and successes, less failures, and for the first time LEAN seems to clearly be working.

4-	In the final phase, change is now the accepted norm.

Similar to the opinion of Kotter, Koenigsaecker believes that leaders should shepherd an organization through this transition, not by managing, but by leading. It's about a leadership style that is, *"knowing the questions, not the answers"*. For a successful LEAN transformation, he believes you need;

1.	Principled leadership,

2.	A People focus,

3.	Policy Deployment- that leads to goal alignment, ownership, and accountability at all levels,

4.	Practice- the application of LEAN tools for the right problems.

He reinforces that the commitment of leadership and management is critical. In LEAN transformations leadership must focus on limiting staff distractions and promoting engagement in the "greater" team; on the organization and in societal goals (Koenigsaecker 2013).

©Glasbergen
glasbergen.com

"This is a major project of utmost importance, but it has no budget, no guidelines, no support staff, and it's due in 15 minutes. At last, here's your chance to really impress everyone!"

Reproduced with permission and licensed from Glasbergen

Figure 3.2 Budgets, Funding and Commitment (see figure legends)

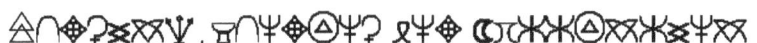

Leadership Management in Business Basics as They Affect Change

Because a LEAN transformation will fail if pursued in a piecemeal fashion and because it requires the entire organization's commitment, it follows that basic business management will have an impact on implementation. An important role for LEAN Leadership in Transformations is to review the organizations basic business management practices. As an example for an approach, using the 8 key management practices associated with business success as described by Nohria et al, leaders can ask critical questions and consider assessments:

Strategy- When was the last strategic plan created? Was the success or failure of that plan analyzed? Have you updated your information on your Market changes, competition, financial health and the predicted changes for the near future? Where are your organizations strengths and weaknesses, opportunities or potential losses (SWOT)? Have you demonstrated growth?

To implement a LEAN program requires the modification of an existing strategic plan to build upon. If a typical business strategic plan is not in place, it must be created prior to the implementation. Katherine Clubb gives a clear recommendation of how leaders should approach strategy differently in a LEAN implementation. They must *"abandon that notion that leaders can plan their way to success, and instead adopt a directionally correct strategy geared to action and adjustment by all employees"* (Clubb 2002).

A critical decision in the implementation of LEAN will involve assessments of when and where to start. Most healthcare organizations start with the delivery of services; a healthcare service line such as the Emergency room or the Operating Room. Part of the strategic planning will be to decide how the other value streams will support the first service line and at what point will they be considered to be incorporated into the LEAN process. A LEAN implementation can be conducted through value streams in:

1. Development of goods and services,
2. Demand Generation and Capture- marketing and sales,
3. Delivery- actual services,
4. Support systems- IT, Finance, HR.

Execution- What type of metrics does your company have on how your organization is executing on its goals and objectives? In what areas has your company been successful in execution and where has it failed? What is the explanation for the results- resources, logistics, planning or personnel? A critical consideration in the LEAN implementation will be to take advantage of the organization's execution strengths and adjust or improve the areas of weakness.

Culture- What efforts have been instituted to assess culture and to improve it? The LEAN transformation will start on the foundation of the existing culture; is it antithetical to change? Have change efforts succeeded to some degree? Understanding where you are starting from is an important key concept in how to introduce the transformation and how to educate for change.

Structure- When was the last time a review of organizational structural effectiveness was undertaken? What parts of the organizational structure is helping or hurting and what is missing? A LEAN implementation will require structural changes in personnel reporting, in healthcare activities such as work shift distributions, in educational programs, in performance reviews and in promotion and hiring. What policies and guidelines will require amendment? Amending organizational structures to enhance change is a necessary part of the transformational process.

Nohria's second tier of business practices associated with successful companies, while not as critical in some industries, are of greater importance in healthcare.

Leadership

In the Assessment and planning phase, Leadership effectiveness and the leadership employee relationships should be considered. The leadership should conduct their own exercises on their activities as previously mentioned, focusing on their value added work and planning for delegation. A LEAN implementation will require the leadership to change their daily activities; to change the manner in which they conduct business and in some cases project a new type of leadership style. For this process, self-reflection is critical; understanding where you are and where you need to go to, is a critical issue in preparing for the LEAN transformation.

Talent

Have you assessed your employees for talent, expertise and for succession? For healthcare organizations you should have quality metrics concerning the quality of your peer review and medical leadership oversight. In what services are there talented staff that are underutilized? Conversely, staff that are too busy or being pushed too hard will be unable to embrace any change, particularly something as difficult as LEAN. Who are the staff that need your help and how can leadership intervene before the LEAN implementation?

ⓞ✾℃~:O:O☆

Innovation

Does your company innovate, if so what percentage of your company's services represent new innovations within the last 5 years? Is the organization an environment that supports innovation? Who is innovating? A LEAN transformation should be a process of innovation. If your company is foreign to innovation, as are many healthcare organizations, then additional efforts will be required during the start of the LEAN Transformation to understand innovation and how to support it.

ⓞ✾℃~:O:O◉

Partnering and Mergers

What is the state of your partnering and recent mergers? What mergers are in the planning phase? The introduction of a new company into an organization undergoing a LEAN Transformation can be a disruptive event that will require additional control from leadership. The additional activities required will represent too great a competitive interest to successfully undergo a LEAN transformation simultaneously.

It may be obvious that the better your business management fundamentals, the easier it is to mobilize resources to implement a change program. As pointed out by Handy and Argyris, the second loop of learning that is critical to improvement should start before the organization is in decline and adopting defensive practices (Handy 1995, Argyris 1994). For most healthcare organizations their resources are so limited that they are in a perpetual Catch 22 of not improving because improvement require resources that they don't have, but without improvement they will always have limited resources. Understanding better business management practices may provide resources for improvement and break this vicious cycle (Nohria et al 2003).

Leadership Personal Development in Change

Toussaint and Perry note the "biggest challenge" in a successful LEAN healthcare implementation may be that leaders may have to personally demonstrate the greatest change (Toussaint and Perry 2013). For many leaders, a LEAN transformation will mean that they perform a deep self-reflection to better understand themselves, the position that they are in and the changes that may be necessary to lead. Goldsmith notes that some leaders have difficulty with change to the point of being "delusional" (Goldsmith 2002). The "paradox of success" is that their prior successes inhibits their ability to see the need for change. Another potential obstacle in leading change is that some Leaders maintain a separation from their staff; they don't look to their organization for their own definition. Leaders are often more self-reliant with limited close relationships as opposed to managers that are more dependent on widespread associations. This is an explanation of why some leaders handle change better. Isolated leaders that do not identify with their organization are more likely to embrace the risk of change. However, for LEAN, leaders must identify fiercely with their organization and extend and develop relationships throughout the organization. If they do not, their efforts will seem superficial and synthetic; they must feel the risk of change equally with their staff.

⊚✄〜:○:○〇〇

"To be even minded is the greatest virtue, Wisdom is to speak the truth and act in keeping with its nature"

Heraclitus

What are the other characteristics of successful Leaders in a LEAN Transformation?

❖ Empathetic and Expert

They demonstrate vulnerability and good judgment consistent with, soft leadership (Peace 1991). Leaders often have talent in an area important to the business but if they don't delegate and focus on promoting the vision as opposed to promoting their own talents, they will be unsuccessful. They must understand how to extend their expertise through others for LEAN.

❖ Emotional Intelligence

For a LEAN Transformation, successful leaders require a high degree of emotional intelligence; meaning that they demonstrate higher levels of self-awareness, social skills, are highly motivated, empathetic, and perform self-assessment. Higher levels of self-awareness are also associated with greater flexibility; also required in the transformation, as are understanding the needs and reactions of others (Thompson 2014). Social skills that support innovative thinking are key to a LEAN transformation; leaders must understand the adage that *"Leadership is listening to people you would rather not listen to"* to gain external insight. The leadership challenge will be to accomplish the organization's purpose and highest priorities in a principle centered way with expertise and empathy.

❖ Framing and Trust

A study by Higgs and Rowland emphasized how important the leadership role is in framing meaning and to subsequently define value during change (Higgs and Rowland 2000). This is similar to the concept promoted by Weick, that a role for leadership is as a "sense maker", for the creation of meaning (Weick 1995). This is problematic in healthcare because of the dichotomy between non-medical administrators and physician leaders. In general, neither understand or can do the other's job well. This means that a new type of leadership dynamic must occur in which *"partnered leadership"* is equally shared by physician leadership and a medical organization administration. This approach requires a suppression of egos, suppression of the need for control and for both to, as Max DuPree says, *"surrender themselves to the voices of others"* (DuPree 2011). This may require changes in a leader's personal attributes to achieve the most important ingredient for success; trust. Studies have demonstrated that trust in leadership is the strongest factor in accepting change (Coyle-Shapiro 2003, Eby 2000). Many physicians, physician leaders and organizational administrators, may be required to change on a personal basis to be considered trustworthy. It may require seeking feedback from colleagues and their direct reports about their short comings. This may be required to provide the ability to go out into the organization and convince the staff that there is a genuine interest in them and of a willingness to sacrifice for them. As Covey has said, leaders must find their voice and inspire others to find theirs; voices enunciating talent, conscientiousness and passion (Covey 2004). This idea is stated succinctly by Clubb who promotes that for leaders to embrace change and innovation they must *"First develop a new understanding of how human nature works and why people think and act the way they do"*. She feels this is the first step toward exploding the limitations that keep leadership from innovating and improving. Clubb also points out that innovation only happens with learning. She feels that leaders must challenge their own assumptions and models to be able to support the innovation that a LEAN transformation in healthcare requires (Clubb 2002). This sentiment is echoed by Covey in his belief that leaders need to understand their own responses and develop the *"distance between the stimulus and the response"* that avoids reaction and encourages cooperation (Covey 2004).

۞ﬡℂ~:O:O₤

"God damn it we forgot the silent prayer"

President Eisenhower at his cabinet meeting

Leadership Personal Paradigms

If we use Steven Covey's format, he would outline the important personal paradigms for leadership to succeed in healthcare transformation as follows;

Vision- the critical issue for leadership to help generate and to promote the transformation.

Discipline- to enact change against obstacles and resistance and to provide the sometimes dull but necessary work to change policies and guidelines to allow change.

Passion- The emotional component for change can come from many sources, one can be infused from leadership by personal presence and story-telling.

Conscience- to move forward with integrity and honesty in implementing change.

⊚⧓〔~:〇:〇 ∝

In summary, Personal leadership development means to improve self-awareness, empathy and genuine identification with the staff through personal relationships. Leaders must be able to delegate, trust and most of all, be trustworthy. The key concept is for the leader to understand who they are; it is their integrity and concern for others that is a critical component in a period of crisis for the LEAN Transformation to succeed.

⊚⧓〔~:〇:€ 𝓡

" WELL I WOULD HAVE EXHIBITED MORE LEADERSHIP QUALITIES IF SOMEONE WOULD HAVE TOLD ME TO."

Figure 3.3 It requires vision and judgment (See figure legends)

⊿⧓ ⊚⧓𝓎⌒⊙⊚⧓Ѵ Ѵ⊙Ѵ⊙𝒥𝒞Ѱ 𝓁Ѱ⊕ ⊲𝒢⋀⊕𝒫⧓Ѱ⧓

Leadership in LEAN Healthcare Innovation; Innovation Laboratories

To support a successful LEAN transformation in healthcare requires more than improvement or adaptation but using innovation as an approach. How do leaders create an environment for innovation? First, Margaret Wheatley promotes that *"all change begins with meaning"* and creativity comes from involvement and the importance of meaning at work. (Wheatley 2002) Second, leaders in a successful LEAN transformation will need to create a review system for innovation to promote success and to seek and develop innovators. Third, leaders will need to link strategy to innovation such that *"innovation then becomes an answer to a set of strategic questions"*; it sets the direction for innovation. Fourth, as Collins points out, the most powerful and profound innovation that a leader can support is *"social innovation"* in clarifying the rights or expectations of the employees and the way that the staff interact (Collins 2002). Fifth, a leader can affect the environment for innovation by arranging circumstances to promote innovation. Mintzberg describes it as providing the staff *"with the freedom to act in places where detailed knowledge is held"* (Mintzberg 2002). To get there, leadership must support activities such as *"try anything"* improvisation. Sixth, as Ulrich notes the leadership should encourage an innovation environment as one that is encouraging, questioning, challenging, pushes curiosity and focuses on problem identification while demanding the regular work continues (Ulrich 2002). Can this approach work? Consider the example of the treatment of postoperative pain by pain management specialists; treatment that has changed medicine with the concept that instead of treating pain as it occurred, to prevent it from occurring in the first place.

Leadership Roles and Behaviors in LEAN Healthcare Innovation

Pollard has said in innovation, a leader *"cultivates, champions and supports the new ideas through their behavior"* promoting that innovation and empowerment goes hand in hand; reinforcing the LEAN principle that a leader empowers the staff (Pollard 2002). Rich Karlgaard notes that a critical role for leadership in innovation is trust; the leadership must create an atmosphere of trust and security in which the sharing of ideas and experimentation is a comfortable event (Karlgaard 2014). In addition, leadership supports the innovation process by demonstrating integrity and courage. It has been estimated that out of 3000 ideas, one possible successful change is generated. Innovators need to trust their leaders to support them, through both good and bad ideas and to demonstrate the courage to follow through; as Peter Drucker has said, *"When you have real innovation, don't compromise"*. The 3M Company provides an example of execution and follow through in their commitment to innovation. 3M maintains the goal that 25% of revenue will come from new products developed in the last 5 years.

Collins states that *"innovative leaders are also innovative in the way they lead"*; echoed by Covey in the importance of modeling (Collins 2002, Covey 2004). This is the concept of "leadership in background" the quiet work of inspiring and promoting innovation that is behind the scenes by innovating in their own activities. Such an activity is when leadership orchestrate regular innovation symposiums or events with external sources for ideas. This activity can serve to review progress, achievements, the implications of change and future directions. A key point on leadership behavior is that a leader must genuinely delight in the wild ride of innovation, both good rides and bad.

❾✖︎℄~⊙꞉℄△

Leadership Actions to support innovation

Kanter notes that to start a system of innovation, leaders must start by looking for where innovation is needed. Part of the standard work for leaders is to connect the work, the exploration and the observation of change throughout the organization. For innovation you need to provide examples of openness, imagination and acceptance through the organizational communications. For logistics, Kanter recommends that the leader set up a system for innovation that includes fast approval, open communication, cooperation across units and the tolerance of uncertainty mixed with faith and security. In addition, leaders must support innovation by removing obstacles (Kanter 2002). Ulrich suggests that LEAN Leaders can support innovation by providing a process for filtering of ideas, incubating those that are supported, investing in the new projects followed by integration and improvement of those projects (Ulrich 2002). Equally important, Pollard notes a key role for leaders in innovation is monitoring innovation projects and knowing when to pull the plug on innovations that are not successful (Pollard 2002). This occurs in LEAN by a disciplined review and follow-up on Rapid Improvement Events. Finally, for any innovation you need "new and different", this emphasizes the need to go to other sites and to other LEAN organizations to learn. In the same fashion, Kanter recommends that organizations use "idea scouts" to fuel innovation (Kanter 2002). In summary, the steps for creating an innovation program include;

1. Creating the innovation environment,
2. Creating a system for innovation suggestions,
3. Monitoring and Filtering innovation efforts and suggestions,
4. An execution program to trial or pilot innovation suggestions,
5. An innovation rewards program.

❾✖︎℄~⊙꞉℄□

An Example of LEAN Leadership Innovation: A New Definition of Waste, Political Conflict

LEAN has many definitions of waste; defects, waiting, transportation, over production, etc. A suggestion for a new waste definition that may have value is <u>political conflict.</u> Political infighting is one of the most wasteful activities in healthcare. It is particularly destructive because of the unstructured reporting and limited accountability between physicians and organizational administrators. Leaders in healthcare can add an innovation in leadership by actively looking for and addressing political conflict as nonvalue added activities. Examples of waste related to politics include staff members that are suppressing colleagues to further their own careers or fighting over resources such as control of budgets, staff or office space. Leaders should recognize and resolve conflicts in alignment, incentives and resources between different groups within the organization. An exercise or retreat to review political conflict within the organization, led by leadership has the potential to address and improve one of the major problems preventing efficient and high quality healthcare.

SUMMARY

1. The leadership style that best fits LEAN is that of servant leadership with partnered management; transformational leadership.

2. Leaders must plan and assess known problems as a first step; The problems in business management basics, personnel resistance factors, physician alignment and partnering.

3. Leaders must make structural changes such as creating LEAN time and processes like LEAN education, LEAN Communication and LEAN Data at the start of an implementation.

4. Leadership must approach a LEAN implementation with a specific focus on managing the change itself and its impact.

5. The context of change, the magnitude and time frame can all affect the leadership approach to change and should be accounted for in the planning phase.

6. Leaders should understand that simple tool kits for change fail, a linear approach to change fails, a directed approach to change and a *"do it yourself"* change approach, all fail. (Sammut-Bonnici and Wensley 2002, Stacey 1996, Harris and Ogbonna 2002, Senge 1997).

7. In Healthcare most change is complex and for successful management it requires leaders to use a system approach in managing complexity of the multiple elements and approaches, the wide range of tools, of project management and for identification of emergent properties.

8. Leaders should use; "*An Informed emergent*" approach; Big rules, Gemba walks, novel mixes of team members, the establishment of best practices and "*lateral communication*" for success in change.

9. Leaders in a LEAN transformation will need to create 2 guiding coalitions, one in administration and one of healthcare providers; aggregated to support the organizational change.

10. Leaders should focus on cultural change through visioning, campaigning, modeling and promoting passion.

11. Leaders should consider if their personal attributes and habits are consistent with LEAN and if they have demonstrated integrity, empathy and commitment.

12. Leadership in a LEAN transformation entails understanding the appropriate management of knowledge workers; this requires emotional intelligence.

13. Leaders should consider a new approach to the problem of administrator-healthcare provider partnering.

14. In healthcare organizations, leadership action steps should focus on framing, increasing capacity and enabling.

15. Leadership ordering of behavior and not using relationships for change implementation is associated with failure. Prior to implementation leadership should focus on relationships. (Higgs 2003, Kouzes and Posner 1998, Gill 2002)

16. Leadership behaviors that focus on position, role, and power should be described as detrimental.

17. Leadership should apply a complex and evolutionary approach to change with less centralization and a greater focus on creating an environment that promotes innovation for success.

18. Leaders should consider if the environment is supportive of true innovation and push for innovation, not just improvement.

"Run out of the tunnel, put the team on the field, unleash the force, and hope you can adjust"

Pugh Decision Analysis of Leadership Styles for a LEAN Transformation

This Pugh Analysis was designed to look at the importance of leadership characteristics versus leadership approaches as they apply to LEAN transformations.

Characteristic	Multiplier	Laissez- faire	autocratic	participatory	transactional	transformational
Promoter	2	-1	-1	0	0	1
Monitoring	1	1	-1	1	1	1
Enabling	2	0	-1	0	0	1
Trust	3	0	0	0	0	1
Empathy	2	-1	-1	0	0	1
Expert	1	0	1	1	1	1
Vulnerable	1	-1	-1	0	0	1
Good Judgment	3	0	1	1	1	0
Disciplined	2	0	1	1	1	1
Emotion Intell	3	-1	-1	0	0	1
Talent	1	0	1	1	1	0
Mentor	2	0	-1	0	0	1
Industry	1	0	1	1	1	1
		-9	-2	9	9	20

Table1. Leadership style on the horizontal axis versus Leadership Characteristics on the vertical axis rated for application to a LEAN Transformation on a scale from -3 to 3.

Characteristic	Multiplier	Tyrant	Pacesetter	Innovator	Charismatic	Servant
Promoter	2	-1	0	0	1	0
Monitoring	1	1	0	0	0	0
Enabling	2	-1	0	0	1	1
Trust	3	-1	0	0	0	1
Empathy	2	-1	-1	0	-1	1
Expert	1	0	1	1	0	0
Vulnerable	1	-1	-1	0	0	1
Good Judgment	3	1	1	1	0	0
Disciplined	2	0	1	0	0	0
Emotion Intell	3	-1	-1	0	1	1
Talent	1	1	1	1	0	0
Mentor	2	-1	0	0	0	1
Industry	1	0	1	1	0	0
		-9	2	6	5	13

Table 2. Leadership Approaches on the horizontal axis versus leadership characteristics on the vertical axis rated on a scale from -3 to 3.

Character	Multiple	talent /industry	skill /team	Organizing /objectives	vision /performance	humility /determined
Promoter	2	0	0	0	1	1
Monitoring	1	0	0	1	1	1
Enabling	2	-1	0	1	1	1
Trust	3	-1	-1	0	0	0
Empathy	2	-1	-1	0	0	1
Expert	1	1	1	0	0	0
Vulnerable	1	-1	-1	0	0	0
Good Judgment	3	0	1	0	1	0
Disciplined	2	1	0	1	1	1
Emotion Intell	3	-1	1	0	0	1
Talent	1	1	1	0	0	0
Mentor	2	-1	0	0	1	0
Industry	1	1	1	1	1	1
		-6	3	6	13	17

Table 3. Leadership approaches based on Jim Collin's Definition of Leadership Levels on the horizontal axis versus leadership characteristics on the vertical axis rated from -3 to 3.

Conclusions: As might be expected Determined Leadership with Humility, Servant leadership and Transformational Leadership are all significantly more supportive of a LEAN transformation then other approaches. What is also of note are the negative ratings of Lasse faire, Autocratic, Tyrannical leaders indicating they can be a detriment to any Transformational efforts. This also applies to "level 2" Leaders based on Jim Collins definitions, indicating that leaders that have considerable talents related to healthcare management and that are hard workers can actually be an inhibitor of a healthcare organization's change efforts because they may lack the focus on the more critical leadership characteristics needed for change.

Leadership Mission Statement

To see the essential problem

To remember what it means

To anticipate their need

To improve healthcare

and enable new treatments to come

To be the best for them

REFERENCES

Argyris, C. Good Communication That Blocks Learning. Harvard Business Review 1994.

Balle M. A LEAN leap of faith. LEAN Enterprise Institute 2013. http://www.lean.org/LeanPost/Posting.cmf?LeanPostId=82.

Beckhard, R., & Harris, R.T. (1987). *Organizational transitions: Managing complex change* (2nd ed.). Addison-Wesley series on organization development. Reading, MA: Addison-Wesley Publishing.

Buchanan D and Boddy D. The expertise of the change Agent. 1992 Prentice Hall.

Cady, S.H., Jacobs, J., Koller, R., & Spalding, J. (2014). The change formula: Myth, legend, or lore. *OD Practitioner*, 46(3), 32–39.

Chapman J. System Failure. 2002 Demos.co.uk.

Clubb MK. Inviting Innovation, in Leading for Innovation, Hesselbein F, Goldsmith M, Somerville I. (Ed) 2002 Jossey Bass.

Collins J. The Ultimate Creation. in Leading for Innovation, Hesselbein F, Goldsmith M, Somerville I. (Ed) 2002 Jossey Bass.

Coyle-Shapiro, J and Morrow PC. The role of individual differences in employee adoption of TQM orientation *J Vocational Behaviour* 2003;62: 320-340.

Conner D. Managing at the speed of change. 1992 John Wiley.

Covey SR. The 7 Habits of Highly Effective People. 1989 Fireside, Simon and Schuster.

Covey SR. The 8th Habit: From effectiveness to greatness. 2004 Free Press, Simon and Schuster.

DDI 2013 Driving health care patient satisfaction (HCAHPS) through talent management practices.

DuPree M. Leadership is an Art. 2011 Random House.

Eby LT, Adams DM, Russell JEA, Gaby SH. Perceptions of organizational readiness for change: Factors related to employees' reactions to the implementation of team-based selling. Human relations, 2000;53:419-442.

Giglio L Diamante T, Urban JM. Coaching a leader: Leveraging change at the top. J Management Development 1998;17:93-105.

Gill R. Towards an integrated theory of leadership. EIASM Leadership Conference 2002.

Gallagher J. The Three Must-Have attributes of leadership in LEAN. http://www.johngallagherblog.com/Global Leadership Forecast www.ddiworld.com/gfl2013

Goffee and G. Jones Why should anyone be led by you? What it takes to be an authentic leader.

Goldsmith M. Changing the Behavior of *Successful* People. In Leading for Innovation, Ed Hesselbein F, Goldsmith M, Somerville I. 2002 Jossey Bass.

Handy, Charles. The Empty Raincoat, Making Sense of the Future. 1995 Random House Business Books.

Hanrion M. LEAN healthcare challenges: Will you succeed? LEAN Healthcare Exchange 2013. Harvard Business Review Press 2015).

Harris LC and Ogbonna E. The Unintended Consequences of Culture Interventions: A Study of Unexpected Outcomes. British J Management 2002;13:31-49.

Hesselbein F, Goldsmith M, Somerville I. Leading for Innovation 2002 Jossey Bass.

Higgs MJ Developments in leadership thinking. J Organizational Development and Leadership. 2003;24:273-284.

Higgs MJ Rowland D. Building change leadership capability: "the quest for change competence". J Change Management. 2000;1:116-131.

Higgs MJ Rowland D. Developing change leadership capability. The impact of a development intervention. Henley Working Paper Series, HWP 2001/004.

Higgs M and Rowland D. All changes great and small: Exploring approaches to change and its leadership. J Change Management 2007; 5:121-151.

Jacobson RD. Leading for a Change: How to master the 5 challenges faced by every leader. 2011 Butterworth-Heinemann.

Jaworski J and Scharmer CO Leadership in the new economy. Sensing and actualizing emerging futures. Working Paper, Society for Organizational Learning 2000.

Kanter R. Creating the Culture for Innovation in Leading for Innovation, Hesselbein F, Goldsmith M, Somerville I. (Ed) 2002 Jossey Bass.

Karlgaard R. The Soft Edge: Where Great Companies Find Lasting Success 2014 Jossey-Bass.

Kim WC and Mauborgne R. Blue Ocean Leadership. Harvard Business Review. May 2014.

Koenigsaecker G. Leading the LEAN enterprise transformation. 2013 CRC Press.

Kotter J. Winning at Change. Leader to Leader 1998;10:27-33.

Kotter J. What leaders really do. Harvard Bus Review 2001.

Kotter J. Leading Change: Why transformation efforts fail. 2007 Harvard Bus Review.

Kouzes JR Posner BF. Encouraging the Heart. 1998 Jossey-Bass.

Litchenstein BM Evolution or transformation: a critique and alternative to punctuated equilibrium in: D. Moore (Ed) Academy of Management Best Paper Proceedings 1996 291-295. (Vancouver: Academy of Management).

Litchenstein BM Grace, magic and miracles: a "chaotic logic" of organizational transformation. J Organizational Change Management. 1997;10:393-411.

Mintzberg H. Managing to Innovate in Leading for Innovation, Hesselbein F, Goldsmith M, Somerville I. (Ed) 2002 Jossey Bass.

Nohria N, Joyce W, Roberson B. What Really Works. Harvard Bus Review 2003.

Pagonis WG. Leadership in the combat zone. Harvard Bus Review 2001.

Pascale R. Managing on the Edge: How successful companies use conflict to stay ahead. 1999 Viking.

Peace W. The Hard Work of Being a Soft Manager. Harvard Bus Review 1991.

Pendlebury, J., Grouard, B. and Meston, F. (1998) The Ten Keys to Successful Change Management, John Wiley, London.

Peters T. Leadership sad facts and silver linings Harvard Bus Review 12 2001.

Pettigrew, A. M. (1985) The Awakening Giant: Continuity and Change in ICI, Blackwell, Oxford.

Pollard CW. The Organization! Is it a Friend or Foe of Innovation? in Leading for Innovation, Hesselbein F, Goldsmith M, Somerville I. (Ed) 2002 Jossey Bass.

Rowe A. Iris Murdoch: A reassessment. 2006 Palgrave MacMillan.

Sammut-Bonnici R Wensley R. Darwinism probability and complexity: Market-based organizational transformation and change explained through the theories of evolution. International J Management Reviews 2002:4:291-315.

Schein EH. Organizational Culture and Leadership. 1985 Jossey-Bass Publishers.

Selznick P. Leadership in Administration: A Social interpretation. 2011 Quid Pro Books.

Senge PM. The Fifth Discipline: the art and practice of the learning organization. 1990 Doubleday Currency.

Senge P.M Communities of leaders and learners. Harvard Bus Review 1997;75:30-31.

Senge, P., Kleiner, A., Roberts, C., Ross, R., Roth, G. and Smith, B. 1999 The Dance of Change, Nicholas Brealey, New York.

Shaw P. Intervening in the shadow systems of organizations: consulting from a complexity perspective. J Organizational Change Management 1997;10:235-250.

Stacey R. Management and the science of complexity: if organizational life is non-linear, can business strategies prevail? Research and Technology Management 1996;39:2-5.

Studer Q. Hardwiring Excellence 2003 The Studer Group.

Thompson R. For a more flexible workforce, hire self-aware people. Harvard Bus Review 2014.

Toussaint JS and Berry LL. The promise of LEAN in Health Care. Mayo Clin Proc 2013;88:74-82.

Ulrich D. An Innovation Protocol in Leading for Innovation, Hesselbein F, Goldsmith M, Somerville I. (Ed) 2002 Jossey Bass.

Weick, KE Sense-Making in Organizations, SAGE 1995.

Welch J. Jack: Straight from the Gut. 2001 Warner Business Books.

Wheatley M. Leadership and the New Science 1992 Brerrett-Koehler.

Wheatley M. Leadership and the New Science 1993 Brerrett-Koehler.

Whealey M and Kellner Rogers M. A Simpler Way 1996 Berrett-Koehler.

Wheatley M. We are all Innovators in Leading for Innovation, Hesselbein F, Goldsmith M, Somerville I. (Ed) 2002 Jossey Bass.

Womack JP and Jones DT. LEAN Thinking: Banish waste and create wealth in your corporation. 2003 Free Press.

Womack JP, Byrne AP, Fiume J, Kaplan GS, Toussaint J. Going LEAN in Healthcare 2005, Institute for Healthcare Improvement.

Zaleznik Managers and Leaders are they different? Harvard Bus Review 2004.

Chapter 4

Managers in a LEAN Healthcare Innovation

"It is not the strongest of the species that survives, nor the most intelligent that survives. It is the one that is most adaptable to change"

Leon C. Megginson interpreting Charles Darwin

Experts say that the most common reason for LEAN transformation failure is a failure of leadership. But in this chapter we will make the argument that the most common reason for failure in a LEAN transformation is not the upper level leaders but it is the failure of management by middle level leaders, managers and supervisors. In a LEAN transformation managers must become more active, make more decisions, and may have to make the greatest change in their approach. As a consequence of their day to day activities, managers are the most visible representation of the transformation which may be the hardest, most important job in the transformation. As noted by Steven Smith, compounding these challenges for managers is that they often do not have formal management training; most learn from their predecessors, inheriting both their strengths and weaknesses (Smith 2014). In general, manager training research has shown that between 40 to 60 percent of first time managers lack basic management skills or actually do not have the critical capacities to perform their job (Mintzberg 1990). Sixty percent would be a generous underestimate of management incompetence in physician healthcare managers. The impact of this lack of training is poor management performance with the expected reduced productivity, poor staff satisfaction and high employee turnover. As noted by Buchanan et al, change situations compound poor manager performance, in that managers have neither the expertise nor capacity to implement change successfully and the alternative of managing change by text book theory is difficult and usually fails (Buchanan et al 1999). As noted by Stacey, to be successful in change efforts managers must be able to choose successful "mutations" of processes anticipating environmental change. Since organizations evolve toward stable equilibriums that resist change, the identified mutations are the least likely to support transformation, representing another challenge for managers (Stacey (1996). These deficiencies in problem solving, training, and addressing emergent system events compromise a manager in understanding and participating in change (Senge 1990, Beer and Nohria 2000). Additionally, with a LEAN transformation, all the limitations in managers are magnified; they must learn new skills and in most cases learn to manage differently. Is it any wonder most managers are generally against the change efforts (Sirkin et al 2005)?

"So much of what we call management consists in making it difficult for people to work."

Peter Drucker

Plan, Organize, Coordinate, Control

To consider the specifics of just how a manager's job must change for a LEAN implementation, we can use Henry Mintzberg's outline of management activities to explain what managers really do and the required differences for LEAN. Dr. Mintzberg used detailed diaries, records and personal experiences involving all kinds of managers from multiple countries and industries to study what managers really do and don't do. Dr. Mintzberg was able to determine that, despite current impressions, managers don't do the following;

1. Reflective thinking and planning- What Dr. Mintzberg found was that 50% of manager's activities were less than 9 minutes in length and they started a new activity on average every minute over the course of a day. They found that a manager had only one uninterrupted 30-minute period every other day. He found managers participated in general planning less than 1% of the time and as might be concluded from above, managers spent their day just responding to acute issues. This type of management approach is a problem as a foundation on which to add change efforts and change management, particularly with something as overarching as LEAN.

2. Open schedules free of regular activities- Dr. Mintzberg found just the opposite; managers have regular activities because of being short staffed or because of the necessity to shield workers from other duties. This implies that a manager's time is consumed with regular activities and putting out fires. To create time for LEAN will require managers to formally

change the logistics of their position for the 10-20% of time needed for LEAN. A case can be made that managers are so critical to LEAN success that they should be devoting 25 to 40% of their time to the change effort.

3. Managers use aggregated information from a formal data system- In reality, most managers spend the majority of their time in conversation, obtaining "soft" data through personal interactions. For LEAN, visible metrics, which are centrally collected and updated are a critical feature to moving the organization forward. This will be a change for most managers.

4. Use of a scientific approach to problem solving and decisions- Dr. Mintzberg points out that most managers operate based on intuition confirmed by internal judgment. This approach will conflict with LEAN which focuses on using tools, the scientific method of testing and a team based trial and error approach. This issue will have to be resolved for LEAN success.

    (Mintzberg 1990)

When one considers what managers actually do, they are often addressing their work in a superficial, fragmented fashion and use verbal communication as a primary approach; they also find it difficult to delegate. These characteristics of a manager's job are incompatible with a LEAN implementation. A manager in LEAN will need to have a more in-depth focus on issues and to use real data and rapid improvement experiments that require a scientific method. LEAN requires the managers to participate in a much more inclusive and extensive communication approach. To be successful in LEAN requires managers to provide focused time with their reports to address change. Finally, in LEAN, managers must innovate as well, but with the current situation as noted above, it would be hard to believe managers could participate in innovative activities instead of fighting fires. To address these issues, a LEAN implementation will require restructuring the manager's work, to provide new tactics to address their obligations and to perform LEAN operations. The Covey time management matrix is a good initial exercise for managers. This is a Kano Model that plots out activities based on urgency and importance. In evaluating and prioritizing their activities, managers should be able to reorder, delegate and focus on duties that they can stop doing to be able to do

LEAN (Covey 1989).

The Manager's Role in LEAN Healthcare Innovation

What are the roles of managers and how should they be adapted to support LEAN success? Through Mintzberg's own studies (and those of others), he compiled a list of management categories and related roles:

1. Interpersonal-related to their position of authority

   a. Figure head- In many businesses, this role means representing the company in ceremonies, for a LEAN implementation, the manager is the "figure head" of leadership, modeling the new behaviors in LEAN; a critical task, if not performed properly, the effect may lead to that business unit's failure.

   b. Leadership- In LEAN, managers must reinforce leadership's vision, help translate the mission statement and strategic plan into work place values and behaviors. Managers motivate and encourage their direct reports; often they make hiring and promotional decisions. In the LEAN implementation, managers promote and hire based on concurrence with LEAN principles and practices. An additional role in LEAN for the manager is to be at the fore front of LEAN education. In LEAN, managers are educators, promoters of improvement through education and assessors of the effectiveness of education.

   c. Liaisons with peers- The business literature reflects that managers spend as much time with peers as they do with their direct reports. For a LEAN implementation and transformation, managers must shift their focus to the workplace and the personal development of their direct reports.

⊚✄〖~:♨:☐

2. Informational- managers serve a key role in informational dispersal in an organization.

   a. Monitor- Managers are a primary source of new external and internal information from their contacts across units in the organization. In LEAN a critical function for managers is to incorporate into every communication the message of change by constantly alluding to positive evidence of LEAN improvements. Because LEAN focuses on staff inclusiveness and empowerment, managers fill critical roles by providing the staff's feedback to leadership on policy deployment, planning and program progress.

   b. Disseminator- As noted above, managers have access to information that the rest of the staff do not; their attention to communicating important messages about LEAN activities is paramount. This is particularly true in organizations which are siloed or fragmented, like healthcare. Managers need to convey images and impressions that enhance strategy, culture, intuition and insight and they have a critical role in explaining metrics and improving the visual impact of progress.

c. Spokesperson- A key role for managers is the representation of leadership to staff and for the staff, to the leadership. In LEAN, this communication responsibility is enhanced and more difficult. The message from leadership must be translated into a positive message for the staff and then the manager organizes and summarizes the input from the staff back to leadership.

◉✖ℂ~:♉:O

3. Decisional Roles- The manager plays the critical role in logistical decisions for their units.

a. Entrepreneurial- Managers should be entrepreneurial in improving their section or unit and in applying new innovations. While this is often a small role in some management positions, in LEAN this becomes the priority. Management of a new suggestion system that supports innovation is a major new metric for each manager.

b. Disturbance handler-For any manager, this is an important role, but in a LEAN implementation this becomes even more critical. The disruption from change is an additional challenge that must be managed. The manager is the first line of defense to help staff cope and to keep LEAN moving forward. This often means balancing competing personal interests or personalities as LEAN moves forward. *"Managing insightfully depends on the direct experience and personal knowledge that comes from intimate contact."*

c. Allocator- Most managers control budgets and resources. As LEAN is implemented, all budgets, staffing, resources and structures must be adapted by the managers (with the input from their staff) to adjust for LEAN activities. The manager is also a critical decision maker on managing LEAN projects. Mintzberg notes that for managers to be effective they need help from data analysts. Data is critical for managers to not only assess their personal effectiveness but to also assess their unit in the context of the whole system. For the LEAN implementation, managers' assessments are critical to creating priorities in the LEAN transformation.

◉✖ℂ~:♉:℃

"Remember when I walked past your desk this morning and didn't fire you? In today's economy, that counts as a raise and promotion."

Figure 4.1 Devoted, engaged and committed (See figure legends)

⬦⬰♡〇⬰⬰⬰⬦, ⬰⌁⥜⌀⬰⌀⬰⬦ ⥜⌁⬦ ⟳〇⌁⬰⬰⊖⬰⬰⬰⬰⬦

"No job is more vital to our society than that of the manager. The manager determines whether our social institutions will serve us well or whether they will squander our talents and resources."

Henry Mintzberg

Failure Modes for Managers in LEAN

How do managers in LEAN implementations fail? Considering the scale and the range of the impact that organizational change has on the staff, it is easy to understand why managers cannot rise up to the difficult tasks for implementation of LEAN initiatives. Michael Balle and Daniel Jones document *"the 5 biggest mistakes managers make that hinder a LEAN startup"*. Three are particularly important to healthcare. First they sight the overdependence on systemic fixes or new technology approaches as opposed to using tacit knowledge and local solutions for specific plans. Second, they condemn system approaches that ignore the staff as a source of solutions and innovations. Third, they note that managers underestimate how important morale and trust is to success. These mistakes are particularly important to healthcare managers because of the lack of engagement and fragmentation in their organizations; both poor morale and lack of trust further supplement staff mismanagement in a LEAN implementation (Balle and Jones 2014).

Included below are additional examples of manager failure in change related activities, similar to LEAN.

1. Lack of Delegation-The inability to adjust or accept staff empowerment. As noted by Dickson, managers will need to take a subordinate role in some change processes, a position many will be unable to accept (Smith 2014). As teams and individual employees become empowered, many managers feel their position and responsibilities threatened. At Porsche, during their LEAN implementation, there was a shift in power from product engineers to operations managers, which was not anticipated or communicated optimally; this developed into a major issue. The problems for the LEAN implementation at Porsche is a good parallel to healthcare because of the focus on service, production details and entrenched hierarchies in both industries (Womack and Jones 2003). There is no room for micromanagement in LEAN. Managers must be able to delegate. If their ego, need to control or inability to trust others, compromises their ability to delegate and empower, LEAN will fail.

2. Taking Short Cuts- *"Short cuts never work."* A common failure mode for managers is to look for short cuts to expedite the process of change. As noted by LEAN experts and business management professors, this routinely fails in change initiatives.

3. Monitoring-Monitoring is a critical managerial function that is particularly important in LEAN transformations. Managers should confirm that the staff is converting to LEAN and they must confront the *"Antibodies"*, those individuals that undercut the initiative. Managers should address these problems from a process design approach with controls to create hard stops for poor progress or lack of compliance with the LEAN initiatives. This is often missed.

4. Poor work Environment-Another important role of managers is control of the work environment; equipment, facilities, etc. If managers do not explore, review and adjust the work environment for the changes required in the LEAN transformation, they will not remove obstacles that will impede the LEAN initiative and thereby promote its failure.

⑨✖ℂ~:👁:ℰ

"Almost all quality improvement comes via simplification of design, manufacturing... layout, processes, and procedures."

Tom Peters

5. Neglecting Redesign-Part of the accountability of managers includes assuring jobs are re-defined for LEAN, at all levels. If you redefine jobs and responsibilities, then appropriate resources can be provided. The initial problem with the LEAN transformation at Pratt Whitney was that the initiative was short of resources and the authority to redesign. The response to this problem was to reorganize by function and then create a "New Norm" which required participation in job redesign, standard work determination and the appropriate resource allocation (Womack and Jones 2003).

⑨✖ℂ~:👁:ⵝ

6. Lack of Resources- Good managers create structures to allow for logistics to succeed. In LEAN, creating a "Project Manager" will fail without staff or authority. The healthcare *"Quality Assurance Nurse"* is an example, this is an individual that does not have the authority to act on any of the findings necessary for improvement and is consistently reporting on processes without making progress despite their best efforts.

⑨✖ℂ~:👁:△ℛ

7. Not providing time for LEAN- Matt Hanrion notes in his writing "Divided Focus" that a common failure in LEAN implementations is to not make the structural changes that provide time for LEAN activities. A good example of this error is to initiate LEAN efforts by just adding on the LEAN activities to the staff's other jobs. There is no such thing as "making time" in healthcare; this approach for busy healthcare workers routinely fails (Hanrion 2015). Managers must reinforce the leadership's commitment to make time available for LEAN.

⑨✖ℂ~:👁:△△

8. Poor Governance-George Koenigsaecker promotes that governance is <u>the</u> key issue with a LEAN implementation. The organization must change the way it looks at work, performance and achievement and then subsequently how the work is organized and overseen and possibly most importantly, who decides! Koenigsaecker considers not adjusting the organizational governance to be the biggest reason for LEAN implementation failure (Koenigsaecker 2013). Managers have a key role in this reform of the organization's governance process.

9. Lack of Trust-In "the soft Edge" by Richard Karlgaard, the author emphasizes that creating trust is a manager's critical function that creates a culture that supports a successful company. He lists the following approaches to instilling trust;
   o Walking the walk,
   o Being predictable,
   o Trusting your employees,
   o Identifying and communicating the company goals and objectives,
   o Banishing fear as a means to motivate,
   o To use newer technologies like social networks and real-time customer feedback.

Each of these approaches support LEAN success and conversely, their absence can exert the opposite effort; without trust, implementing change is almost impossible (Karlgaard 2014).

⚙✳℃ ~:👹:△□

"The manager's effectiveness is significantly influenced by their insight into their own work"

Henry Mintzberg

Managers in LEAN Transformations

Having sited multiple ways to fail, this next section will focus on manager behaviors for success.

Organizational interface

The manager is critical to the cultural conversion that is the foundation of a LEAN transformation. They are on the front lines with the staff providing the coaching, mentoring and promoting of LEAN. By communicating both to the staff and then providing feedback to the leadership, managers become models for LEAN values and demonstrate the LEAN transformational behaviors. Part of the organizational integration is the critical managerial function of utilizing a guiding coalition of the staff that supports inclusiveness, that can address new problems and to reinforce change (Koenigsaecker 2013). Managers help implement the transformation by creating the complementary teams that make up the coalitions and by organizing their activities. As noted by Smith, the construction of teams and the subsequent relationships helps to develop new roles, align structures and processes that will then empower their staff for change (Smith 2014).

Rewards and Acknowledgement, Staff empowerment

For many staff, the manager is a significant source of respect. As promoted by McGregor, respect given to employees produces better results; by not micromanaging, managers demonstrate the ultimate respect for their employees (McGregor 2006). By helping the employees find meaning and enjoyment in their work, managers demonstrate respect and promote the cultural transformation. This may mean job redesign to increase responsibilities and autonomy, by doing so, it demonstrates true respect and concern for the staff; it demonstrates trust. It's understandable why a LEAN transformation is tougher on managers than any other group. It goes against their nature to give up control; control of details, control of process, control of behavior and change. As Max DuPree explains managers must *"surrender to the voices of others"*. They must guide not control, adjust, not overrule and sometimes apprehensively support. A vision killer for managers is when they seem to find every excuse or reason to delay or not implement LEAN and the related staff autonomy. Managers have to present the same degree of commitment to a LEAN culture as the leadership or they become "lethal antibodies" to a LEAN transformation.

Probably the most critical skill for managers in a LEAN transformation is their management of the staff through their personal relationships. Ideally this is a positive nurturing relationship that is more like a family dynamic then a work relationship. However, even if the relationship is not that positive, at a minimum it must demonstrate respect, support and empowerment (DuPree 2011). In addition to the personal respect rewarded to staff my managers, the managers should also oversee a rewards program that matters to the staff and acknowledges conversion to LEAN.

The Manager's Influence on Business Practices

Most managers don't know the key successful business practices critical for their organization's success. Referring back to Nohria's conceptualization and findings on the business practices of successful companies, we will outline the critical focuses required of managers that supports any change effort (Nohria et al 2003).

Structure –Managers must modify the existing organizational structures to assure a sound work environment; this is accomplished through assessment and elimination of "hated" rules and regulations that impede performance. Additionally, they must assure that there are appropriate rewards and punishments. Managers should assure that the performance review is productive with a real time feedback approach. Most of all, managers need to keep work interesting and to remember what has value for the patient and co-customers and to continue to push for LEAN.

◉✂℃~:🖐:△☆

Execution- Following through on execution is a key management responsibility. A Pareto charting is a good exercise for managers to identify the 20% of departmental activities that are critical to adding value; it provides a focus for performance. Additionally, Managers are critical for accountability, without it there is lack of achievement. Manager's oversight of the workplace includes completing processes, delegating to increased responsibilities and to demonstrate that they understand the jobs they supervise by confirming the successful execution of a task.

✂✗✂◉~:🖐:□

Culture- For managers to promote culture it takes a humanistic approach combined with critical thinking, clear communication and the managing of complex problems. Managers should aim to encourage thinkers not laborers. This humanistic approach may require a manager's self-exploration, abstract self-contemplation and artistic appreciation as change occurs. Managers must take a philosophical, almost spiritual approach that builds on prior history to support culture change. This is accomplished by using ceremonies, music, art and environment to translate what change will look like.

◉✂℃~:🖐:△☉

Strategy and Leadership- As mentioned earlier, managers must model and promote LEAN values, the organization mission and strategy by translating these directives into values and behaviors. Managers monitor and reinforce the consistent demonstration of these values and behaviors in the work place.

◉✂℃~:🖐:△∞

Innovation- Managers are critical to innovation in establishing an environment that encourages innovation and to assure its regular use by managing the suggestion system and creating events for innovation efforts. Managers monitor the execution and follow-up of the innovation program.

Talent- A critical role for managers is to manage talent, promote job enrichment and, in appropriate cases, to increase the scope of a position. To maximize talent, managers should hire by assessing positive attitude, expertise, accomplishments, positive recommendations and fit for position. They should also assure that there are good job descriptions with definitions of standard work, clear and specific work responsibilities, ideal job qualifications and check lists of required skills.

Motivation- Managers assure that the staff has meaning in their work and they use public recognition and promotion to support work accomplishments. Managers should provide additional staff education and training for personal development; this is also critical for LEAN education. An example of how to support motivation is through performance reviews by using "responsibility Tables" -first column job responsibilities- second column metrics and due dates. These tables are used to determine accomplished goals, to assess workloads and overall performance. Goals in performance reviews are to provide support, discussions and to provide personal interest in an employee's success. LEAN goals should be included in these reviews.

> *"It is during challenges or severely compromising events that innate efficiencies and effectiveness are most necessary"*

Personal Development for Managers in LEAN Healthcare Innovation

Like leaders, managers are a source of the organization's vision, but managers bring vision and mission into reality by working with their staff; by pathfinding the new activities specific to their department. If Leaders must be identified as "true believers", campaigning like politicians and visionary "sellers of faith in the organization", then managers are the campaign managers and field directors. Managers must be organizers, environmental controllers, expeditors, and like LEAN leaders, they must be innovators (in management). LEAN managers must also be experts at judging character and the responsible delegation of autonomy. It is too easy for managers to do the "Pratt salute", pointing with both arms in opposite directions simultaneously to blame leadership on one side and the staff on the other for failure. A middle level manager is often rewarded for doing as little as possible with problems; for being quiet and demonstrating no courage in any decision. To properly support managers in LEAN, they will need support for personal development to accept their new roles, take on decision making and demonstrate courage. In LEAN, they must be proactive and look for situations to change; they must be loudly heralding LEAN activities, LEAN accomplishments and LEAN progress. Middle level managers must have the courage to try, to fail and to speak up for change. For many, this change will require *"personal development"*; to expand their capabilities to be comfortable exhibiting these behaviors publicly. The levels of uncertainty, ambiguity and stress that accompanies change is in conflict with most manager's personal traits. Helping managers adjust their personal attributes and to cope with stress or anxiety should be a focused effort for their personal development.

Another area that may require managers to leave their comfort zone is to work with other managers across the organization. This role is critical in organizational assessment, for providing feedback to leadership and for new innovations at an organizational level. Understanding how to work productively with colleagues that may be competitors for resources or positions may require education and mentoring for managers in healthcare.

Another way to consider the personal changes required of managers transitioning to LEAN is outlined by Steven Covey. Managers should be:

➢ Pathfinding- to be a role model and to have the courage to explore and promote change

➢ Aligning- To look at process and consider how structures, policies and staff are in sync with change and to act as necessary.

➢ Empowering- To act as a coach and mentor to staff, to take a genuine personal interest in them, their success and their wellbeing.

➢ Modeling- To have the personal discipline to live the values and behaviors of respect, integrity and trustworthiness necessary to support change.

An approach to help implement these roles include; education on new behaviors, discussions on change, and providing tools for personal development (Covey 2004).

"At many US companies, product and process innovation are not the main bottleneck to progress. The bottleneck is management innovation. We have to ask ourselves, as a company and a nation, are we investing enough in management innovation."

Ray Stata

Management innovation in a LEAN Healthcare Innovation

For healthcare organizations in a LEAN Transformation the most important role for managers is supporting and creating an environment for innovation. Management innovation is;

> *"the invention and implementation of a management practice, process, structure or technique that is new to the state of the art and is intended to further organizational goals"* *(Brikinshaw et al 2008).*

Innovation is a new and different entity; accepting it is a challenge to managers and the staff. Additionally, the existing organizational culture will be an obstacle to change particularly if the innovation has abstract and/or technical components or if the innovation has an uncertain outcome (Knights and McCabe 2000, Stjernberg and Philips 1993, Zbaracki 1998). To add to these problems, as noted by Zbaracki, the personal reaction of employees to innovation is usually negative; they are often intimidated by the change, particularly if new technology or new skills are involved. All these factors make up the resistance component in the proposed formula for change that leadership and management should consider.

A suggested approach for the afore mentioned problems, is considered in the article, "How management innovation happens" by Birkinshaw et al. This study was conducted in two parts. First it included analysis of 100 management innovations that occurred over the last 130 years. In the second part, the authors performed detailed case studies of 11 new management innovations through interviews. Their review demonstrated some unique aspects of management innovation and several consistent patterns. The first commonality was that there was always some dissatisfaction with the current state of affairs that started the process; often the change was considered necessary for survival. Second, they found that the inspiration of new management innovation is unlikely to occur from within the company or the company's industry. Third, they found that "Eureka moments" are rare. The authors found that the most common process in management innovation was a progression from aggregating problem elements to then generating possible solutions through an interactive process. They found a valuable interactive role of "external change" agents. These agents can provide initial inspiration, help shape and legitimize innovation; they can help with experimentation and later validation. They also found that management innovation is more diffuse, gradual and locally or organizationally specific then in other activities. The authors noted that key factors influencing the innovation process included:

➢ An "Influencer" of attitudes and conditions,

➢ That the "New" ideas be considered legitimate,

➢ The existing organizational culture,

➢ The key individuals driving process.

They also noted that adding a change in technology may accelerate progress. Finally, there was a commonality in dealing with resistance and validation. While external agents can provide legitimacy of the innovation, they noted that internal acceptance required promotion by a "champion" with a senior executive supporter. They found that for success in management innovation that managers need to focus on early victories, creating clear metrics and developing a supportive coalition. They also noted an additional value of external validation, which entails acceptance by outside entities such as academics, consultants, media and industrial associations. The authors and others recommended that management innovators must *"seek out distinctive approaches to building legitimacy of the new practice to make it acceptable"* (Birkinshaw et al 2008, Ashforth and Gibbs 1990).

These authors list 10 core activities of the innovation process, which they group into four management innovation categories as follows;

1. Motivation- the authors identified two conditions that supported management innovation initiation. First a formal innovation process that allows an activity or problem to be identified as "new" and which requires a new solution. Second, organizational support of innovation that enhances the freedom to increase change. This can be accomplished by; creating an informal context for an employee to take initiative (Ghoshal and Bartlett 1994), by input from outside sources (Oldham and Cummings 1996) or through a more formal organizational innovation program. External agents can help with stimulation and by providing new and different ideas. Success with LEAN can be increased from any and all of these efforts.

2. Invention- Managers can help create new ideas through several approaches; a problem driven search, trial and error or idea linking with external agents. The process of invention often works better with a combination of the 3 approaches. Idea linking is connecting a new idea with an experimental effort, for example, to revamp the front office registration process, we considered the introduction of an electronic registration card with kiosks. An external source like a LEAN sensei can provide idea contextualizing, the speculation on new ways of

working to address problems or by idea refining. This is often described as disciplined imagining (Weick 1989) on how the innovation might work for specific circumstances and by ideation trial and error connected to idea linking (Campbell 1974).

3. Implementation- Managers must convert the ideas into actions. This can be accomplished by trial and error, during which the manager will be monitoring and adjusting for success (LEAN Rapid Improvement Experiments). Zbaracki notes that innovation processes are typically complex, recursive and occur in nested repeated cycles of variation, selection and retention (Zbaracki 1998). During the implementation phase, managers must address groups that are indifferent to the ideas proposed, build coalitions of support, and mobilize resources. This requires an honest interaction between the manager and staff and it depends on their base relationship. If the managers work through their relationships with the staff to create an iterative process that synthesizes the different viewpoints, innovation can move forward (Knights and McCabe 2000, Zbaracki 1998). Consultants can contribute to the implementation phase by conducting; *"Gedankenexperiment"* or thought experiments, reflective theorizing based on their knowledge and by idea refining. They can also influence the implementation by facilitating and acting as sounding boards.

4. The final phase is Theorization and Labeling. Theorization is the link between the organization values and how problems are resolved. Labeling is the naming process that has been shown to legitimize the new idea and has been found to have a significant effect on organizational acceptance (Eccles and Nohria 1992, Kieser 1997). Managers build legitimacy, promote value and translate how the innovation will integrate with organizational values. Suchman's model is a practical approach that can be used to promote new innovation legitimacy by having the employees consider a pragmatic self-interest approach on the innovation's value while the managers use an organizational moral consistency tactic to create alignment (Sushman 1995).

Manager Activity in a LEAN Healthcare Innovation

Birkinshaw et al recommends that managers incorporate real time research on the innovation process by; documenting the process, identifying it is non-linear, recording the process changes through the iteration of events, documenting the sequence of activities, identifying the sources of initiation, noting the activities of external and internal agents and their coordination. The insights gained from this approach can encourage later innovation success in other areas (A3, Box 9 approach).

The authors provided the following outline for accelerating the process of management innovation.

1. Create an awareness of the need to innovate with supportive structures,

2. Create a questioning culture with mechanisms to go deeper into problems, such as LEAN rapid improvement experiments,

3. Use examples or information from outside sources to stimulate and support innovation,

4. Use low risk experimentation, such as the LEAN "Just do its",

5. Use external Change agents, such as LEAN Senseis,

6. Make innovation part of culture and competitiveness.

(Birkinshaw et al 2008)

⦿✖⦅~:♥:▢◯

How do these studies and their findings support the implementation of LEAN? The LEAN structure to organize problem solving is the A3, a series of steps on one piece of paper to generate actions (see Appendix). In LEAN gaps are identified (A3, Box 4) and staff solutions are proposed (A3, Box 5). It is at the solution step that there is often a stumbling block to progress. LEAN Healthcare Innovation focuses on addressing this problem by moving to an innovation approach utilizing the suggestions above. Bringing these innovation elements together into a LEAN transformation represents a new solution to improve LEAN healthcare success.

Summary

1. For the LEAN implementation consider retraining managers; end the "Fire Fighting" focus and instead focus on delegation, empowerment and coaching. Use the Time Management Exercise and Pareto Charting as an educational aid.

2. Managers should use staff relationships to encourage change and decrease politics.

3. Managers should translate business strategic plans into behaviors integrated with the LEAN implementation.

4. Managers should consider making their own personal changes to be better able to; encourage LEAN, control politics, suppress egos, echo leadership vision, enjoy the success of the staff and model the values and behaviors required in LEAN.

5. Managers must take on a key role in LEAN by supporting innovation. Provide new ideas, idea linking, monitor innovation progress and adjust for success. They should provide education on innovation and support an environment that encourages innovation.

6.   Managers should promote the legacy of innovation and support the labeling process for organizational acceptance.

7.   Managers should perform research on the innovation process in their company and disseminate these lessons for future success.

Analysis of A Manager's Activity: Pareto Chart Prediction of Necessary Changes in Manager Activity in a LEAN Healthcare Innovation

Pareto charts are used to look at the manager activities before and after a LEAN implementation. Using Mintzberg's categories of manager's roles outlined in the chapter, the percentage levels for activities are grafted. In the prior to LEAN chart, "Firefighting" is considered disruption control and the dominant activity. The Pareto concept is that 20% of activity determines 80% of the results. These 20% of activities would then constitute the areas where we can "leverage" for the best results.

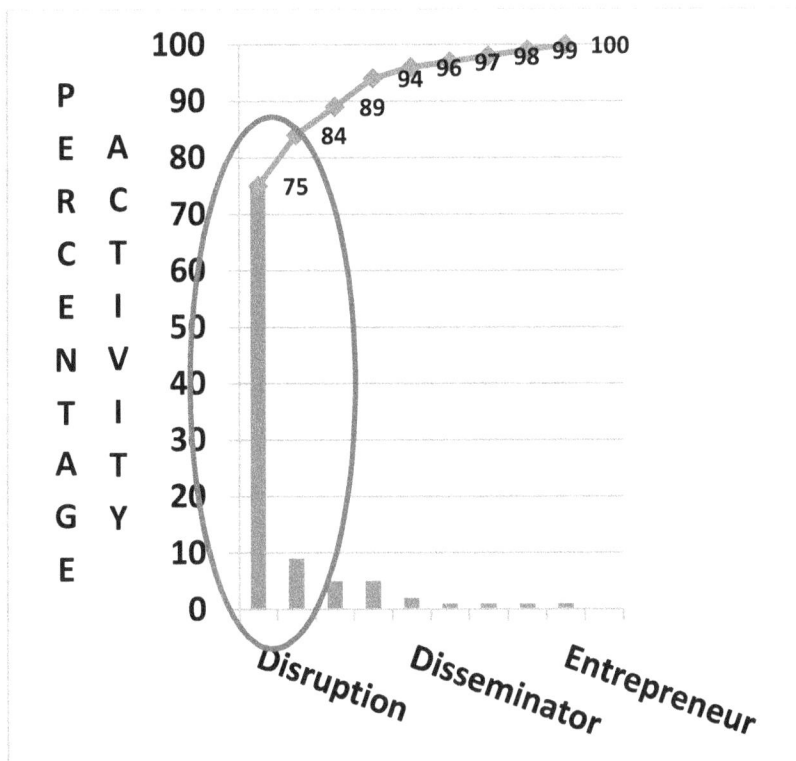

Figure 4.2 Manager Activity before LEAN implementation

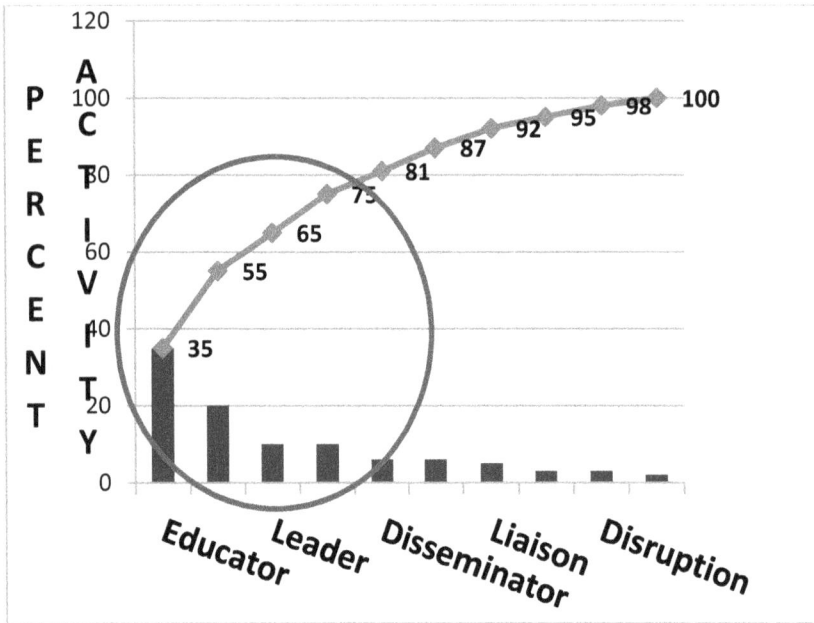

Figure 4.3 Changes in manager activity levels after LEAN.

The assessment of the "Before LEAN" graph would infer very little time for critical activities related to allocation, communication, monitoring, innovation or for education. An analysis of the change in activities after LEAN implies more control of problems through employee empowerment, more educational and leadership activities and a better overall distribution for productive work.

REFERENCES

Ashforth BE and Gibbs BW. The double-edge of organizational legitimation. Organizational Science 1990;1:177-194.

Balle M and Jones D. The 5 Biggest Mistakes Managers Make That Hinder a LEAN Startup. Fast Company 2014.

Beer, M, and Nohria N. "Cracking the Code of Change." *Harvard Business Review* 2000;78:133–141.

Birkinshaw J, Hamel G, Mol MJ. Management Innovation. Acad Management Review 2008;33:825-845.

Buchanan D, Claydon T, Doyle M. Organizational development and change: the legacy of the nineties. Human Resources Management Journal. 1999;9:20-37.

Campbell DT. Evolutionary epistemology. In P.A. Schlipp (ED) The philosophy of Karl Popper. 1974;14:413-463, Open Court.

Covey SR. The 7 Habits of Highly Effective People. 1989 Fireside Simon Schuster.

DuPree M. Leadership is an Art. 2011 Random House.

Eccles RG and Nohria N. Beyond the hype: Rediscovering the essence of management. 1992 Harvard Business School Press.

Ghoshal S and Bartlett C. Linking organizational context and managerial action: The dimensions of quality and management. Strategic Management Journal 1994;15:91-112.

Karlgaard R. The Soft Edge: Where Great Companies Find Lasting Success 2014 Jossey-Bass.

Kieser A. Rhetoric and myth in management fashion. Organization 1997;4:49-74.

Knights D ad McCabe D. "Ain't misbehaving"? Opportunities for resistance under new forms of "quality" management. Sociology 2000;34:421-436.

Koenigsaecker G. Leading the LEAN enterprise transformation. 2013 CRC Press.

McGregor D. The Human Side of Enterprise. 2006 McGraw Hill.

Mintzberg H. The Manager's Job: Folklore and Fact. Harvard Bus Review 1990.

Nohria N, Joyce W, Roberson B. What Really Works. Harvard Bus Review 2003.

Oldham G and Cummings A. Employee creativity: Personal and contextual factors at work. Acad Management Journal 1996;39:607-634.

Senge PM. The Fifth Discipline: the art and practice of the learning organization. 1990 Doubleday Currency.

Sirkin H, Keenan P, Jackson A. The Hard Side of Change Management. Harvard Bus Review 2005.

Smith S. Managing for Success. 2014 Cambridge Hill Press.

Stacy R. Management and the science of complexity: If organizational life is non-linear, can business strategies prevail? Research Technology Management 1996;39:2-5.

Stjernberg T and Philips A. Organizational innovations in a long-term perspective: Legitimacy and souls-of-fire as critical factors of change and viability. Human Relations 1993;45:1193-1219.

Suchman MC. Managing Legitimacy: Strategic and institutional approaches. Acad Management Review 1995;20:571-610.

Womack JP and Jones DT. LEAN Thinking: Banish waste and create wealth in your corporation. 2003 Free Press.

Weick KE. Theory construction as disciplined imagination. Acad Management Review. 1989;14:516-531.

Zbaracki MJ. The rhetoric and reality of total quality management. Administrative Science Quarterly 1998;43:602-638.

Chapter 5

Organizational Change in a LEAN Healthcare Innovation

"To be successful a healthcare organization must repeatedly accomplish its high hazard mission while avoiding catastrophic events despite significant hazards, dynamic tasks, time constraints, and complex technologies."

A High Reliability Organization in Healthcare

In the leadership section we noted that leadership failure was the most common reason for LEAN programs to fail. In the management section, we proposed a different opinion that manager performance was more accountable for the failures of LEAN programs. But now, after additional contemplations and review, we will make the case that the primary reason for LEAN program failures is the behavior of the organization itself, specifically the employees as individuals.

A LEAN transformation is a transformation that occurs with each employee in the place of work. No matter what leaders do, or what managers promote, if the staff do not make the change in their daily work, change their habits and values, then LEAN fails. This opinion is supported by studies from Mckinsey and Deloitte in which they determined that the employee resistance to change ranged from 39% to 60% (McKinsey and Deloitte). In this section, we will address those staff issues that are critical for a successful LEAN transformation including resistance, engagement, modeling, education, the timing of change, the use of evidence based practices, and dealing with low performers.

General Considerations: Chronic Organizational Problems

In their book, *"Lean-Led Hospital Design: Creating the Efficient Hospital of the Future,"* Grunden and Hagood cited research that more than 50 percent of hospital based organizations in America have attempted some form of a Lean Healthcare initiative. Unfortunately, they found less than 10 percent were successful (Grunden and Hagood 2012). This is similar to John Kotter's estimate of success for any type of change effort at 30% (Kotter 2007). To understand why LEAN fails at the staff and organizational level starts with considering the basic definition of an organization. As defined by Covey, an organization is "relationships with a shared purpose and the purpose being to meet someone's needs". He promotes that to be a successful organization, it should allow members to sense their innate worth and potential for greatness. They should be able to contribute their unique talents and passion to achieve the organization's purpose. For all the staff, their goals should be to accomplish the organization's goal's and highest priorities in a principled centered way (Covey 2004). An exercise in the planning phase of the implementation is to survey the staff on Covey's definitions of a successful organization and on their roles and relationships. A LEAN transformation will require the organizations core elements and relationships to improve and for a greater realization of shared purpose. By creating a group understanding of new purpose and by identifying staff with relationship issues such as lack of work meaning or purpose, early problems will be identified.

Steven Covey outlines four chronic organizational problems that are very applicable to healthcare and may provide an insight into improvement activity failures. In the categories, as defined by Covey, the problems are;

1. Spirit/Conscience- Healthcare organizations are dominated by low trust of leaders, managers and of diverse siloed groups. For a LEAN initiative, the lack of trust or of engagement creates an impossible environment for change.

2. Mind/Vision- A conceptual approach, explained by a well-defined vision and mission statement creates the necessary structures leading to behaviors for success. Unfortunately, they are usually missing in healthcare. The void is filled by hidden agendas, bad politics, poor decision making and frequently chaos. This is the opposite of what a LEAN program needs for success.

3. Body/Discipline- this category reflects the need to formulize, through the hard work of reviewing and adapting, the organizational protocols, policies and structures. Often, this does not occur or occurs too late in a change effort. For LEAN to succeed, the alignment, compensation rewards and hiring process must all change to allow for success.

4. Heart /Passion- In healthcare, there are major problems in how most organizations coordinate functions and activities; it is the old style command and control structure that treats healthcare providers as machines that produce patient care. This leads to organizational fragmentation resulting in a discontented and a disempowered staff. A dysfunctional disorganized organization is the norm in healthcare and this kills passion and commitment. This might be the most critical problem for LEAN implementations which require a higher level of coordination, employee empowerment and most of all a passionate committed staff that wants to improve (Covey 2004).

ⓞ✘ℂ~: ✍ :△

"Ailing organizations cannot see their problems"

John Gardner

To expand on why an organization has difficulties with a LEAN transition, Dave LaHote, President of Education at the LEAN Enterprise Institute, believes that it is *"a lack of agreement"*. Dr. Dave Munch reinforces this point by citing that a primary failure for LEAN implementations is the failure to achieve staff buy-in and their commitment to make the time necessary for a successful outcome. Dr. Munch recommends using dialogue, reasoning and the scientific method to reach agreement with employees (Munch 2013). This point is reinforced by the McKinsey Global Study that found 85% of managers felt that information about organizational change was inadequate and 91% felt that the metrics about change were not clear (Mckinsey). These organizational issues; lack of trust, limited vision, structural malalignment, lack of buy in, lack of empowerment and disagreement epitomize healthcare organizations. For those considering bringing about organizational change these issues must be addressed at the staff level in an organized and planned fashion.

"People don't resist change. They resist being changed!"

Peter Senge

ⓞ✘ℂ ~: ✍ :□

Resistance to Change

Rosabeth Kanter has listed the 10 specific reasons that people resist change. They are:

1. Loss of control
2. Excess uncertainty
3. Surprise
4. "Everything is different"
5. Loss of face
6. Concerns about competence
7. More work
8. Ripple effects
9. Past resentments
10. "Sometimes the threat is real"

The multitude of possible issues for the staff that Kanter lists provides an insight into the overall complexity and extensiveness that is part of change (Kanter 2012). The magnitude of the problem for healthcare providers is also illustrated in Alan Deutschman's book, "Change or Die: Three keys to change at work and in Life". He points out something every physician knows, that even when faced with dire health consequences, people still cannot change. To overcome these problems, he recommends focusing on 3 areas to improve change efforts; "relating, repeating and reframing". "Relating" means to make the change applicable to a person or cause that inspires hope. This supports the concept of the leadership "*selling*" change by politicking with the staff to believe in change. For managers this entails explaining change in terms the staff understands. Deutschman uses "repeat" to mean repetitive training to support or provide new skills or habits. The third key to successful change is personal "reframing" which is creating a new way of thinking about the problem, change or life in general. His basic premise is that change fails not based on effort or positive intent but based on a lack of understanding of the change process itself and for not applying tools to support change. He emphasizes that change comes from changing the emotions of the individual, usually through a relationship or situation (Deutschman 2009). We can propose that these lessons about personal change are just as applicable for healthcare providers changing for LEAN.

The Patient Centered Health Improvement Approach: A New Definition of Successful Patient Outcomes

Another explanation for failure in LEAN initiatives is the failure to realize that LEAN will be moving from the standard healthcare approach of assessment, diagnosis and treatment to a patient centered "*improvement approach*"; a subtle but important difference. Because the practice of medicine is individualized, the focus has always been specific to the patient or clinical situation and the primary definition of success, a patient health outcome, is primarily controlled by the patient's specific clinical characteristics. This specificity has led healthcare providers away from more general approaches to healthcare process improvement and innovation. What is required in LEAN is a new definition of "successful patient outcome". This is a shift in focus from not just providing good care, but to focus on innovating to provide even better more reliable care in the future; which is a critical conceptual difference. If the patient care given is already the best it can be; perhaps it could be provided faster, could have been more accessible or could be better coordinated with other healthcare issues or the patient's life style. This difference, the change in the goals to Anticipatory Nursing Care, continual improvement, innovations and improving the value of care in the patient's terms is often not clearly communicated to the staff in LEAN implementations.

Staff Engagement, The #1 Issue

The core or primary issue related to staff participation in change, improvement effort or innovation is the staff's level of engagement. More importantly, the motivation to overcome resistance originates from their engagement. As summarized by Kevin Sheridan, to be engaged means the staff is intellectually committed and emotionally bonded to their organization. If the staff believes in their organization; they would recommend their healthcare organization to others. This represents a good survey question in the planning phase. He stresses the importance of engagement with the following facts. Engaged employees are;

- 10 times more likely to feel their good work is recognized and feel senior management is concerned about them as individuals,

- 8 times more likely to feel their supervisor encourages their growth,

- 7 times more likely to feel they receive regular feedback,

- 4 times more likely to be satisfied with their job and less likely to consider leaving.

Additionally, there is a very high correlation between employee engagement and customer satisfaction. (R=0.85, Figure 5.1). Unfortunately, in general, only 27% of employees are actively engaged, 60% are ambivalent and 13% are actively disengaged. (HR solutions normative database 2011 of 117,868 employees).

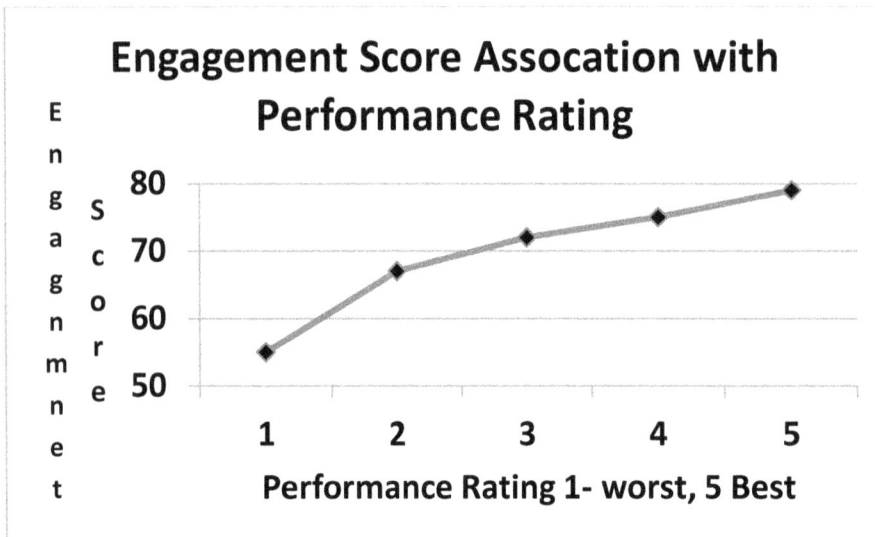

Figure 5.1 Employee engagement score correlated with performance assessment (adapted from Sheridan 2012)

When we consider that engagement is the indicator of the relationship that the employee has with the organization; it follows that it reflects the desire to be part of organizational value and it reflects the intellectual and emotional bond to the employer. This then translates to the degree of eagerness to exert extra discretionary effort and creativity for change. An additional component to consider in addressing employee engagement is that most employees (73%) agree in joint ownership of this relationship. David Zinger, an engagement expert, notes that leadership can help their staff by supporting them in owning their engagement. These employees should exert ownership over their jobs; they can be organizational promoters and demonstrate passion about the vision and mission. They can be self-motivated performers at a high level, can be good coworkers that are optimistic and with whom it is a pleasure to work (Zinger 2015). As is outlined above, an engaged employee that owns their relationship with their organization is the foundation for successful change efforts like a LEAN transformation, but how does that level of engagement occur?

"An empowered organization is one in which individuals have the knowledge, skill, desire and opportunity to personally succeed in a way that leads to collective organizational success"

Steven Covey

Creating Employee Engagement: Sheridan outlines 11 factors linked to engagement:

1. Recognition- Fifty-six percent of the engagement level is related to recognition. A program should be instituted to determine what performance will be recognized, how it will be promoted and how often it will occur. A specific LEAN recognition program acknowledging employees that are embracing change is additionally important. Unfortunately, recognition programs in healthcare are generally less then authentic.

2. Career Development-This represents the opportunity to move up within the organization. Ninety-four percent of companies offer education for advancement, but this is uncommon in healthcare. Additionally, a career development program should include a mentoring process; also rare in healthcare. Using LEAN and embracing improvement through change can be a center piece for career development.

3. Manager relationship- Thirty percent of employees do not feel valued or feel they do not "belong" because of their manager relationship. This relationship is critical because the first two issues noted above are dependent upon it. This emphasizes the critical nature of managers in cultural transformations. Managers must put others first, increase confidence, promote open communication and provide guidance for staff. In LEAN this should be an initial assessment and manager exercise.

4. Strategy and Mission-Employees need to be empowered for change activities to be successful; employees want to be part of something that matters, to be of value. However, 36% don't know the organization strategy and mission and 31% don't think they contribute. The staff needs a connection with values and mission, to know

how to be "best in class" such that their personal goals contribute to department and organizational goals. Assessing this should be a staff exercise in the planning phase.

⬫✕⬫◉ ~: ⬫:₵

5.   Job content-To improve engagement, the staff and manager should review (together) the results that different tasks generate. The manager should know, for each employee, what causes pride, what do they like or dislike about the work. Changes in job content can increase engagement through considering new tasks and roles.

◉⬫₵~: ⬫:∞

6.   Senior management and leadership relationship with employees-For the employees, the belief that leadership is concerned about them is correlated with leadership visibility (R=0.9). In part, this explains the success of Gemba walks, and Tom Peter's "management by walking around". Visibility of leadership is a key factor in engagement and successful change efforts.

◉⬫₵~: ⬫:Ɛ

> *"We know that communication is a problem, but the company is not going to discuss it with the employees"*
>
> *Scott Adams*

7.   Open and effective communication- Only 68% of employees believe their organization's policies are clearly communicated. For successful cultural change efforts, this result must be improved. The improvement starts with a consideration of where the staff gets their information; huddles, social media and personal meetings can all be used to verify that the priorities are clear.

◉⬫₵ ~: ⬫:✗

8.   Co-worker satisfaction, cooperation and sharing- Eighty-seven percent of employees indicate they have friendly helpful coworkers; a key driver in engagement. This perception supports the idea that promoting social events and to have "fun" with co-workers is not superfluous but an important part of culture.

◉⬫₵ ~: ⬫:Δℓ

9. Providing available resources – Fifty percent of employees don't have the proper equipment to complete their tasks at work. This emphasizes the value of Gemba walks or as Quint Studer recommends *"rounding for outcomes"*; these are meetings in which these issues can be unearthed by direct observation and staff interactions.

    ⊚⚡☾~: ⚡ :△△

10. Organizational culture and core values -Shared values anchor culture. There is a need for a framework to support values that are aligned to initiatives and then subsequently behaviors. The framework must be clearly communicated through multiple sources and efforts. Another exercise in the planning phase is to survey the staff on vision, mission and core values and to discuss their everyday application.

    ✷✕✷⊚~: ⚡ :☆

11. Pairing-To increase engagement, pair the ambivalent staff with the engaged employees and focus on a workplace environment that makes engagement thrive.

    ⊚⚡☾ ~: ⚡ :△☐

An Engaged Workforce for Excellence in Practice

Quint Studer in his book *"Hardwired for Excellence"* provides another source for practical principles that enhance an engaged effective work force.

1. Excellence and commitment required – In healthcare, to provide value means to believe you are providing excellent care. When employees feel valued, physicians feel that their patients are getting good care and the patients feel that they getting great service and high quality. By requiring excellence in practice it creates value for both the patients and the staff; to *"Be the Best"* should be translated during the LEAN implementation into quality and patient satisfaction metrics.

2. Service Culture-Studer emphasizes that culture is living out the values through behavior. This is reflected in social norms like providing elevator space for patients by moving out. He recommends a team approach to dealing with values by creating teams such as a patient satisfaction team, physician satisfaction team, service recovery team, etc. He recommends that employees sign an affidavit that commits them to the organization's standards of behavior (the decision stage in change implementation, see below). In a LEAN transformation; the change in

philosophy, the strategic deployment and an innovation program replace the need for these committees because it becomes the mission and ingrained values for each employee.

3.   Leadership- Leadership excellence is demonstrating the appropriate behaviors and to develop a form of re-recruitment of the existing staff. Re-recruitment means to confront the staff about problems or behaviors and in so doing, use that as an opportunity to communicate values and better behaviors. This process is continued by following results and metrics with a reward and recognition program. Those employees that demonstrate the ability to change and improve are re-recruited. Success does not happen by chance, it is achieved through basic cause and effect relationships. Every action made by employers reflects their perceptions of the leadership values and the values the organization requires. Leadership actions either reinforce or sabotage the necessary cultural change for improvement (Studer 2003).

LEAN Staff Education and Staff Modeling Failure: The LEAN "Rollout"

Just as pushing the staff to embrace practice excellence is an engagement process so too is the changing and modeling of daily behaviors. Modeling in the staff's daily behavior is another important area of failure in LEAN transformations that effects the entire organization. LEAN is a process that is visible every day in all situations by everyone. As LEAN begins, if you don't embrace this and live LEAN, then you are compromising the vision of the LEAN transformation by "*a thousand betrayal behaviors*". It is through small daily changes that leadership and staff move the mission forward or conversely kill the transformation. This failure in modeling is directly reflective of failures in the LEAN educational processes. LEAN education should focus on creating LEAN philosophy and tool competencies such that the staff has a comfort level to start change. The staff must feel a level of sophistication in LEAN methods, problem solving and philosophy. This educational program must be uniformly distributed throughout the organization in an extensive and widely disseminated manner to initiate a shared understanding of the new philosophy. This requires special planning for the needed educational sites and coordinated scheduling. Unfortunately, some LEAN education programs take too long to achieve wide dissemination or the program uses poor or antiquated educational approaches. Additionally, there is often a failure to educate in basic or critical areas such as team training, listening skills and how to initiate continuous improvement, which then undercuts the LEAN implementation. But the biggest failure is to not demonstrate to the staff why the incorporation of LEAN is in their best interest during the "Roll Out".

ᗝᗡᙧᗡᙏᙧ~: ꜀ᗡ꜀ :Δᙏᙏ

Timing; It Can Be Everything, Especially if it's Bad Timing

Another area to consider to prevent failure in the LEAN organization implementation is related to the timing of the role out. If you conceptualize an organization's success as a plot against time, it will rise steadily and at some point level off and curve downward to a lower level (the Handy Curve, Handy 1994). The time to implement a major change initiative is at the top of the curve when the organization has the most resources and abilities to make change occur. Missing this window of opportunities has been termed the "failure of success". It is a common error during this phase to use the current successful approach to try to improve as opposed to embracing a new tactic. Understanding how to change and identifying what and when to change is not obvious if the old approach that has led to success is applied. So, how do you improve if you are on the downward curve as an organization? The first step is to realize it will now be more challenging to improve and will require additional or special efforts which may have not been previously applied. The second step is to summon the courage to marshal the resources necessary for change at a time when it's risky to devote any resources; in gambling terms, <u>it's time to double down</u>. Third, and possibly most importantly, it is necessary to identify, that it is now really the beginning of a crisis and to respond with immediacy, even though it seems like business as usual. A good organizational exercise at the beginning of the implementation is to plot the organization's position on the "Handy Curve" and then adjust the LEAN implementation approach to the organizations circumstances.

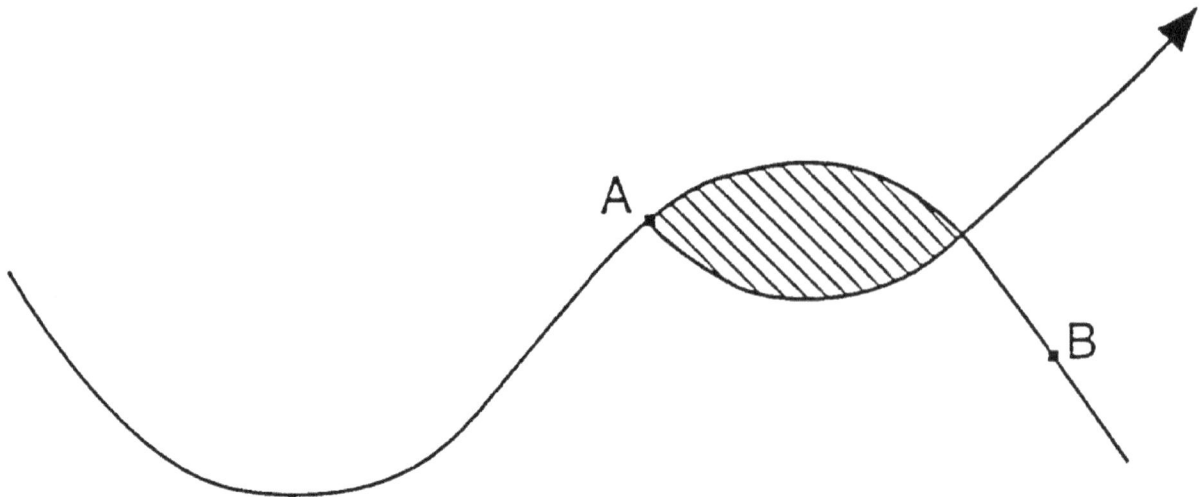

Figure 5.2 The Handy Curve demonstrating at point A, the time to start a new approach for continued success. Unfortunately, point B is the typical time that most organizations realize they need to change to improve, inferring why so many fail.

As Demonstrated in Figure 5.2 of the organizational Handy Curve, the vertical access is a summary assessment of organization success versus a time frame, usually 5 to 10 years. The cross hatched area represents the impact of an improvement process, such as LEAN, aimed at continued improvement for the next 5 to 10 years. The figure demonstrates the necessary drop in productivity during the implementation and then subsequent later improvement and sustained success (Handy 1994). At the start of any improvement process, knowing whether your organization is at point A or point B will change the approach.

Evidenced Based Medicine and the Scientific Method

Just as staff engagement is a critical factor in a successful change effort, so too is staff education and skill preparation. Another problem in healthcare change efforts is that most organizations have been slow to adopt evidenced based practices and scientific approaches to problem solving. Studies have demonstrated a lack of use of evidence by healthcare managers in decision making in both the UK and Canada (Lavis et al 2003, Canadian health services research foundation 2000, 2004). Based on these studies authors recommended that managers;

"Find more effective ways to organize and communicate priorities and when dealing with problems, simplify findings and demonstrate application…screen and appraise information".

Part of the explanation for the poor EBM application has been blamed on the *"Rapid Cycle"* (Kovner 2005). As explained by Kovner et al in their study of 68 US healthcare manager's practices, *"Rapid Cycle"* is the concept of how the rapid changes in medical treatment, healthcare regulations and policies represent a special challenge for medical providers to deliver up to date and complete care. To address this problem, they recommended;

- ❖ Forming committees to assure EHR application,
- ❖ A communication system to disseminate new information throughout the organization,
- ❖ Developing a culture that uses and values research,
- ❖ Training in research application.

The lack of a scientific approach to problem solving in healthcare organizations has also been pointed out by the National Center for Healthcare Leadership in 2004. This group recommended an "Evidence Based Health Services Management Program (EBHSM); a more formal approach to identifying problems and applying evidence for improvement. In their goals for healthcare "Leadership Competency" the group described a need for:

- o *"Analytical thinking"*
- o *"The ability to understand a situation, issue, or problem by breaking it into smaller pieces or tracing its implications in a step by step way…"*,
- o Organizing systematically,
- o Comparing different features systematically,
- o Prioritizing,
- o Identifying time sequences,
- o Understanding causal relationships or if-then relationships.

The healthcare staff's lack of experience and rigor in problem solving represents another obstacle to a transition to LEAN. Prior to the LEAN implementation, time and effort may be required to develop fundamental problem solving skills that utilize EBM and the scientific method blended with LEAN tools.

"The Wall", The Failure to Address Poor Performers

Another reason for failure in LEAN implementations is the response to poor performers during change. This occurs when an organization reaches "The Wall" as conceptualized by Quint Studer; a state that occurs during 5 phases of organizational change. He summarizes them as:

1. "The Honey moon" phase-At initiation this period starts with success related to leadership rounds and thank yous for the staff. The employees begin standardizing key behaviors and the reward and recognition program is promoting a new accountability. Values are moving to be hardwired and leadership can see a change in performance.

2. "Reality Sets in" phase-Resistance to change is now evident in a "we versus them" mentality, ambiguity seems more prevalent and ambivalence has increased. Efforts to address this response is through training, improved communication, the further hardwiring of values, and conversations about performance.

3. "Uncomfortable Gap" phase- Now "The Wall" appears, it is the gap in performance between the high and low performers, which is widening. Process improvement is seen to increase; there is still a need for more standardization and inconsistencies seem more obvious. There is realization that the performance gap between the high or good performer's from the lower performers now seems unfairly addressed, such that the high performers will leave, disengage or slow down if it is not addressed. This is approached with more training, re-recruitment, additional communication, promoting winners, adjusting the staff to the right jobs and most importantly to move high performers up or low performers out, if necessary.

4. "Consistency" phase-There is now high system performance, the right leaders and managers are in place and they understand the keys to success; they are disciplined and proactive leaders. There is now a push for innovation based on reliable standardize behaviors.

5. "Leading the way"-The organization now functions based on results, employees know their purpose and the organization is an institution of choice for patients and physicians. The organization is improving care; the seemingly impossible has been achieved.

Studer's conceptualization of change in healthcare organizations points out a critical area in which many organizations fail. It is the inability to face "The Wall"; that is, to manage the staff through change, specifically the low performers. This is a critical problem in change implementations and cultural transformations, such as LEAN.

> *"The range of what we think and do is limited by what we fail to notice. And because we fail to notice that we fail to notice, there is little we can do to change; until we notice how failing to notice shapes our thoughts and deeds."*
>
> *RD Laing*

Modeling in Organizational Change and Transformation

A recommendation for successful organizational change is provided by Cawsey et al in their book, Organizational change: An action oriented toolkit (Cawsey et al 2011). The authors recommend proceeding based on several conceptualizations of organizational change models. In their conceptualizations, the "goal setting model" is most like LEAN in that it involves gap analysis, defining a future state, setting goals and measuring results. The authors note that there is *"clear evidence that recognition of complexity of change is important in formulation of effective change strategies."* This emphasizes the importance of organizational assessment and planning in a LEAN healthcare implementation (also a good leadership exercise). The authors provide eight categories of initial actions to lead to successful organizational change:

1. Consider a change mission or purpose,
2. Redefine strategy,
3. Consider shifts in objectives or performance targets,
4. Make alterations in organizational culture, values, beliefs,
5. Consider organizational restructuring,
6. Seek technology changes,
7. Consider task design,
8. Evaluate and change people,

They and others also point out that organizations interested in change must also decide "how to change" and "what to change" (Higgs and Rowland 2000).

Their point is that change is not simple; *"it is complex, interactive and emergent"*. All these areas must be addressed as a separate concern. In addition, there should be a consideration of the rate of change; if change is constant, the organization will require a balancing to maintain stability and to assure coherence of direction and purpose. Providing organizational balance is a key role for leadership and management in LEAN (Higgs and Rowland 2007). The Authors drew upon the Beckhard and Harris and Lewin models to recommend the following action steps to institute organizational change, which included;

1. Discuss the need for change with the staff with consideration of performance gaps,

2. Create teams and taskforces for desired outcomes and better utilization of data on organizational performance,

3. Seek expert advice,

4. Evaluate the costs of change and budget appropriately,

5. Consider the necessary staffing and training related to the change.

(Beckhard and Harris 1987, Lewin 1947)

The "Unity Organizational Model for Change"

A LEAN transformation is a cultural change. The current business literature is overwhelmed with books and articles on organizational cultural change, but there is still very little success in achieving this in healthcare. Since the failure rate is so high, it may be useful to look at conceptualizations about cultural change from other fields. In general, the first step, as noted above, is to identify the need to manage the change process itself as a unique organizational event. As noted in Deloitte's Organizational Acceleration program, *"There is no single process by which people or organizations change. Organizations often respond more effectively to change programs that are tailored to the way they operate."* The next reasonable step is to adopt an approach or model to conceptualize the change efforts. The Transtheoretical Model proposed by Prochaska and DiClemente is the most popular of the "step models" for change in personal health behaviors and has been applied to organizations (Prochaska and DiClemente 2005, Armitage and Conner 2000, Prochaska et al 2001, Levesque 2001, Mayeno 2007). Their model included five stages of change: precontemplation, contemplation, preparation, action, and maintenance which the authors proposed as a required sequential progression. Most of the evidence for this model comes from studies of health behavioral change programs related to alcohol, drug abuse, and smoking cessation. A modification that may help healthcare organizations in a transformational change builds on the step model concept with stage matched interventions. Organizational coordination is provided by integrated management of step progression, behavioral performance metrics indicating success and group/team activities to actuate new cultural norms. In a sense the staff's education about the model and its subsequent application constitutes an organizational exercise of facing a struggle together. A suggestion for how the model could be applied to healthcare organizations includes the following phases;

1. Reflection- As the process starts, there is no conscious intention of making a change, but awareness and interest which may be sparked by communication of stories, experiences and success; there may be resistance to even considering change related to past failures. To move past reflection, the staff, by reviewing their goals together, will sense that their behavior is at odds with important personal and organizational aims. The promotion of the organization's vision and the communication about the need for change is the critical issue in this phase. Similar to the TTM model, surveys are used at this phase; metrics and an educational program to support successful change are developed as group and organizational activities.

2. Deliberation- the staff often vacillates for a period of time in this stage. They should be aware that their behavior is a problem and are now considering change but still aren't committed to taking action. Ambivalence may lead to reconsidering the costs and benefits. Certain decision techniques may help the organization move to the next stage. A force Field diagram is a good group exercise to weight strengths and weaknesses or opposing forces for change. The impact of this exercise can be extended to considering the forces on obstacles or barriers to overcome. Another group exercise to consider is a Fear Deposition Chart, in which, the staff list their fears related to the change and try to prioritize. The fears are discussed by examining the root causes the fears represent. The public airing of fears and concerns can be a powerful exercise to improve organizational relationships and in creating a group identity. The process of planning for change, changing structures and education about change are all important during this phase. Managers, through staff meetings prepare an estimate of the staff resistance to change (application of "Change Formula").

3. Preparation. At this stage the organization now agrees it must change, and has considered the ramifications and believes it can change. The date for formally starting the change process is agreed upon. The focus is now on potential obstacles or situational challenges associated with failure (see below). Exercises to help with this phase include a 5S approach aimed at improving the work environment or a reverse fishbone exercise to consider the categories of

structures that will need to be modified for change. LEAN education about methods and tools and continued planning for change are critical at this stage. An affinity diagram that focuses on the obstacles to change is a good exercise for leaders, managers and staff that includes both the organizational changes and changes for them personally (personal development). The results at the end of this phase are the creation of a realistic action plan with achievable specific goals and alternative behaviors implemented through small steps for each staff member, department and the organization as a whole. This is shared with the entire organization.

4. Decision- Is a formal process or ceremony, in which a signed commitment or affidavit in which the personal decision and commitment is formalized. This process involves a public comment with the work group or the organization as a whole explaining the personal reasoning for the decision and includes a confirmation of the date for change to start.

5. Execution. At this stage, the organization has started to change and started to experience the challenges at work without the old behavior. The staff will need to practice the alternative behaviors identified as necessary during the preparation stage and to remember their importance to reinforce motivation. Reinforcement techniques include; a daily review of their decision document, "self-talk" as a technique to bolster resolve as an independent practice rehearsal and networking to talk about the new experiences. The staff should focus on attaining support from the managers and Senseis for repeated training and refining of goals. Exercises used at this time include the LEAN standards of Just Do It, Rapid Improvement Experiments and Project management; the processes that support the implementation phase of LEAN. Metrics that demonstrate changes in behavior such as suggestions for improvement, innovations tested, process improvement and patient related outcomes are reviewed with the staff by managers through visual metrics for feedback. Departmental and organizational meetings are held to review progress and problems.

6. Sustain. Once the new organizational changes are in place for at least six months, the sustain stage should start. The key is to prevent relapse and to assure integration of the change throughout the organization and in the habits of the staff. This requires monitoring for relapse and the introduction of new cues to identify the recurrence of old behaviors. This also means to look for "*UFOs*", the emergent and unexpected dynamic system changes. The focus is to continue to build on change and reach for additional improvements. Group activities for

assessment and comment, metrics on change performance and cross departmental coordination are now regular activities. Surveys are used for comparisons about improvement in work related satisfaction.

꘎X꘤◉~꘎ ⤳꘎OO

◉꘤꘍~꘎ ⤳꘎△◌

"Just as with patients, you can't heal an injured company by just telling it what is wrong, the organizational needs must be addressed; it needs treatment, commitment and concern."

Foundational Support for a Cultural Change model

A Team Approach and a Questioning Culture

John Womack points out that a "LEAN cultural approach" to problems is significantly different than in other approaches. This approach applies interdisciplinary teams, not departmental silos and it uses a focus on group goals. An important part of the LEAN cultural approach is about enabling managers to try to improve through problem management, root cause analysis and the sharing of information within a team structure (Womack et al 2005). For a team approach to be effective it requires an open interaction for all team members; a "Questioning Culture".

"Questioning Culture"

In his book, "*A more beautiful Question; The power of Inquiry to Spark breakthrough ideas*," Warren Berger promotes that the key cultural change for organizational improvement is to create a "Questioning Culture". The author interviewed 100 creative thinkers from multiple different businesses and based on his research, he recommends that questions like; "why", "what if", and "how", can themselves become the process of change. Berger also emphasizes the need for "relaxed or reflective" thinking to generate new or innovative answers and that leadership support is critical to create the culture of "*beautiful questions*" (Berger 2014). This fits with the LEAN methodologies such as using the "5 Whys", gap analysis (A3, box 4) then moving to the "*What if*" approach (A3, Box 5) with an in-depth consideration of "*How*" in Box 7 of the A3 project plan. A focus on "*a questioning organizational culture*" has shown to improve knowledge transfer within the organization and supports evidence based decisions (Kovner and Rundall 2006). However, this approach may necessitate a change in the leadership and management approach to the staff. A questioning culture can generate anxiety for leaders and managers; the questioning may make them feel inadequate or not trustworthy. To deal with the new challenging questions may require managers to pursue personal development to be able to be comfortable with this type of culture. Additionally, a questioning culture may initially decrease efficiency because of the interactive engagement, which can be time consuming, contemplative work. (Lavis 2003) The adjustments for leaders and managers may require training and restructuring of work duties. For the staff, they may need training on how to apply questioning in a positive and productive way.

⊚✸ℂ~: ⌁ :☐�ᴿ

"If you change your thinking, you can change your life"
William James

If we apply these recommendations, how will we identify that a LEAN transformation is occurring? Jim Luckman addresses this by crystalizing what it means to really move to a LEAN transformation in his article "Doing lean versus becoming LEAN." He acknowledges that there is a 79% failure rate for LEAN implementations, which he believes is related to a focus on methodological application of LEAN tools but failing to change culture. He defined *"doing LEAN"* as tracking lean training, performing Kaizen (improvement) events and considering LEAN application across the organization as it impacts on cost. Conversely, he believes that *"becoming LEAN"* can be identified when it is clear that you are *"creating a complete organization of problem solvers who are engaged in solving the right problems at the right level every day."* He notes this requires a mindset of curiosity and experimentation, a commitment to learning and reflection and high quality relationships. He proposes that you know you are *"becoming LEAN"* when you have small groups excited about problem solving, when value streams are aligning systems, when the organizational dialogue has changed to be more respectful, when trust is building and real problems are exposed (Luckman 2014).

Business Management Practices and Staff Incorporation
For the staff, business management practices are normally not the primary concern, however it is important that the staff understand the organization's basic business practices as they are translated from the vision statement, strategic plans and organizational details. Many healthcare organizations have value statements that are very similar; they include teamwork, integrity, compassion, respect, community service, etc. Few employees have translated those values into work related behaviors or

more importantly, excluded conflicting actions. The translation of proposals from leadership and management into real behaviors is critical for successful cultural change. Additionally, the response and feedback from the staff back up to leadership about central values is equally important in a change event like LEAN. This is the capitalization of the value of knowledge workers; a fundamental business practice for success that should be initiated early in a LEAN implementation.

ⓞ✗ℂ~: ⚡:□△

Business Models in Healthcare and Organizational Culture Change

A major problem in healthcare as opposed to other industries is the organization's structural model. As previously mentioned, basic functions of reporting structures, role accountability and linked reimbursements are different in healthcare when compared to other businesses. Nurses in hospitals do not report to the physicians that give them orders, nor do their supervisors. Often physicians do not work for the hospitals in which they practice, however legally the hospital has accountability for allowing these physicians to practice there. Physicians regardless of the organization are primarily accountable only to themselves and their patients and usually do not report or accept supervision from an administrator. A medical organization is usually reimbursed differently than the physicians they work with, and at times their interests are at odds, however hospital cost and reimbursements are in large part dependent on the attending physician's decisions and their documentation of the same. This business model requires a different approach then those used for other types of industries when considering a LEAN implementation. In healthcare, the critical feature of the LEAN implementation is to align physicians and administration and to then coordinate their management; maybe the biggest challenge in healthcare. Adding to this problem as noted the McKinsey Global study of organizational change, surveys demonstrated that 88% of respondents felt that the business structural changes were not successfully defined (McKinsey). Steven Covey's recommendations on how to manage fragmented groups may provide some guidance for this difficult situation. His approach includes pursuing the win-win solution. To start by trying to understand your colleagues and only then, to ask them to try to understand you. To look for new ways to synergize the different groups concerns. Although very basic, these recommendations are critical to allow for a cultural transformation to progress for the entire organization (Covey 2004).

ⓞ✗ℂ~: ⚡:□□

"We are what we repeatedly do, excellence then is not an art, but a habit"

Aristotle

Personal Development of Staff and the Organization in LEAN

Since organizational culture is the translation of leadership values and plans into staff behavior, it then follows that a change in organizational culture will require a change in personal values at work, reflected in work related behaviors and habits. This section will start with a discussion of the theories about how individuals begin the process of deciding to change, such as by being open minded or reflective. We will then consider how individuals approach these decisions; to change their values, personal behaviors and how social norms effect habit change. The effort to help healthcare providers with their own personal change is a critical event for cultural change that is often neglected in a LEAN implementation. It must be addressed with each tech, nurse and physician if there is to be success in terms of transformation.

"One does not 'manage' people. The task is to lead people. And the goal is to make productive the specific strengths and knowledge of each individual."

Peter Drucker

Because of the challenges that accompany a LEAN transformation, a focus on personal growth is required for most staff to fully embrace LEAN behaviors and to deal with the pain of change. The challenge is to promote self-learning and self-motivation for each staff member. This is where directing versus leading the staff is a clear difference. For those who want to apply Peter Drucker's concepts related to initiating progress and improvement, it's about enabling the staff as knowledge workers and freeing them to deal with the new problems such as value-based purchasing (VBP), heart failure readmissions and bundled payment schemes. Rick Morrow echoes this sentiment; for healthcare to be more efficient and effective, it will require capitalizing on the strengths and knowledge of each staff member (Morrow 2013). This sentiment starts with open mindedness and reflection as a means to initiate LEAN empowerment.

"A mind is like a parachute; it doesn't work if it's not open"

Frank Zappa

Reflection, Deliberation, Open mindedness and Engagement

Social cognitive theory suggests that self-monitoring, self judgement and self-reaction are necessary parts of the process for personal change (Bandura 1977, Bandura et al 1997). To reach a state that supports these activities requires us to be open minded; to reflect on our situations and to engage in considering change. We know from studies in healthcare, that the required engagement that would support this activity is a problem. The Advisory Board Company used their National Engagement Database from 250 healthcare organizations, to focus on 5 key clinical areas related to 15 best practices in healthcare. The Advisory board estimated that 7.4% of registered nurses (RN) are disengaged. The numbers are worse for LPNs and physicians at 38.4% and 37.8% disengagement respectively. More troubling is that only 32.6% of RNs consider themselves really engaged. Without engagement, there is no connection or motivation to improve, which means that a large percentage of the staff are not focused enough on their job to be supportive of a LEAN Transformation (Virkstis 2014). To break this vicious cycle, the first step will be an initiative aimed at generating reflection, self-evaluation and open mindedness.

"The measure of intelligence is the ability to change"

A. Einstein

"Those who cannot change their minds cannot change anything"

George Bernard Shaw

A Reflective Approach to Support Change

An important point about engagement and open mindedness is that it requires a reflective approach. An example of increasing reflective thinking and open mindedness in medical practice was sited in a study by Shaw et al. This article emphasized the value of a structured reflection technique used by a staff of 4 Family Medicine Practices in an attempt to improve colorectal cancer screening. The study methods included using meeting notes and recordings from office staff. They categorized the reflections into; First organizational reflection, which promoted buy in, and that provided motivation and feelings of inspiration. The second type of reflections were those that enhanced team problem solving and change management. The third type of reflections was on the dynamics in relationships related to implementing QI changes. They noted the use of "Helicopter Vision", to rise above the situation for an overview of context and component interaction as a valuable technique for improvement. This is an approach that also encourages double loop learning. This study and others emphasize that being reflective or open minded can be a valuable approach in the process of change that can work in healthcare (Shaw et al 2012, Antonacopoulou 2004, Gould et al 2004).

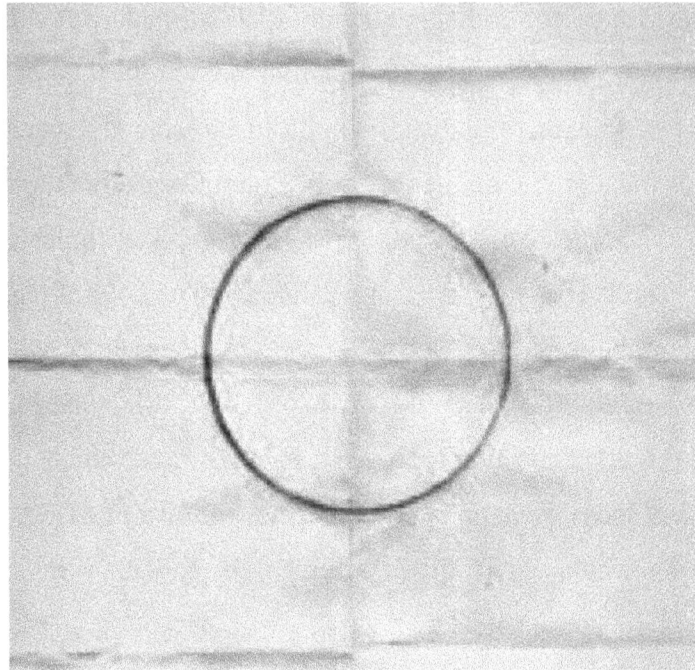

"You know, for kids"

Norville Barnes

Figure 5.3 How Many entities does this represent? Suggestions in the Appendix.

The pathway to openness and reflection may require help with mood and emotions. This is particularly important when we consider how procrastination and mood can inhibit the deliberation of change. According to research, 20% of adults acknowledge they are chronic procrastinators (Ferrari 2010, Shellenbarger 2014) and studies have shown that negative emotions or moods can disrupt self-control and increase procrastination. An approach to stop procrastination includes; first to ask the individuals to reflect on how procrastinating is compromising performance. Second, to then ask them to project themselves into their future free of procrastination. Third is to pick an area in which they are procrastinating and to take action, even if it is a small step. Fourth, ask them to stop self-condemnation about procrastination and focus on the forward action taken. An additional note is to consider an emotional influencer to help start the process. As we noted in the manager's section, managing an emotional influence is part of the formula in the change equation to support a LEAN transformation; in this case, it may help to end procrastination.

"A different species, a different set of values a world completely unlike your own. There is a feeling you can only get when you meet the unknown and open your mind"

Nakajima

Engagement and Cultural Change

As noted by Blumenthal, to create cultural changes through personal development requires a multimodality approach which draws upon multiple sources such as; the science of systems, psychology, education, prediction and experimental statistics (Blumenthal and Kilo 1998). The goal of these personal and cultural changes is to create a healthcare system that insists upon providing the best possible care for that particular patient in the best possible way as its' cultural standard. In addition, there must be a belief, a determination and a momentum that is taking the quality culture to a new level (a philosophy). To quote Donabedian *"the single requisite is a commitment to quality, an unequivocal desire and determination to dedicate oneself to the best one is capable of..."* (Donabedian 2002). The critical point of importance about engagement is that it represents a willingness to move forward and consider personal change, not just an intention, which is why this change may require personal development and management help (Gibbons et al 2003).

◉⚔☾~: ⤲:□☆

Personal Norms, Social Norms and Social Principles in Change

To convince the staff to commit to the change effort, there are many influences and activities that contribute to that obligation. The influences include behavioral decision making, habit change, social norms, group identification and social principles, which may all play a part in encouraging commitment to change. The following sections will address the importance of these influences.

Using Behavioral Models and Theories of Change

As outlined by Andrew Darnton in their review of healthcare behavioral change, there are certain basic behavioral principles that support promoting personal behavioral change. These principles may be applicable to healthcare cultural transformations. The theories are based on the conceptualization of personal norms; feelings of moral obligation that originate from innate values. Values represent broad based dispositions for beliefs and attitudes; beliefs that are the foundation of behaviors. Personal norms determine actions such as altruistic behaviors, decision making and the response to change (Darnton 2008, Stern 2000).

Because behavioral change is an extensive field of study, we will only superficially address the primary theories that might be helpful in promoting personal development that would support a LEAN transformation.

Some of the principles to consider include:

Principle 1   Behavior is rational but strongly influenced by emotions, habits and routines.

Principle 2   Behavioral models can identify which factors are the most significant in determining behavior and the process of change.

Principle 3   Change is a process, not linear, but incorporates feedback loops.

Principle 4   The models suggest that you need a process of engagement and partnering; learning by doing is a good example.

Principle 5   Model applications require a local context and is specific for a process. The implementation of behavioral change requires;

    1.   Assessment of past experience,

    2.   A realistic approach,

    3.   Possible trial and error,

    4.   Monitoring with good judgment.

When we consider applying these principles to support personal development in change, it helps to clarify how important an individualized, hands on, interactive approach is to successfully supporting cultural change. This subject matter can be used as an educational event for managers followed by their meeting with each of the staff at the start of the implementation.

Behavioral Theories in Decision Making

As we noted earlier, change requires a decision. There are many theories on personal behavior and decision making; listed in the appendix are some of the more prominent theories or truisms to consider when an organization or an employee is being approached to change. When one considers these theories on personal decision making they suggest that to promote decision making in change, clear directions and consequences should be described. Potential specific actions should be presented as an individualized approach that is easily implemented and without conflict with personal interests. Just presenting arguments that are rational may not be convincing and an emotional request may have more impact. The benefits of change should be carefully described that emphasize short term gains. Overall managers should help make difficult decisions simple and easy.

Conclusions

When considering theories on behavioral change as it affects cultural change and support for a transformation, we can generate several conclusions. First, it is clear that change may not be based on a rational decision, prior education or best information. If decisions are made in a rush, they will reflect attitudes as opposed to thoughtful deliberation. In considering change, the expectations about success or failure should be explored to enhance consideration of potential value. Second, the need for individualization is pronounced; the barrier to changing behaviors may be different for each individual based on their own personal responsibilities and personality traits. Third, changing routine behaviors or habits takes time and techniques like visual management of results and projected outcomes may help promote progress. In summary, this amounts to promoting change that is practical, specific and positive as the best approach. These recommendations are reinforced in a review from The Economic and Social Research Council (UK) on 129 different studies of behavior change strategies. The researchers note that experts agree that habit change is most successful if it is self-motivated and rooted in positive thinking. The survey found that the least effective strategies were those that aroused fear or regret in the person attempting to make a change. Studies have also shown that a few, specific and practical goals make habit change more successful (Sheeran et al 2005). These results reinforce the concepts that change is a process, not an event and can be improved by good management from a human behavioral and developmental approach; a concept reinforced by Deloitte in their article "Humanizing change: Developing more effective change management strategies" (Deloitte 2).

Reproduced with permission and under license Mike Keefe, Intoon.com

Figure 5.4 Culture is a wave of momentum (see figure legends)

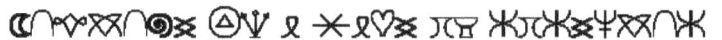

⚏⚏⚏⚏⚏⚏ ⚏⚏ ⚏ ⚏⚏⚏ ⚏⚏ ⚏⚏⚏⚏⚏⚏⚏

Execution of Cultural Change and Habit Change

This section started with a consideration of open mindedness, self-reflection and engagement; all components that start the consideration for personal behavioral change. When an individual has gone through a decision process and starts acting to make change; part of that modification will require addressing personal habits. In the Theory of Interpersonal Behavior, habits can be defined as a primary determinate of behavioral action based on automatic actions, intention, and the facilitating conditions (Traindis 1977). A habit is an intersection of knowledge, skills, and attitudes; all of which will need to be addressed in habit change; an effort that requires a higher purpose. Lewin makes the point that, by definition, a habit is resistance to change. To change a habit will require the re-creation of conscious control with the identification of conscious clues and goal setting (Lewin 1947). This is a learning process about the space between stimulus and response, as a way of enabling behavior change (Covey 2004). For managers and leaders, assessing employee's abilities to change habits is part of changing organizational culture and is a core requirement for a LEAN transformation. In that regard, it is important to realize that habit change takes time. Lally et al investigated the process of habit formation for everyday life activities. In their study, 84 volunteers chose a daily habit which they self-recorded. They found it took between 18 to 254 days to develop a true habit through repetition of a behavior in a consistent context. This study emphasizes that for changing habits, one must consider how old and established the habit is and to realize that to change a habit may require weeks and months (Lally et al 2009).

The Lewin model for habit change is conceptualized by the phrase; unfreeze-change-refreeze. The first step is to dislodge beliefs and assumptions and to disrupt the prior balance of values, to create thinking fluidity (Lewin 1947). A common impediment in healthcare to the Unfreeze phase occurs if the staff are too busy just doing their jobs; they can't stop to help themselves or others to change or improve. The "change" phase requires that you capture attention; often through new activities that promote behaviors. These new actions often create uncertainty and may require a tolerance of ambiguity. An approach to help this process could be a **"LEAN Evaluation Day"**. On this day, there is regular work but at a slower pace with a "research eye". The staff is focused on asking the right questions, "why do we do it this way", "why not this or what about that?" and allowing time to talk to patients about changes. Later they will need to take time to re-consider the process, fill out evaluations, etc. LEAN days are optimal times to consider how to adjust work pace and flow to allow for improvements without compromising patient care (LEAN Takt Time).

"Culture eats strategy for breakfast"

Peter Drucker

Emotional Messaging

Lewin notes that breaking habits requires an emotional "stir up". This can occur from externally applied approaches that effect comfort, cleanliness and convenience. Leadership has the opportunity to improve, or by neglect, inhibit change by the environment it provides. The additional hurtles of inconvenience; discomfort or distastefulness that might accompany change can lead to behavioral lock in and prevent change. The opposite impact can be enacted by removing the external obstacles to improvement (Lewin 1947). Bandura notes in his theory *"Mastery Modeling"*, that external conditions can also act as critical cues. The practice of creating behavioral cues from certain situations and then translating them into an identification reinforcing change can strengthen the refreeze process (Bandura 1997). This is why the LEAN tool of identifying waste can be so critical to changing habits and culture; it can be the critical behavioral cue. This approach can be part of the process of a LEAN transformation by the identification of waits, actions on hold, piles of paper or supplies, unclear organizational schemes, a missing "error detection system" or repeated errors. All of these forms of waste can be visual cues for the need for change.

Personal Development, Changing Habits and "Schelling points"

Steven covey recommended a series of steps to change habits. The first and possibly the most important step is to create an atmosphere in which it is safe to talk about the organizational values and the forces driving behavior and habits; this can support "unfreezing". The next step is an introspective reassessment, which leads to creating new insights to transform restraining forces into driving forces for new behaviors. He emphasizes this requires an acceptance of personal accountability. The final step is to then create new shared goals and opportunities and then a new way of interacting; a new culture. The refreezing will involve a new standard for teamwork communication, feedback and evaluation for employees. For each employee this approach starts as a negotiation by asking "would you accept change that is a "win-win" solution for you and for the organization". This is similar to the concept of looking for "Schelling points", mutual independently derived points of compromise in future expectations of change (Covey 1989, Schelling 1960). For managers and staff, the implementation of this approach is through a focus on meaningful communication; to try to understand and then, to be understood. This subsequently leads to working together and seeking synergy in the new solutions (Covey Habits 4, 5, 6). Covey felt that breaking habits required an "internal will" and a desire to realize your own natural talents and strengths (finding your voice). He felt it all begins with "breaking free", reiterating the unfreezing concept of Lewin. Covey felt that managers and leaders must discover their own meaningful voice and their "unopened birth gifts" to then enable the staff to change their lives. Behaviors Covey cited that will lead to staff refreezing include; to make and keep promises, to push to leaving their "comfort zone", and to take initiative (Lewin 1949, Covey 1989). If one agrees that change is realized by these influences and the personal changes in the staff, then it should be clear why this approach is critical to a LEAN implementation.

Commitment Devices

Another approach that may help with changing habits comes from research on changing personal health behaviors. Studies have demonstrated that 90% of large employers provide incentives for healthy behavioral change but despite these incentives there is a high failure rate (Volpp et al 2009, Rogers and Bazerman 2008). A technique to try to improve these results is *"Commitment devices"*. Commitment devices are voluntary, behavioral restrictions prior to goal achievement or penalties for failing to meet goals. As described by Dubner and Levitt, it is a self-imposed " *means with which to lock yourself into a course of action that you might not otherwise choose but that produces a desired result*" (Levitt and Dubner 2009, Dubner and Levitt 2007). A famous example of a commitment device was when Cortes scuttled his own fleet off the coast of Veracruz to prevent the abandonment of their mission against the Aztec empire. A more modern approach to these devices is that they must be voluntary and self-imposed and the individual must know the current performance gap. The value of this commitment must be clear and there must be accountability (performance reviews). This is very similar to the recommendations of Milkman; to create a simple starting process for habit change, by providing feedback, by keeping goals challenging but achievable and by providing support (Milkman et al 2009, Rogers and Milkman 2014). A final point on coaching for staff behavioral change is that managers should consider how to obtain the "yes answer". To start habit change the managers should create convincing arguments that feature the following characteristics to gain agreement from that staff; reciprocity, liking, social proof, commitment/consistency, authority, scarcity (Goldstein et al 2008).

☉✖ℂ~: ⤳ :O𝓡

"It's what we do that defines us"

Sustain: Social Norms, Group Identity and Social Principles

If we have been successful in changing habits and behaviors, the critical issue then shifts to how to sustain the impact of these changes. This requires changes in the social system, social norms and group identity. The cumulative efforts of personal habit changes in the organization transforms into change for the organization as a social system; the social norms and group identification. Social norms are defined as a pattern or trait taken to be typical of the behavior of a group. There are two types of social norms; injunctive norms and descriptive norms. Injunctive norms are perceptions of acceptable and unacceptable behaviors. Descriptive norms are the behaviors that are typically performed; a perception of the behavior of others (Berkowitz 2005, Cialdini 2006). Both types of norms are constructed from observed behavior, communication and self-knowledge (Miller and Prentice 1996). Meshing these concepts together infers that in a change effort, the aim is to try to operationalize descriptive norms, both positive and negative to support change and to standardize and enforce injunctive norms for cultural change. There are several obstacles to this process. First, the fundamental attribution error, which is the tendency of individuals to view other's behavior as a trait rather than a result influenced by situational variables (Ross 1977). Second, the false consensus effect which is when a person misunderstands what others believe and then acts in concert regardless of reality (Mullen and Hu 1988). And third, Pluralistic ignorance; the false assumption that the attitudes or behaviors of a group are different from one's own, even when in fact they are similar, which then leads to a divergent group behavior. The cumulative effect of these different influences on norms can lead to inaccurate perceptions about the organization's behaviors, attitudes and standards and represent a major impediment to cultural change (Miller and Prentice 1996).

The concepts and findings above are of critical importance because part of a LEAN transformation includes a transition in group identity. Lewin notes that habits are generated from group standards or values, reinforcing the concept that to change habits you must also consider changing group behavior (Lewin 1947). The concepts of Social proof, Social Identity Theory and Self Categorization Theory all include identifying with an "in group" and contrasting with the "out group". These group prototypes are formed from shared values, feelings, beliefs, actions and shared behavioral standards, all of which determine group identification. This creation of a new "in group" which the staff wishes to be part of; a group which reflects LEAN transformational culture is a critical goal. This conversion requires a change in group behavior, usually through indoctrination of the attributes that reflect group "*new*" social norms. Social norms and group identification are instrumental in maintaining the coherence of groups; "*we do that here*" and "*at our hospital, that is not acceptable*", they mediate the individual's identity in the group, which is why it is critical to a LEAN Transformation.

For most healthcare organizations fragmentation limits group social norms. Hence a focus on creating new social norms and new group identity is another way to move a healthcare organization toward engagement, supporting a LEAN transformation and a continuous improvement culture. Staff that do not identify with their organization or only identify with their department or unit will not be able to consider organizational values as their own. They will not commit to the difficult struggle of a LEAN transformation or consider sacrifice for their colleagues and organization.

Changing Social Norms: Hand Washing

The first step in addressing social norms and group identity consists of surveying the staff regarding perceived norms and actual behaviors and what change is required. In Norm Activation Theory there are 2 stages; first awareness of the consequences of not changing and second on the cost of acting versus denial of responsibility (Schwartz 1977). To change social norms based on this theory requires a prominent role for options and consequences for inaction. In addition, managing a social norm change requires consideration of the staff's control of the process and of the ease of performing the behavior reflecting the new norm; both can constitute a limit to change (resistance theory). The programs aimed at improving handwashing practices illustrates the principles above. While some institutions have been successful in instituting consistent handwashing practices, most have been ineffective. Handwashing is perceived as easy to do, but the external constraints; lack of time and inconvenience has limited handwashing performance. Conversely, efforts that focused on increasing convenience and minimizing time constrains (moving hand washing facilities, increasing lotion dispensers), have been more effective (Bishop et al 2013). Part of the explanation for failure in handwashing behavior is that most efforts do not focus on changing hand washing as a habit or a social norm. Social norms can be reinforced through the orientation processes, modeling by administration and leadership, and by the recognition and rewarding of handwashing behaviors. Rehearsal of the behavior may make the response more accessible and easier to initiate, such as when attendings demonstrate handwashing during teaching rounds or when administrators wash their hands on walk throughs. Additionally, a focus on enhanced self-efficacy has not been consistently applied to change habitual handwashing. This is the *"if then approach"* to improvement and projecting the consequences of behavior into the future. The realization that if by washing, an infection is prevented or if by failing to wash, it causes an infection in your patient (Clostridium Difficile), emphasizes how self-efficacy may impact on behavior. Behavioral change programs that focus on improving the environment, enhancing the staff's options for changing the behavior and providing consequences for changing or not changing the behavior are more likely to be successful. These processes can then lead to consistent hand washing to be a requirement to be part of the "in group"; *"we pay attention to hand washing guidelines here"*.

Enhancing Self Efficacy Linking to Changing Group Norms; The Agency Exercise

When considering change in social norms the term "agency" or self-efficacy is used in most theories. Agency is the intention to act based on:

- the probability of reliable success
- the power to act
- the ability to take meaningful action for positive outcome.

The focus on why personal development is necessary for successful change is related to the belief that by enhancing agency or self-efficacy, personal change will be more likely. This is conceptualized in Deloitte's Organizational Acceleration program as *"a person's stance toward change begins with two states: being able to change and being willing to change"* (Deloitte). It is the key to the initiation and continuance of change behavior; in applying and sustaining efforts. An exercise for Leaders and Managers is to assess the self-efficacy for each employee to make the necessary changes for a LEAN transformation based on the definitions of agency. An individual's self-efficacy can be increased through supportive behavior, verbal persuasion and emotional arousal; but there must be follow through with consistent organizational support. While self-efficacy may arise from personal experience, it can also be acquired or learned from other group members or outside groups; groups that have already made changes for success. Group activity can enhance agency to support change by identifying simple achievable goals that are consistent with the "new culture" and new group identity. This points out the critical nature and need for providing education and appropriate resources in a group setting even for a personal change effort; this particularly applies to LEAN, which is so foreign to most staff.

Addressing Social Principles as Part of Cultural Change

Social principles are part of our culture; the basic shared human traits that are ingrained in all the staff. Social principles affect behavior in the same way peer pressure changes personal actions. In the "3-line experiment" as described by Asch, it demonstrated that peer pressure will change behavior even when the behavior is clearly wrong (Asch 1951). Cascade effects and the theory of social proof indicate that sequential events will lead to behaviors that demonstrate a herd mentality and pluralistic ignorance (behavior based on the misimpression of the group behavior (Goldstein 2008). To change culture, social principles should be considered, in addition to social norms. In Milgram's subway seat exercise, his students asked New York subway riders to give up their seat without a reason. Surprisingly 50% of subway riders complied. The results demonstrated the internalized social norms of justice and altruism (Milgram and Sabini 1978). In the economic game called the "Ultimate game" proposers and takers split $10 if an agreement is reached, but if there is no agreement, both get nothing. The socially internalized norm of justice is displayed by the fact that bids below $2 are refused, despite the result that both participants lose. (The most common offer is $5). This social norm, the Fairness doctrine has been demonstrated to be true in all cultures and even in primates. In another variant of the game, the rules are altered by the knowledge that the proposer has earned the money being offered. In this case, all offers are accepted and it demonstrates that the Fairness doctrine is altered by the acknowledgement of accomplishment, in other words it reflects a just system (Surowiecki 2004). In failed change efforts, it is common for orders to be directed from above that seem unjustified and unfair to the staff. Acknowledgement of ingrained social principles in managing a change effort is critical; fairness, justice and acknowledgement of accomplishment should be incorporated into how the staff is treated and asked to consider change. A LEAN transformation is fundamentally bound to these principles.

ⓞ✖️ℂ ~: ⟊ :ℴℂ

Foundations for Organizational Change: Employee rights and Physician Engagement
A safe environment for change

One of the most common barriers to successful Lean Healthcare transformations is a lack of staff commitment. LEAN requires that healthcare groups collectively agree to subordinate old habits and create approaches to new ones; a difficult and uncomfortable process. To accomplish this requires a process for open sharing and personal insights about change, and doubt. This can only occur in a safe environment, without criticism or retributions and there must be trust. The *"shadow of the future"* and the *"thickness of the relationship"* are determining factors to allow for the feeling of safety during this process (Axelrod 1984).

This brings up a critical question, *"What are the characteristics of a safe environment for change"*? The staff must be able: to embrace, to be open to the unknown and not be ready to knock ideas. They must first be honest with themselves. They must listen more and more intently, thoughtfully and silently. The staff should be able to start by saying yes, to be positive and to not jump to conclusions. They should be encouraged to use measured judgement, enjoy friendly debate and learn to accept uncertainty. The staff should be open to learning, to think first and to realize that we can all learn from others; to face their fears and still feel they can achieve. They must get to their own *"personal place"* in which they are ready to go forward, to cut back on control and be comfortable with vulnerability. They need to learn that they don't know it all, but that's ok, and that it is ok to fail because you can fail upwards.

How is this type of environment created for the staff? It starts with the introduction of a standard employee bill of rights that indicates these behaviors are accepted and encouraged. Healthcare facilities advertise the patient bill of rights in the charts, on the walls and on their websites, but the concept of basic rights for the staff above standing labor laws are usually missing. The foundation for these rights is the relationship that each individual has with the organization. Those relationships span the range from *"Shut up and do your work"* to *"we are concerned about you and want you to feel successful"*. Which one of these extremes is consistent with establishing a safe environment for change and to support a cultural transformation? The work environment should promote the principles of providing good communication based on facts, on proper acknowledgement that demonstrates respect and appreciation and on promoting the ability to speak the truth (with diplomacy and tact). For most healthcare organizations, the staff or physicians have never participated in such an environment, meaning that if such an environment was to be created, they will need to be educated about their rights and the new expectations about their behaviors. The concept of rights of healthcare staff incorporates;

1. The Right to be needed- This includes a meaningful personal relationship to group goals.

2. The Right to be involved- In a structured way, with problem ownership that includes a system of input, and expected response.

3. A Covenantal Relationship-A relationship that fills deep needs, creates meaningful work, fulfillment and allows for management of conflict and change.

4. The Right to understand- To know and understand the mission, strategy and organizational plans and their role; a sense of place and clear responsibilities.

5. The Right to affect one's own destiny- Clear performance expectations, promotion requirements and the opportunities for career development.

6. The Right to be accountable- To contribute to group goals and share ownership.

7. The Right to appeal-An assurance against the arbitrary.

8. The Right to make a commitment-To be able to do one's best and know there is an impact.

(DuPree 2011)

An important value that is critical for change in a LEAN transformation is a move to organizational *"trustworthiness"* in which *"coworkers believe that others are ethical and the organization as a whole is true to its values and commitments"* (Karlgaard 2014). Without trust, there will be no improvement and only limited short term success. An assessment in the planning phase is for each group; leaders, managers and staff, to grade their organization based on the rights as listed above.

꙰꙰꙰꙰ ~: ꙰ :꙰꙰

Physician engagement: Accountability, Physician Leadership

A critical difference in healthcare verses other industries is the effect physicians have on healthcare organizations; specifically, their organizational engagement. Unfortunately, physicians, in general, are not good organizational members. This is true even within their own organizations like the AMA or professional societies. In his book, "The Logic of Collective Action: Public Goods and the Theory of Groups", Mancur Olson documents the free rider approach of most physicians (Olson 1971). A "free rider" in economic terms refers to someone who benefits from resources, goods, or services without paying for the cost of the benefit (Fehr and Gachter 2000). In general, 70 to 80% of people try to be free riders even if their group loses and the overall outcome is suboptimal. These economic studies demonstrate that people are selfish in 25% of cases; altruistic in 5% of cases and the majority are conditional donators which includes free riders. These percentages change if the person's actions are visible and the consequences of being a free rider are clear. Compounding this problem, studies have shown physicians have limited ability to accurately assess their own behavior (Davis et al 2006). Limitations in self-assessment often lead to inappropriate or unrealistic decisions and expectations by physicians when dealing with their organizations. For physician cooperation and engagement, there is a need for transparency for performance that is linked to recognition and accountability (Surowiecki 2004).

⊚✄⫽(~: ⚔:O☆

By regulation, a healthcare organization's Board of Directors delegates the responsibility for the quality and safety of patient care to the licensed medical staff. An unengaged or resistant medical staff will impede or even reverse process improvements that have been implemented by others. From medical school onward physicians live in an environment that stresses individual responsibility and competitiveness. The current approach to mortality and morbidity conferences and peer review processes further promotes individualism. The results are that the organization and physicians are not aligned for defined goals. This problem with engagement extends to the physician leadership. Physician leaders are generally chosen because of their clinical excellence, not because of administrative, managerial or leadership skills. A lack of leadership and management skills hampers their ability to help the physician staff engage with the organization. An added problem is that engaging in process improvement means time away from the office or operating room which is usually uncompensated. George Palma the Medical Director for Simpler, a LEAN consulting group, summarizes the impact of physician engagement in LEAN initiatives. As he notes, almost everything that occurs in healthcare does so under physician order. To address these issues, Dr. Palma lists these recommendations;

- o   Put the patient first, last and always, at every level of the healthcare organization,
- o   Set clear organizational expectations,
- o   Value physician's time and provide protected time for process improvement work,

- o Create a formal process for educating and mentoring physician champions and structural leaders,
- o Create targets that are meaningful in terms of the patient care experience (timely access, service, quality and safety),
- o Provide good data: Few in number, timely and reliable, to motivate proper behavior,
- o Measure processes that move the organization's strategy forward and make it easy to understand and visual in nature.

Dr. Palma notes that the change should be evident by;

1. Process improvement that is physician led, which in a LEAN approach would entail that physicians are represented on every value stream and improvement event that touches or alters a physician's workflow.

2. Teamwork is valued by physicians, which they demonstrate through their behaviors.

3. Physician leaders and champions have received training in LEAN leadership and support its application.

4. Good data is available to provide timely information relevant to the physician's and team's work processes, and the patient care experience.

(Palma 2014)

A primary lesson from high risk industries is that quality management is a "*culture*". In healthcare the physician culture has the most influence in controlling quality and promoting change. It follows then that by working with the staff and physicians; to educate them to see the bigger picture, is a critical activity for success in a LEAN transformation. For some physicians changing behavior may require personal discomfort, even courage, and may require support from a trusted leader.

> *"The selfishness must be discovered and understood before it can be removed. It is powerless to remove itself, neither will it pass away of itself. Darkness ceases only when light is introduced; so ignorance can only be dispersed by knowledge."*
>
> *James Allen*

Healthcare provider engagement and alignment, particularly for physicians, is the critical difference in healthcare when compared to other industries when we consider change or improvement. The approach involves education, alignment efforts and special structures to increase engagement. In organizations where this has been done, efficiencies and improvement have occurred, but these have usually been temporary and a culture of engagement and alignment has not been sustained. It is through continual efforts at alignment and personal relationships that the gains may be sustained and evolve into a culture, this is a requirement for a LEAN transformation.

ⓞⵊⵛ~: ⵊ :ⵔⵔ

"Our doubts are traitors and make us lose the good we oft might win, by fearing to attempt"

Shakespeare

Organizational and Staff Innovations in LEAN

In her review of the global problems in healthcare innovation, Dr. Regina Herzlinger list 6 forces that drive healthcare innovation;

1. Players- for or against innovation success,
2. Funding- for innovation,
3. Policy- over management or structural impediments,
4. Technology- poor integration of good technology and poor selection of bad technology like dynamic cardiomyoplasty or ventricular reduction surgery,
5. Customers- meeting or not meeting their needs,
6. Accountability- for quality that may impede experimentation.

(Herzlinger 2014)

We have pointed out that the US healthcare system is a complex interaction of competing groups with different agendas that can create these forces to inhibit any systematic efforts at improvement or innovation. While innovation may have been neglected in some aspects of healthcare, this has not always been the case. Innovation has been part of American medicine from the beginning. As expressed by William Halsted, the first surgical chief at Johns Hopkins.

"... the hospital, the operating room and the wards should be laboratories, laboratories of the highest order, and we know from experience that where this conception prevails . . . the welfare of the patient is best promoted. . . . The surgeon and the physician should be equipped and should be expected to carry on the work of research"

(Cameron 1997, Halsted 1904).

James Womack provides an updated confirmation of Halsted's sentiments, *"with our changing times in healthcare, the role of creativity is more important now than ever"*. However, we are faced with many forces that oppose innovation in healthcare. First, it is a common error in improvement events to push for standardization and oversight from a central regulatory authority. Organizational studies have shown strong centralization of authority in a system can discourage innovation (Damanpour 1991). Successful innovation requires the balance of the two opposing influences of central promotion and support versus local application through good management. Second, for Physicians, the memorization of study knowledge, discipline to practice standards and rules, i.e. the practice of medicine, can also limit creative thinking. In addition, healthcare providers are in a *"doing culture"*. The high number of complex tasks required, assessments, diagnosis and complex treatment with time limitations decreases the focus on other activities like innovation. A third element that is different in healthcare compared to other industries that limits innovation is the heighten presence of the "expert culture." Provider experience and judgment is promoted as the most important factor in providing care and in making all decisions. Inquiry and innovation, the exercising of intelligence in the world, the intertwining of thought and action by which we move from doubt to doubt can be suppressed by chasing the expert.

Theoretical Foundation for Service Innovation and Innovation Education

How do we address these inhibitors of innovation in healthcare? In their article "Innovation in Services", Gallouj and Weinstein discuss different types of service innovations that could be applied to healthcare. The authors defined innovation as any change that affects one of the characteristics of the service and radical innovation as a new service such as the transition, from a horse drawn carriage to a motor vehicle. They describe several different types of innovation:

> ➢ Incremental innovation as the addition or substitution of a new element to a service, such as providing additional optional services.

> ➢ An Ad hoc innovation occurs at the provider client interface, not necessarily planned as a rearrangement of existing knowledge and experience, but produces new knowledge and competencies reflected in a change in service (a LEAN principle).

> ➢ They define recombinant innovation as the new combination of service characteristics from other services or by separating service components. They note a benefit of recombinant innovation is that it leads to standardization and formularization; this enables more "innovation in routines" through a better understanding of the components of service.

➢　　In the "Formulization model" of innovation, which is more about standardizing, clarifying and specifying services; the shaping of the whole process creates a "natural trajectory" of service development, which is comparable to the development of Standard Work in LEAN. The process of formulization of a service includes;

1. Naming
2. Definition by methods or characteristics
3. Explicit documentation, which should lead to it being identified as a "social construction" as well.
4. Definition of the components that can be assessed.

The authors note that the capacity for innovation depends on the ability to explore and mobilize existing knowledge and techniques, and utilizing flexible project groups that capitalizes on the different members' competencies or characteristics. These project groups in turn, depend on information, education and organizational support. The authors reiterate that innovation is a counterintuitive process, first rigid, narrow and specific at the beginning which then evolves into flexibility and a more general contextual approach to change. For all members of a healthcare organization, starting with leadership, a specific educational effort early in the transformation should be conducted such that the staff understands what innovation is and how to innovate. (Gallouj and Weinstein 1997, Argyris 1999).

✳✕✣◉ ~: ⚐ :△△

Excellence through Innovation: Initiation and the Inversion Exercise

A LEAN transformation should make excellence through innovation a social norm, a concept previously promoted by Jim Collins. In his studies, he found 50% of great companies focused on institutionalizing the values of excellence and innovation. He concludes successful organizations are innovative in the way they lead, manage and build within the organization. This may start by having innovators from outside groups expound to the staff on how innovation promotes success and thereby reinforce initial innovation efforts. In addition, rewarding the application of innovation will be critical to making innovation part of the organization's and the staff's identity (Collins 2002).

"The more sincere and sustained the participation in analyzing and solving problems, the greater the release of everyone's creativity, and of their commitment to what they create. "

Steven Covey

Multiple business authors have emphasized the importance of creating time to participate in the innovative process. To start to formally incorporate innovation into an organization begins with reflection and contemplation. This in turn will hopefully lead to openness and a willingness to participate. Womack notes that to foster that creativity and participation requires a focus on encouraging innovation by providing resources; "primarily time and training". The evidence that you have reached those goals will be regular open discussions to new approaches, and the expression of innovative ideas during daily activities (Womack et al 2005). An exercise to help this process is the inversion technique. This approach starts with identification of what we do not want to happen in the future, an example would be to ask *"if we were to become worse as care givers, what would that look like."* In healthcare it is sometimes easier to identify negative processes or outcomes and by doing so, the pathway to positive ones may become clearer. This approach can be incorporated into proposed solutions (A3, Box 5).

"When you are inspired by some great purpose, ... project, all your thoughts break their bonds: Your mind transcends limitations, your consciousness expands in every direction, and you find yourself in a new, great and wonderful world."

Yoga Sutras

An Innovation in LEAN; A New Definition of Waste, "Non-flow" and the "Flow" exercise

In, *"Flow: The Psychology of Optimal Experience"* Mihaly Csíkszentmihályi outlines his theory that people are happiest when they are in a state of *"flow"*, a state of focused concentration or complete absorption in the current situation or activity; as he described it, this is the feeling of being *"in the zone"* or *"in a groove"*. This is an optimal state of intrinsic motivation, in which the person is fully immersed in their activity and is accompanied by a feeling of great absorption, engagement, fulfillment, and application of skill. The flow state can be identified by the characteristic that while in "flow" banal and temporal concerns (time, food, appearance, and environment) are unrecognized. Csikszentmihalyi characterized nine components for achieving "flow" immersion including;

1. *"Challenge-skill"* balance
2. Merging of action and awareness

3.   Immediate and unambiguous feedback

4.   Concentration on the task at hand

5.   Paradox of control- a sense of well-being in the activity which may not be real

6.   Transformation of time

7.   Loss of self-consciousness

8.   "*Autotelic*" experience- intrinsically rewarding

To achieve a flow state, there must be a balance or matching of the task challenge and the performer's skill. The experience of "Flow" leads to an "*autotelic*" experience which is one in which the acts or activities performed are intrinsically rewarding. The autotelic personality trait is possessed by individuals who enjoy situations that most would find miserable, such as "*mudder races, diaper changes or surgical internships*". The outstanding autotelic personality traits consist of curiosity, persistence, and humbleness (Csikszentmihalyi 1990).

Identification of "nonflow" or being "out of the zone" should be a new definition of waste in a LEAN transformation. Part of the conversion to LEAN should include increasing the "*Flow*" state for as many of the staff as possible thereby enhancing productivity, staff satisfaction and error reduction. The new definition of waste would be "*Lack of Flow*"; addressed through job re-design for employees that find their positions as either too easy or too hard such that it prevents being in "*Flow*". For the manager the focus is on making jobs intrinsically rewarding through job restructuring, staff input and staff identification of their real values and meaning. The metric would be to consider the percentage of time each worker is "*in Flow*" and for the organization, the percentage of staff "*in Flow*". For physicians, flow should directly reflect satisfaction and proper engagement. It follows that an important early exercise in a LEAN Transformation would include managers and staff working to improve individual employee "*Flow*" as outlined above.

FLOW

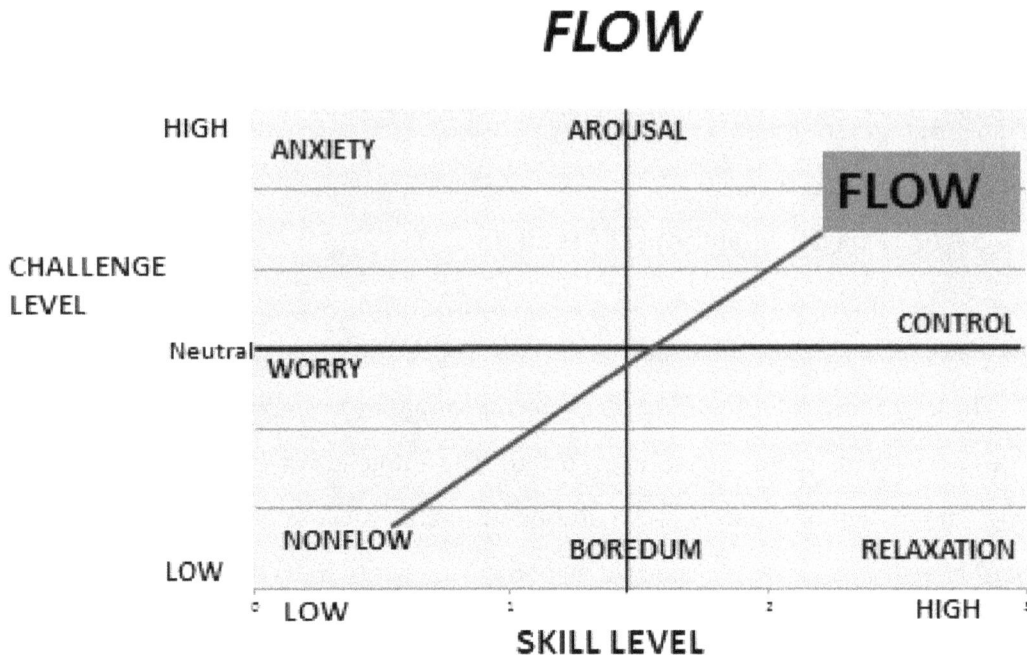

Figure 5.5 A Kano diagram to illustrate the characteristics of the "*Flow*" state. The Challenge level is represented on the vertical axis and The Skill required on the horizontal axis; the interaction of both contributes to the impact on work related engagement.

Summary

1. The staff must trust their leadership and know the organizational vision. For all the staff the organizational structures should be aligned to support these interests and pursuit of meaning at work. The management approach to the staff should be one of enabling and empowering.

2. The leadership, management and staff should be in agreement about change and the efforts and activities to achieve it. Trust in all relationships is the indispensable requirement.

3. In the implementation of LEAN, the staff must have trust in leadership and feel there is agreement to move forward. There may be the need to introduce a new approach or philosophy, which is that improvement is required to define good healthcare. Modeling of this approach will be part of the practice for success.

4. Part of the process of successful LEAN implementation will encompass realizing; the lack of scientific approach in healthcare management, adjusting the approach for appropriate timing for the organizational change and the need for quality educational programs.

5. For the organization, a LEAN transformation should be viewed as a process analogous to personal change that is sequential and time consuming. It requires the acknowledgement of the staff as knowledge workers and to support a "questioning culture".

6. The importance of the basic business management practices should be understood by the staff to help maximize realization of organizational business priorities; the business practices must also be changed to support the implementation.

7. Personal Development- the decision to change is required, a process that can be made easier, by using good communication with information and an emotional personalized appeal. This requires a familiarity with the staff based on a relationship.

8. Cultural change entails changing values, beliefs and habits of the staff. Habit change is a process that requires support from managers and leaders and takes time. Facilitation of changing habits should be a specific plan to enhance change.

9. Social norms should be addressed and the norm that change is a positive, be introduced; with specific personalized action steps that considers the self-interests of the group and the group's identity.

10. Agency and self-efficacy can be reinforced by promoting understanding and the appreciation of how personal effectiveness can lead to success and what that success would look like (Visual Management).

11. The principles of justice and fairness must be part of the process of change if it is to be truly cultural change.

12. Physician engagement is the critical foundational factor for success in the LEAN transformation, a specific approach through alignment and relationships is required.

13. There are many avenues for innovation in healthcare services. The first is to create "standard work" along with a safe environment for the employees to be creative and innovative. An environment which enhances their rights for respect and for empowerment.

14. Physicians and staff will require education, support and an environment for innovation. Excellence through innovation should be introduced as a new norm.

15. A focus on enhancing "*Flow*" for the staff is a new innovation to improve productivity, staff satisfaction and healthcare quality.

FORCE FIELD DIAGRAM FOR STAFF ACCEPTANCE OF A LEAN TRANSFORMATION

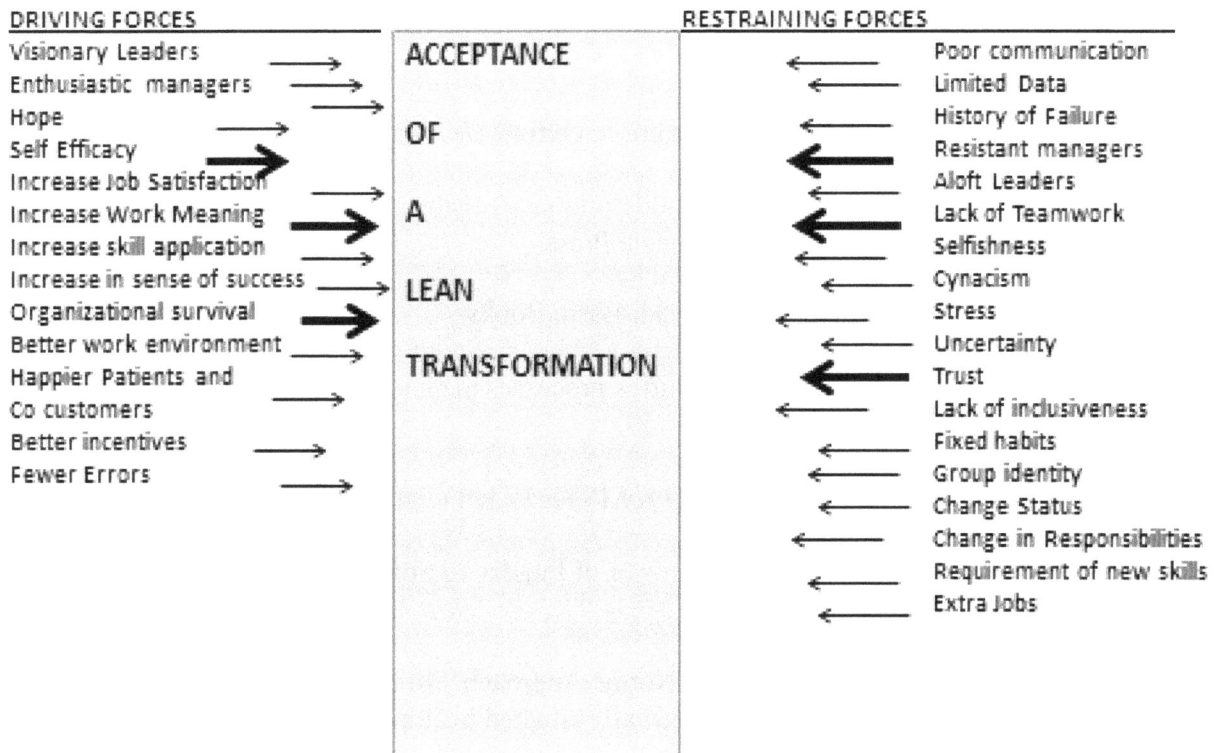

DRIVING FORCES

Visionary Leaders

Enthusiastic managers

Hope

Self Efficacy

Increase Job Satisfaction

Increase Work Meaning

Increase skill application

Increase in sense of success

Organizational survival

Better work environment

Happier Patients and

Co customers

Better incentives

Fewer Errors

ACCEPTANCE OF A LEAN TRANSFORMATION

RESTRAINING FORCES

Poor communication

Limited Data

History of Failure

Resistant managers

Aloft Leaders

Lack of Teamwork

Selfishness

Cynacism

Stress

Uncertainty

Trust

Lack of inclusiveness

Fixed habits

Group identity

Change Status

Change in Responsibilities

Requirement of new skills

Extra Jobs

Figure 5.6 A Force Field Diagram of staff acceptance of a LEAN transformation which shows driving forces on the left and restraining forces on the right.

REFERENCES

Antonacopoulou EP. The dynamics of reflexive practice: the relationship between learning and changing. IN Reynolds M, Vince R (Ed) Organizing Reflection. Burlington, VT: Ashgate; 2004; 47-64.

Armitage CJ and Conner M. Social cognition models and health behavior: a structured review. Psychology and Health;2007;15:173-189.

Argyris C. On Organizational Learning. 2nd edition. Oxford UK Blackwell 1999.

Asch SE. Effects of group pressure on the modification and distortion of judgments. In H. Guetzkow (Ed.), Groups, leadership and men 1951 Carnegie Press.

Axelrod R. The Evolution of Cooperation, 1984, Basic Books.

Bandura, A., Adams, N. E., & Beyer, J. Cognitive processes mediating behavioral change. *Journal Personality Social Psychology, 1977;35*:125-139.

Bandura, A. *Self-efficacy: The exercise of control* 1997. W H Freeman/Times Books.

Berger W. A More Beautiful Question; The power of Inquiry to Spark breakthrough ideas, 2014 Bloomsbury.

Berkowitz, AD. "An Overview of the Social Norms Approach". In L. Lederman & L. Stewart (Eds.), Changing the culture of college drinking: A socially situated health communication campaign 2005 Hampton Press.

Beckhard, R., & Harris, R.T. (1987). *Organizational transitions: Managing complex change* (2nd ed.). Addison-Wesley series on organization development. Reading, MA: Addison-Wesley Publishing.

Bishop J, Parry M, Hall TS. Impact of resident rounding protocols and hand washing initiatives on clostridium difficile infections in surgery. Connecticut Medicine 2013;77:69-75.

Blumenthal D and Kilo CM. A report card on continuous quality improvement. Milbank Quarterly 1998;76:625-48.

Cameron JL. William Stewart Halsted: Our surgical heritage. Ann Surg 1997; 225: 445–58.

Canadian Health Services Research Foundation 2000, 2004.

Cawsey T, Deszca G, Ingels C. Organizational Change: An Action Oriented Toolkit, 2nd Edition 2011 Sage Publications).

Cialdini RB, Barrett DW, Bator R, Demaine LJ, Sagarin BJ, Rhoads KL, Winter PL. Activating and aligning social norms for persuasive impact. Social Influence 2006; 1: 3–1.

Collins J. The Ultimate Creation. In Leading for Innovation. Hesselbein F, Goldsmith M, Somerville I (Ed) 2002 Jossey-Bass.

Covey SR. The 7 Habits of Highly Effective People. 1989 Fireside, Simon and Schuster.

Covey SR. The 8th Habit: From effectiveness to greatness. 2004 Free Press, Simon and Schuster.

Csikszentmihalyi M. Flow: The Psychology of Optimal Experience. 1990 Harper Row.

Damanpour, F. Organizational innovation: A meta-analysis of effects of determinants and moderators. *Academy of Management Journal*, 1991;34: 555–590.

Darnton A. GSR Behavior change knowledge review 2008, www.gsr.gov.uk.

Davis DA, Mazmanina PE, Fordis M, Van Harrison R, Thorpe KE, Perrier L. Accuracy of physician self-assessment compared with observed measures of competence: A systemic review. JAMA 2006;296:1094-1102.

Deloitte. Humanizing Change: Developing more effective change management strategies. https://dupress.deloitte.com/dup-us-en/deloitte-review/issue-19/developing-more-effective-change-management-strategies.html.

Deloitte 2. Organizational Acceleration. https://www2.deloitte.com/global/en/pages/human-capital/articles/organization-acceleration1.html.

Deutschman A. Change or Die: The Three Keys to Change at Work and in Life. 2009 Harper Collins.

Donabedian A. An Introduction to Quality Assurance in Healthcare. 2002 Oxford University.

Dubner SJ and Levitt, SD. "The Stomach-Surgery Conundrum," New York Times, November 18, 2007.

DuPree M. Leadership is an Art. 2011 Random House.

Fehr E and Gachter S. Fairness and Retaliation: The Economics of Reciprocity. J Economic Perspectives. 2000;14:159-181..

Ferrari JR. Still Procrastinating. 2010 Wiley.

Gallouj F and Weinstein O. Innovation in Services. Research Policy 1997;26:537-556.

Gibbons R, Gerrard M, G Lane G. A Social Reaction Model of Adolescent Health Risk. In Social Psychological Foundations of Health and Illness. J Suls and K Wallston. (Ed)2003 Oxford: Blackwell.

Goldstein NJ, Martin SJ, Cialdini RB. Yes!50 Scientifically Proven Ways to be Persuasive. 2008 Free Press.

Gould N, Baldwin M. Farnham Social Work, Critical Reflection and the Learning Organization. Farnham England:Ashgate;2004:134.

Grunden N and Hagood C. LEAN-Led Hospital Design. 2012 Productivity Press.

Halsted WS. The training of the surgeon. Bull Johns Hopkins Hosp 1904; 15: 267–75.

Handy C. The Empty Raincoat. 1994 London.

Herzlinger R. Why Innovation in healthcare is so hard. Harvard Bus Review 2014.

Higgs MJ Rowland D. Building change leadership capability: "the quest for change competence". J Change Management. 2000;1:116-131.

Higgs M and Rowland D. All changes great and small: Exploring approaches to change and its leadership. J Change Management 2007; 5:121-151.

Kanter, R Ten Reasons People Resist Change. HBR Blog Network.

Karlgaard R. The Soft Edge: Where Great Companies Find Lasting Success 2014 Jossey-Bass.

Kotter J. Leading Change: Why transformation efforts fail. 2007 Harvard Bus Review.

Kovner AR, Rundall TG. Evidence Based management reconsidered Frontiers of Health Services Management 2006;22:3-22.

Lally P, Van Jaarsveld CH, Potts HW, Wardle J. How are habits formed: Modelling habit formation in the real world. Eur J Social Psychology 2010;40:998-1009.

Lavis JN, Robertson D Woodside JM, McLeod CB, Abelson J. Milbank Quarterly 2003;81:221-248.

Levesque DA, Prochaska JM, Prochaska JO, Dewart SR, Hamby LS, Weeks WB. Organizational stages and processes of change for continuous quality improvement in health care. Consulting Psychology Journal: Practice and Research 2001;53:139-153.

Levitt SD and Dubner SJ. Freakonomics. 2009 William Morrow Paperback.

Lewin, K. "Frontiers in Group Dynamics: Concept, Method and Reality in Social Science; Social Equilibria and Social Change" Human Relations. 1947;1:5–41.

Luckman J. The Lean Post 2014.

Mayeno LY. Stages of multicultural organizational change. 2007 www.mayenoconsulting.com.

McKinsey What successful transformations share: McKinsey Global Survey results. http://www.mckinsey.com/business-functions/organization/our-insights/what-successful-transformations-share-mckinsey-global-survey-results.

Milgram S. and Sabini J. On maintaining urban norms; A field experiment in the subway. In A. Baum, J. E. Singer and S. Valins (Ed) Advances in environmental psychology. 1978 1:31-40.

Milkman, KL, Chugh D, Bazerman MH. How can decision making be improved? Perspectives on Psychological Science, 2009;4:379-383.

Miller DT, Prentice DA. The Construction of Social Norms and Standards. In: Higgins FT, Kruglanski AW, (Ed) Social psychology: Handbook of basic principles. New York: Guilford; 1996. 799–829.

Morrow R. Knowledge Workers Are Key to Improvement. LEAN Healthcare Exchange 2013.

Mullen B and Hu L. Social projection as a function of cognitive mechanisms: Two meta-analytic integrations. British Journal Social Psychology. 1988;27:333-3.

Munch D, Go Slow to Go Fast, LEAN Healthcare Exchange 2013.

Olson, M. The Logic of Collective Action: Public Goods and the Theory of Groups (Revised ed.) 1971. Harvard University Press.

Palma G. 2014. http://www.simpler.com/publications.

Prochaska, JO.; DiClemente, CC. The Transtheoretical Approach. In: Norcross, JC; Goldfried, MR. (eds.) Handbook of psychotherapy integration. 2nd ed. New York: Oxford University Press; 2005. p. 147–171.

Prochaska JM, Prochaska JO, Levesque DA. A transtheoretical approach to changing organizations. Administration Policy in Mental Health 2001;28:247-261.

Rogers T, Bazerman MH. Harnessing our inner angels and demons: what we have learned about want/should conflicts and how that knowledge can help us reduce short-sighted decision making. Perspect Psychol Sci. 2008;3:324-338.

Rogers T, Milkman KL, Volpp KG. Commitment Devices; Using initiatives to change behavior. JAMA 2014;E1-E2).

Ross L. The intuitive psychologist and his shortcomings: Distortions in the attribution process. In Berkowitz, L. Advances in experimental social psychology. 1977 Academic Press.

Schelling TC. The strategy of conflict 1960. Harvard University Press.

Schwartz S. Normative Influences on Altruism. Advances in Experimental Social Psychology 1977;10:221-279.

Shaw EK, Howard J, Etz RS, Hudson SV, Crabtree BF. How team-based reflection affects quality improvement implementation: A qualitative Study. Qual Manag Health Care. 2012;21:104-113.

Sheeran P, Armitage CJ, Rivis A, Webb TL. Does changing attitudes, norms or self-efficacy change intentions and behavior? http://www.esrc.ac.uk/my-esrc/grants/RES-000-22-0847.

Shellenbarger S. "To Stop Procrastinating, Look to Science of Mood Repair, New Approach Focuses on Helping People Regulate Their Emotions. Wall Street Journal 2014.

Sheridan K. Building a Magnetic Culture. 2012 McGraw-Hill.

Stern PC. Toward a coherent theory on environmentally significant behavior. J Social Issues 2000;56:407-424.

Studer Q. Hardwiring Excellence. 2003 Fire Starter Publishing.

Surowiecki, J Wisdom of the Crowds. 2004 Doubleday.

Virkstis K. Opened Mindedness and Nursing Engagement, Nursing engagement. Advisory Board, The national prescription of nursing engagement 2014).

Triandis, HC Interpersonal Behavior. 1977 Brook/Cole.

Volpp KG, Troxel AB, Pauly MV, Glick HA, Puig A, Asch DA, Galvin R, Zhu J, Wan F, DeGuzman J, Corbett E, Weiner J, Audrain-McGovern J. A Randomized, Controlled Trial of Financial Incentives for Smoking Cessation. N Engl J Med 2009; 360:699-709.

Womack JP, Byrne AP, Fiume J, Kaplan GS, Toussaint J. Going LEAN in Healthcare 2005, Institute for Healthcare Improvement.

Zinger D. Mastering employee engagement: Easy Performance Management Tools. 2015 Halogen Software.

Epilogue
Making the Decision to Start a LEAN Healthcare Innovation

©Glasbergen
glasbergen.com

"We need to make some big changes around here.
The kind of changes where many decisions are
made but nothing actually happens."

Reproduced with permission and license from Glasbergen

Figure E.1 Execution (See figure legends)

We started with the questions; why now, why LEAN and why a LEAN Healthcare Innovation.

We provided an extensive review of the literature about LEAN implementations with a review of Leadership, Managers and Staff in healthcare with examples of why LEAN implementations have been falling short and provided recommendations and exercises to increase the likelihood of success. So what are the compelling reasons to try LEAN Healthcare Innovation as a new exposure to LEAN or to improve the outcome from a prior LEAN effort. Considering LEAN's past history in healthcare, it's understandable that CEOs are hesitant to commit to LEAN. Michael Balle relates that in his discussions with CEOs, they indicate that they are interested in improvements in safety, quality and productivity from a LEAN system, but they consider these issues less valuable then strategy, technology or investment. His opinion is that until these CEOs have experience with LEAN, they don't understand its true value, and consider it a second tier priority (Balle 2013). Interestingly, most of these same CEOs are often fanatical about their own health maintenance, exercise and avoidance of at risk behaviors. Yet the concept of a system to assure the health of their company, like LEAN, seems foreign. We introduced a new concept, "Patient Centered Health Improvement" as an approach for taking the next step to improve patient care through innovation and improvement as a norm. This is a logical compliment to managing the continuum of care and population health management, yet this type of commitment to improvement has not been embraced by medical leadership. Healthcare Leadership also generally likes competitive professional sports; an activity in which veteran athletes continue to practice and work toward improvement even after decades in the sport. In professional sports, it is a standard to continue to improve, otherwise you will lose your ability to compete and yet in healthcare continuous improvement has been a failure. We will make the case that now is the time to make a radical change, to embrace an improvement approach for survival in the new more competitive field of healthcare and that the radical change should be LEAN Healthcare Innovation.

Reasons to Institute a Significant Organizational Change; Do You Smell Smoke?

Dr. Robert Swain in his article, "Nine Reasons Organizations Need to Change" lists common reasons for organizational change, which are followed by healthcare examples.

1. Crisis

2. Performance Gaps- HCAHPS, readmissions, Meaningful Use.

3. New Technology- EMR, virtual and Telemedicine, social media.

4. Identification of Opportunities- Expansion to address market changes.

5. Reaction to Internal and External Pressure- Obamacare, increasing complexity.

6. Mergers and Acquisitions- Increasing recently in healthcare.

7. Change for the sake of change- To respond to a new uncertain environment.

8. Sounds good- Preparation for an uncertain future with value based purchasing.

9. Planned abandonment- Related to a change in the market place or mergers.

(Swain 2011)

Are any of these reasons appropriate for healthcare? What is the current state in healthcare?

1. Current performance gaps- As was previously mentioned, CMS penalties are affecting many hospitals with performance gaps in HCAHPS, readmissions and Meaningful Use.

2. Increase in complexity- The ACA contains 19,368 pages of rules and adds new boards and panels that have undefined purposes; this one new program has introduced additional complexity in healthcare; regulations are at an all-time high (Moffit 2016).

3. Increase in mergers and partnerships. -As reflected in recent articles, in 2015 there was an 18% increase in healthcare mergers and this is expected to increase going forward. Mergers and partnerships change markets and competition (Hiltzik 2016).

4. Increase in government involvement- As noted, the ACA and the insurance industries response has led to increasing bureaucracy, additional administrative requirements and a transition from state control to central federal control.

5. Increase in the rate of change- Dumont et al in their article "*The faster New World of Healthcare*" points out that regulatory reform, changes in the EMR and information technologies have accelerated the industry's "*Clock speed*"; the term coined by Charles Fine, to denote a faster pace of business. Recent changes have; generated more data that will be publicly available, change in which healthcare providers are assuming the role of information aggregators and the use of social media for interaction with patients (Dumont et al 2012).

6. Uncertainty and Politics- Recent elections and the predicted increases in the "poorly insured" are creating more uncertainty. There are now additional requirements for controlling cost, changes in observation status and mental health funding (Meyer and Muchmore 2016, Evans 2013). Additionally, after Obamacare was introduced, 70 supplemental changes were made. Co-Op health plans collapsed, the individual mandate was placed on hold and plan waivers were being granted arbitrarily; all creating new questions (Turner 2016).

7. Need for increased flexibility- Changes in the market place, uncertainty, government involvement, increasing complexity and the increased pace of care, all speak to the need for a flexible responsive organization for survival.

8. Changing market place- The impact of the ACA has led to disruption of insurance coverage; a new process in which the government now determines what is an

acceptable health insurance policy. There has been a significant decrease in available plans, less insurers, more part time workers or workers with benefit reductions.

9. Decrease in revenues- An additional impact of the increase in mergers expected in 2016 is an increase in cost, drop in efficiencies and less innovation. During the 1990s and 2000s, prices increased 40% (to respond to revenue decreases) based on lost competition attributed to healthcare mergers (Kutscher 2016). More predictably, the ACA has increased Medicaid enrollment, which represents a negative impact on revenue and Obamacare payment reductions are expected. On an even more concerning note, CMS chief actuary Richard Foster has predicted that Medicare payment reductions will bankrupt 15% of providers (Foster 2016). These reductions in payments are expected to be progressive, increasing to 40% by 2050 (Shatto and Clemens 2012). In 2015, the CMS actuary report to the Medicare Trustees predicted, based on their simulations, that by 2040 50% of hospitals, 70% of Skilled Nursing Facilities and 90% of Home Health Agencies will have negative margins (Annual Report 2015).

Taking these points together, it is a reasonable proposal that every healthcare organization consider bolstering their improvement efforts even if they are not convinced that this is an impending crisis. But then again, in rural America, the crisis is undeniable, as evidenced by hospital closings at the rate of 1 per month (Depew 2016).

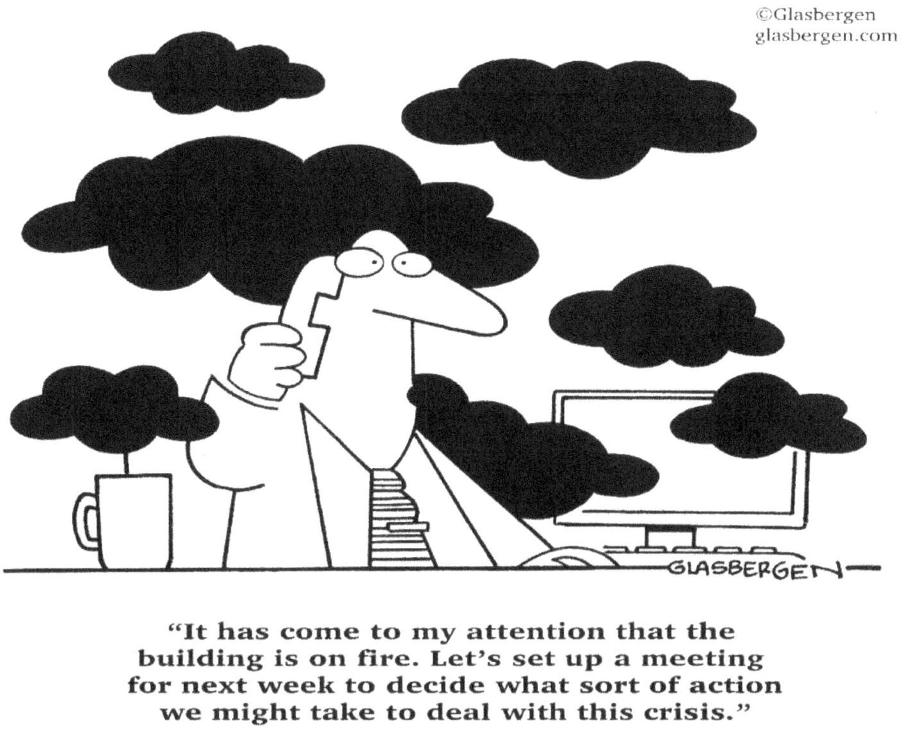
©Glasbergen
glasbergen.com
GLASBERGEN
"It has come to my attention that the building is on fire. Let's set up a meeting for next week to decide what sort of action we might take to deal with this crisis."

Reproduced with permission and license from Glasbergen

Figure E.2 Indecision (See figure legends)

Avoiding the Mistake of Omission

Even with the current state that is predicting a need for radical change, it is still often difficult to commit to a sweeping transformation like LEAN Healthcare Innovation. As noted by Nadina, in the article "*Methods of identification of the need for organizational change as being opportune*", "*proactive change is the surest and most rapid path to success, progress and performance*" but she also notes that it is the most difficult decision because of ongoing stability (Nadina 2011). Reardon et al (and others) have proposed that being proactive in making radical change is the most important factor for future successful leaders; "*The key component of successful leadership now and in the next century is proactive and effective responsiveness to change. Experts agree that successful leaders must be flexible and capable of adapting to new conditions, open to novel alternatives and willing to take greater risks*" (Reardon et al 1998, Kotter 1990, O'Toole 1996). Proactive decisions to make radical change supports Handy's proposal that significant organizational change should occur on the upslope of the organizational success curve, not during decline or crisis (Handy 1995).

Learning from CEO Failures

Another approach to encourage making a radical change comes from learning about the failures of some of the most successful CEOs of recent history. As recounted in the article by Will Bridges "*10 CEOs who made huge Mistakes*," Bill Gates says his biggest error was that he ignored market changes and the growth of the search engine market; the result, Google. Steve Ballmer relates that not making changes early enough was part of his biggest mistakes associated with the failures of Zune and the Surface RT tablet. As noted above, business models and changes in customer profiles or interests are changing in healthcare. Ignoring these type of events was also the mistake of Reed Hastings of Netflix when they changed to separate DVD services which was a business model that also ignored the customers and changes in the market. Jack Welch took control of GE during a period of organizational success, but despite that success, he felt his biggest mistake was that he did not make radical changes quickly enough. To survive Welch promotes that your organization must be on the cutting edge of change because "*someone (or something) is always coming, consumer tastes change, cost structures change and if you're not fast and adaptable, your vulnerable*". Welch also emphasizes that "*the changes are always bigger than you initially sense*" (Bridges).

> "*At any business the revolutionary process starts with an analysis of the business environment and the recognition that radical change is the organization's best response to the challenges it faces*".
>
> *Jack Welch*

In the article "The New Era: A Master Class in Radical Change" several other CEOs express the same sentiments as those lamenting their mistakes. Larry Bossidy took over Allied Signal when it was failing financially and was lacking an identity as a corporation. He made radical changes because "*markets are moving too fast for incremental change*." Michael Walsh also took over at Tenneco during crisis. He also instituted radical changes which included, "*to reassess everything, to move toward delegation, by pushing for mini CEOs ...there has to be something inside the people as well*" (Sherman 1993). The lessons from some of the most successful and famous CEOs is to not let your organization's current triumphs prevent you from making radical change, conversely, if you are in crisis, it may be that radical change is the only hope to save your organization.

"Companies that pursue and embrace change are healthy, growing and dynamic organizations, while companies that fear change are stagnant entities on their way to a slow and painful death"

Mike Myatt

"The problem is I can't tell the difference between a deeply wise, intuitive nudge from the Universe and one of my own bone-headed ideas!"

Reproduced with permission under license cartoonstock ltd

Figure E.3 Stimulus and Response (See figure legends)

ᐯᐟᐟᐤᐠᐤᐯ ᐤᐟᐤ ᐤᐯᐤᐟᐤᐯᐟ

Confirming a Decision to Change: Insights and Action steps

Making a radical change requires overcoming the resistance to change, the anxiety of uncertainty and inertia. Prior psychological research indicates that we are more motivated to respond to impending losses or realized threats as opposed to opportunities for additional success, hence there is a tendency to act only <u>after</u> the negative impact of a crisis occurs. (Kahneman and Tversky 1992, 1984). Chip Eichelberger provides this advice to address the anxiety and confusion; first to accept that the results are not what they should be and then take responsibility. Next you must come to the belief that you can make a change and can take action. At this point it may help to determine the reasons why you will not fail, and what will drive you to succeed. To help overcome resistance he recommends that you review why you are where you are; your accomplishments, results, biggest failures and what it will take to be better. In addition, he recommends that you determine where you are objectively; grade your attributes, identify your ideal state in terms of real results and the changes necessary to get there. With this effort complete, it's time to make a plan; goals and projects on a weekly and monthly basis, without timidity or fear of failure. Next take the step to formulize the action plan, using visual management. The formulization now translates into instituting change; by changing your schedule, change your work and even your recreational habits. It will be necessary to create; time for improvement, time for new opportunities, to create a new feedback system, a new reminder and a communication system. Finally, it is time to start to realize and believe in the future you want (Eichelberger).

To make radical change, Jack Welch recommends that there is a "need *to start with reality, to define values, and understand that change is never ending*" (Sherman 1993). Nadina recommends considering the internal and external environment of the organization and that managers identify what to change, when to change and how to change (Nadina 2011). In addition, metric indicators, a special trigger system or mapping progress changes in outcomes can all serve to generate a radical change. Nadina proposes that if you are considering change, the time to act is as soon as possible by using an action plan that applies the Lewin model of habit change (Nadina 2011). Additionally, Dr. Swain adds that if a company does realize the need to change, they need to identify what they are able to change in the categories; Mission, Vision and Strategy, Technology, Human Behavior, Job design, organizational structure and organizational culture (Swain 2011).

"My job is to make decisions. Your job is to make them good decisions."

Figure E.4 Faith (See figure legends)

An Option to Address the Coming Crisis; LEAN Healthcare Innovation

What are the options if a crisis hits healthcare like the Balance Budget Act of 1997? The impact of that legislation was that 35% of hospitals went to negative margins and10% of nursing homes were bankrupted even after massive layoffs (Pear 2000). In today's environment you can't cut nurses and staff without increasing penalties from readmissions and HCAHPS. Layoffs will also compromise revenues from value based purchasing or managing the continuum of care. To manage Value Based Purchasing and the Continuum of Care requires system management of partners, coordination of services and medical specialties, increases in efficiency and greater effectiveness in terms of patient value. All of these activities will be originating from staff innovation and provider engagement, not cost cutting.

As an example of how provider engagement and innovation can work, we used the LEAN Healthcare Innovation approach to the Total Joint Replacement Value Based Purchasing Program. We started with the typical LEAN A3 process, identified metrics and conducted two Value Stream Analysis approaches for the preparation for surgical procedures and for the immediate and short term post-operative care process. We also included a mapping and waste assessment of the hospital discharge process. This led to multiple immediate changes in practice and policy and new innovations (Just Do Its), process changes (Rapid Improvement Experiments) and new communication standards (Projects) which were created by the staff from multiple departments over an eight-month period. The process involved education about the changes in healthcare, LEAN techniques and the impact of the survival or failure of the program. Communication occurred using multiple different approaches from the traditional small meetings with reflective brainstorming to organizational outreach, Visual Management and Gemba walks by leadership. The aim was to be inclusive, to encourage different points of view and accept skepticism and negativity but to also require participation for a positive outcome from all the staff. An important requirement was that physicians were primary contributors in the LEAN activities. The end result is illustrated in Figure E1. demonstrating the drop in length of stay (LOS) for orthopedic cases while there were simultaneous improvements in HCAHPS. These results demonstrated the great potential impact for improvement from the physicians, physician's assistants, nursing and staff through engagement in a system like LEAN Healthcare Innovation.

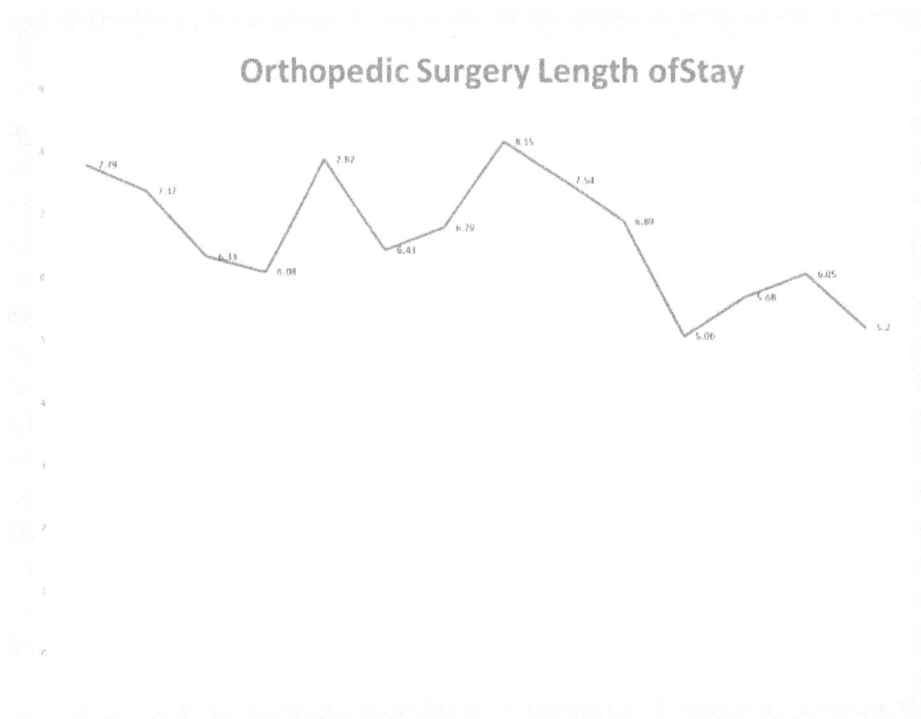

Figure E.5 Drop in Length of Stay during the implementation of LEAN Healthcare Innovation with the simultaneous improvement of HCAHPS scores.

Conclusions

Looking forward, the future for healthcare looks dismal and the options to address these problems are limited. The limited success of prior LEAN implementations in healthcare serves as an indication of why a different approach is required; a LEAN approach that is adapted for Healthcare, LEAN Healthcare Innovation. It is the answer for increasing flexibility, speed of response to market, regulatory changes and dropping revenues. LEAN Healthcare Innovation provides a response to the new paradigms related to patient centered outcomes, managing the continuum of care and value based purchasing through physician and nursing engagement and culture change. LEAN Healthcare Innovation will improve your organization for the patients, the staff and your community for the uncertain times to come.

A Tool for Determining the Method for Consensus Organizational Decision Making

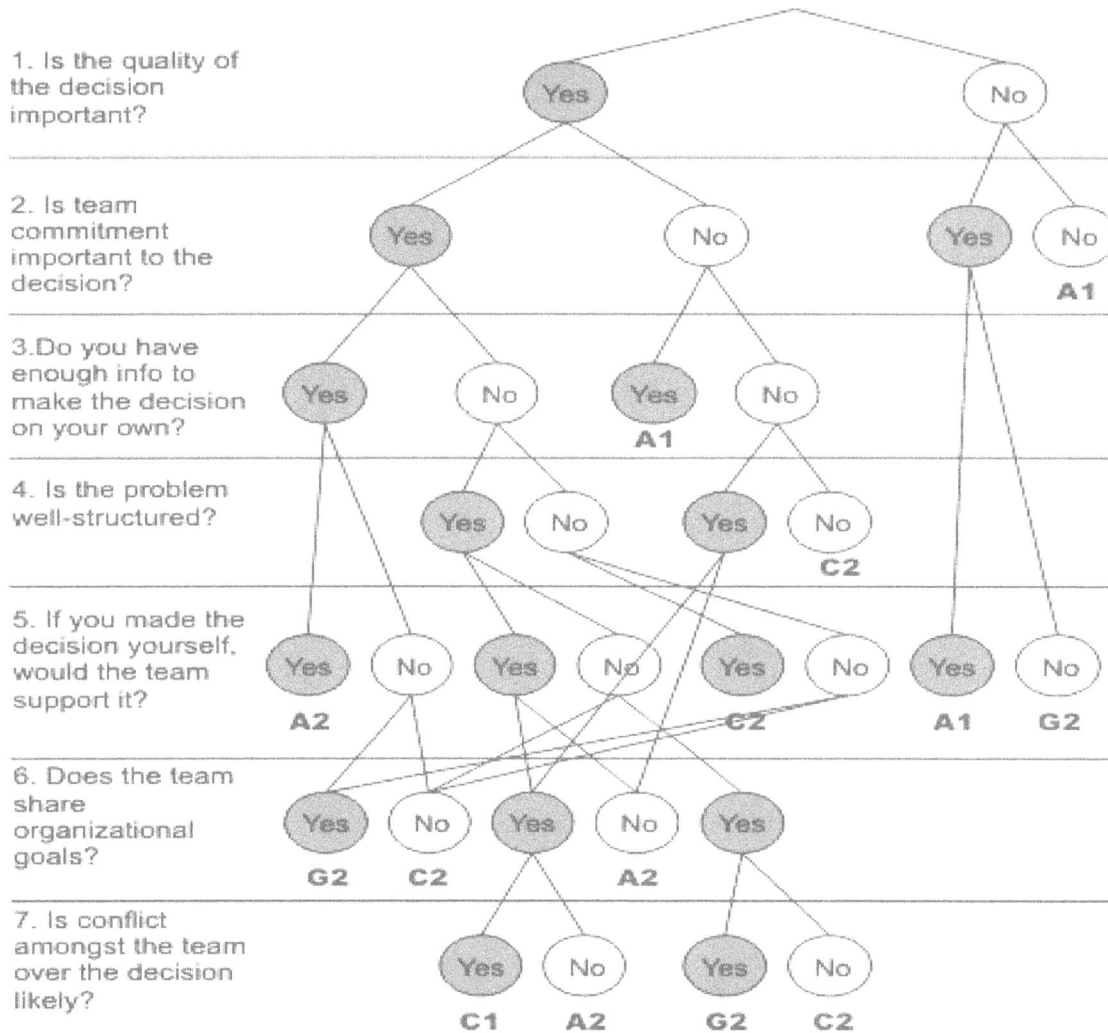

Figure E.6 The Vroom–Yetton contingency model is a situational leadership theory of industrial and organizational psychology. A1-Leader decision required, A2- Leadership decision with input, C1-Individual team members provide decision support, Leaders make the final decision based on recommendations, C2- Group meeting for input recommendations the decision made by leadership, G2-A team decision, approved by leadership. By following the decision tree, it will identify the best process to make a successful and accepted organizational decision (Vroom and Yetton 1973).

References

2015 Annual Report of the Boards of Trustees of the Federal Hospital Insurance and Federal Supplementary Medical Insurance Trust Funds, transmitted to the Speaker of the U.S. House of Representatives and President of the U.S. Senate July 22, 2015, p. 192, https://www.cms.gov/ResearchStatistics-Data-and-Systems/Statistics-Trends-and-Reports/ReportsTrustFunds/Downloads/TR2015.pdf (emphasis added).

Balle M. A LEAN Leap of Faith. The Lean Post 2013.

Bridges W. 10 CEOs Who Made Huge Mistakes/ articles.bplans.com.

Depew B. Rural Hospitals closing at rate of 1 per month. Center for Rural Affairs. 2016.

Dumont C, Kaura A, Subramanian S. The Faster New World of Healthcare. Issue 66, Booz and Company 2012.

Eichelberger C. www.getswitchedon.com.

Evans M. Outlook 2015: Financial pressures, reform uncertainties. Modern Healthcare 2015.

Foster R, "Estimated Financial Effects of the 'Patient Protection and Affordable Care Act,' as Amended.

Grace-Marie T. "70 Changes to Obamacare…So Far," Galen Institute, Health Policy Matters, 2016, http://galen.org/newsletters/changes-to-obamacare-so-far/.

Handy CB. The Empty Raincoat: Making Sense of the Future. 1995 Random House.

Hiltzik M. Mergers in the healthcare sector: why you'll pay more. Los Angeles Times 2016. 2015 18% increase in healthcare mergers.

Kahneman D. and Tversky A. Advances in prospect theory: Cumulative representation of uncertainty. Journal of Risk and Uncertainty. 1992;5: 297–323.

Kahneman D. and Tversky A. Choices, Values, and Frames. American Psychologist. 1984;39:341–350.

Kotter J. A force for change. 1990, Free Press.

Kutscher B. Healthcare merger and acquisition activity likely to stay strong in 2016. Crain communications.

Meyer H and Muchmore S. Outlook for 2016: Election uncertainty clouds business climate. 2016 modern healthcare.

Moffit RE Year Six of the Affordable Care Act: Obamacare's Mounting Problems. http://thf-reports.s3.amazonaws.com/2016/BG3109.pdf.

Nadina R. Methods of identification of the need for organizational change as being opportune. Annals of the University of Oradea, Economic Science Series. 2011;20:707-712.

Pear R. Health Providers and the Elderly Clash on Medicare Funds. Issue in Depth: Health Care. New York Times 2000.

Reardon KK, Reardon KJ, Rowe AJ. Leadership styles for the five stages of radical change. Acquisition Review Quarterly 1998;129-146.

O'Toole J. Leading Change: the argument for values based leadership. 1996 Jossey-Bass.

Shatto J and Clemens M. Projected Medicare Expenditures Under an Illustrative Scenario with Alternative Payment Updates to Medicare Providers," U.S. Department of Health and Human Services, Centers for Medicare and Medicaid Services, Office of the Actuary, 2012. p. 6, https://www.cms.gov/research-statistics-data-and-systems/statistics-trends-and-reports/reportstrustfunds/downloads/ 2012tralternativescenario.pdf.

Sherman S. The new era a master class in Radical Change. Only a few CEOs have attempted corporate revolution. Meet the masters- Jack Welch, Larry Bossidy, Bill Weiss and Mike Walsh and learn from their secrets. Fortune Mag 1993.

Swain R. Nine Reasons Organizations need to Change. Drucker Today. Process Excellence Network 2011.

Vroom V, Yetton PW. Leadership and Decision-Making. 1973 University of Pittsburgh .

Appendix

1.   **Suggestions for Figure 5.3**

   How Many entities does this represent?

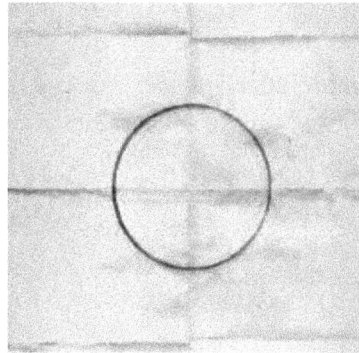

2.   **Behavioral Theories in Decision Making**

3.   **A3 Example**

4.   **Figure Legends**

Figure 5.3 Suggestions

Straw- end on	Oxygen
Frisbee (or dingus)	Contact lens
Hula Hoop	Top of a Bottle
Orange (or other rounded fruit)	Tire
Gun Barrel on end	Basketball (or other round athletic ball)
Cut Carrot (or other rounded	Earth
vegetable)	Ring
Sun	Camera lens
4th most common letter	Halo
Monocle	Sphere
Manhole	Bracelet
Wheel	Open Mouth (and other orifices)
Button	Water Ring Stain
End of a Noose	Basketball Hoop
Saucer	Lasso (on end)
Piston Ring	
Newton Ring	

Behavioral Theories in Decision Making

1. Doctrine of Necessity- (Hume) We primarily do what is needed

2. Bounded rationality- (Herbert Simon) Decisions are bounded by constraints of information, reasoning ability and time,

3. Principle of Least Effort or the Path of Least Resistance- Promotes the concept of situational decision making with a low level of deliberation.

4. Homo Economicus- Humans are rational and self-interested acting only for economic gain, limited by tyranny of small decisions, in other words missing the big picture.

5. Behavior can be irrational, self-harming and habitual- This is where rational choice based models fail.

6. Elaboration Likelihood Model of Persuasion-Messages with an emotional appeal can create attitude formation, and may create stronger and more durable attitudes.

7. Assumption of Rationality- We assume the rules are fair, which accounts for the sometimes very negative response to unfair rules.

8. Hyperbolic Discounting- Valuations fall very rapidly after limited delays, and then more slowly over longer periods. This implies that individuals using hyperbolic discounting reveal a strong tendency to make choices that are inconsistent over time and to discount the value of future rewards.

9. Message Framing- Presentation affects decisions and the assessment of losses versus gains.

10. Prospect Theory of Decisions in Uncertainty- This is a behavioral economic theory about risk assessment. The theory states that people make decisions based on intuition and potential value of losses and gains rather than the final outcome.

11. Inertial in Decision Making- Difficult decisions or those with too many choices promote no change or the easiest change.

12. Behavioral Economics- Preferences are not static and change.

13. Representativeness and Conjunction Fallacy- Decisions are based not on probability but on history or categories and when people rely on representativeness, they can fall into an error which breaks a fundamental law of probability.

14. Elaboration Likelihood Model -Decision making dual process- System 1/system 2 intuition/reasoning run simultaneously, the peripheral- unconscious, central deliberate- balance creates motivation and ability modified by context and messaging

15. Judgement Heuristics – Rules of thumb that reduce calculations to simpler judgements often creates biases that lead to errors.

16. Availability- Consideration based on ease of recall or what is more memorable; a mental shortcut that relies on immediate examples that come to mind have greater influence over decisions.

17. Adjustment /Anchoring and Expected Utility theory- Anchors serve as points of reference and the anchor contaminates the estimate, even if it is clearly irrelevant.

18. Attribute Substitution-When somebody makes a judgment which is computationally complex, a rather more easily calculated simpler problem is substituted. This explains why individuals can be unaware of their own biases, and why biases persist even when the subject is made aware of them. It also explains why human judgments often fail to show regression toward the mean.

Theories on Personal behavior specific to decisions about personal change include;

1. Logic in decision making (Fliegenschnee and Shelokovsky-1998)-80% of factors influencing personal behavior are not related to knowledge or awareness.

2. Time pressure and decision making- (Fazio)- With time pressure, accessible attitudes determine behavioral outcomes; with less pressure, decisions are more deliberate.

3. Theory of Reasoned Action- Beliefs about outcomes of personal behaviors determine supportive attitudes

4. Information deficit models (the AIDA model of market theory) - In general, information is not enough for change. The model implies that communication should focus on improving the transfer of information and understanding from experts to non-experts.

5. Value Action Gap Theory -The disparity from attitude versus actions is created by barriers such as individuality, responsibility and practicality.

6. Routine Behavior- Particularly habits requires weeks to months to be created and a similar time frame to change.

A3 Format

Description:	Value Stream ID:	e / Locati:vent Numbe	Revision:
Sponsor:	Process Owner:	Facilitato:Sensei:	

Event Date: / Current Date: 4/17/2013
Team Members:

1. REASONS FOR ACTION

Incorporating Vision, Mission and Core Values with context, importance and the critical reason why.

2. INITIAL STATE

TRUE NORTH METRICS-
1. Quality Metric-
2. Delivery-
3. Flow-
4. Productivity-
5. Revenue-
6. Human Development-
7. Growth-

Standards missed, critical problems

3. TARGET STATE

TRUE NORTH METRICS-
1. Quality Metric-
2. Delivery-
3. Flow-
4. Productivity-
5. Revenue-
6. Human Development-
7. Compassionate Relationship-
8. Growth-

Who and how

4. GAP ANALYSIS

1. Defects
2. Over-processing
3. Waiting
4. Non-utilized or underutilized staff
5. Transportation
6. Inventory
7. Motion
8. Excess Processing

Root causes, Sources, applied tools, cause of results

5. SOLUTION APPROACH

General approach
3 options down to 1

6. RAPID EXPERIMENTS

Just Do its
Rapid Improvement -Hypothesis statement
Projects- outline approach and goals

7. COMPLETION PLAN

Dates and Accountability
Gantt Chart

8. CONFIRMED STATE

Unintended Consequences from Box 5
Confirmation of goals attainment

9. INSIGHTS

Realtime submissions
Reviewed at Report out

① ② ③ ④ ⑤ ⑥ ⑦ ⑧ ⑨

© 2014 SURGICAL SYSTEMS   (www.surgicalsystems.org)

ACTION PLAN: Title

Executive Sponsor   Team Leader

Team Members

#	VSA	RIE	Proj	JDI	Description	Accountability	Due Date	Comments	Status
1									
2									
3									
5									
6									
7									
8									
9									
10									
11									
12									
13									
14									
15									
16									
17									
18									
19									
20									
21									
22									
23									
24									
25									

Final Thoughts

©Glasbergen
glasbergen.com

"In an increasingly complex world, sometimes
old questions require new answers."

Reproduced with permission and license from Glasbergen

Figure F.1 Limits and evolved thinking (See figure legends)

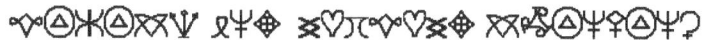

"If you want to be in the world I live in, which is a creative world with new ideas, then you've got to get away from the norm. You've got to go for it."

Jerry Weintraub

"There's no need to sharpen your pencils any more. Even the dull ones can make a mark."
Ze Frank

"Twenty years from now you will be more disappointed by the things that you didn't do than by the ones you did do, so throw off the bowlines, sail away from safe harbor, catch the trade winds in your sails. Explore, Dream, Discover."

Mark Twain

"We can easily forgive a child who is afraid of the dark; the real tragedy of life is when men are afraid of the light."

Plato

"First, have a definite, clear practical ideal; a goal, an objective. Second, have the necessary means to achieve your ends; wisdom, money, materials, and methods. Third, adjust all your means to that end."

Aristotle

"You can't use up creativity. The more you use, the more you have."

Maya Angelou

©Glasbergen
glasbergen.com

GLASBERGEN—

**"Ignore the lifeboats in the parking lot.
Everything is fine."**

Reproduced with permission and license from Glasbergen.com

Figure F.2 Lifeboats (See figure legends)

"You are far too smart to be the only thing standing in your way."

Jennifer Freeman

"When something bad happens, you have three choices. You can either let it define you, let it destroy you or let it strengthen you."

Unknown

"Without change there is no innovation, creativity, or incentive for improvement. Those who initiate change will have a better opportunity to manage the change that is inevitable."

William Pollard

"Change is vital, improvement the logical form of change."

James Cash Penney

"Human improvement is from within outward."

James Anthony Froude

"Patience and experience, A man can do anything if he has those."

Helmut Zemo

"Practice without improvement is meaningless."

Chuck Knox

"The biggest room in the world is the room for improvement."

Helmut Schmidt

"The supreme quality for leadership is unquestionably integrity. Without it, no real success is possible, no matter whether it is on a section gang, a football field, in an army, or in an office."

Dwight D. Eisenhower

"Excellence is the unlimited ability to improve the quality of what you have to offer."

Rick Pitino

"The quality of a person's life is in direct proportion to their commitment to excellence, regardless of their chosen field of endeavor."

Vince Lombardi

"Surgery is a lesson that must be lived to be learned; the essence of that lesson is quality, improvement and the pursuit of excellence."

TSH

"LIFE is short, and Art long; the crisis fleeting; experience perilous, and decision difficult. The physician must not only be prepared to do what is right himself, but also to make the patient, the attendants, and externals cooperate."

Hippocrates

"Writing in English is the most ingenious torture ever devised for sins committed in previous lives. The English reading public explains the reason why."

James Joyce

Figure Legends

Figure 1.1 Denial is rampant in healthcare

Figure 1.2 Improvement is a punishment. Why?

Figure 2.1 It's about execution

Figure 3.1 The energy to move the organization

Figure 3.2 Budgets, Funding and Commitment

Figure 3.3 It requires vision and judgment

⬠⚹ ◉⚹⚐⌒⬠◉⚹⟅ ⟅⬠⟅◉⌒⟒ ⟆⟊⬦ ⬳⟍◉⟁⚶⚹⟊⚹

What is leadership? It requires vision and judgment and internal commitment and a dedication to hard work through others. True leaders are hard to find, most act like free riders on the title.

Figure 4.1 Devoted, engaged and committed

⬦⚹⟅⟍⚹⬦, ⚹⟊⟁⟆⚹⬦ ⟆⟊⬦ ⟎⟍⚶⚶◉⚹⚹⬦

Leaders are devoted, staff engaged, managers are committed. They live the vision and mission. They make things work through a focus on details in the trenches and keep the staff on track.

Figure 5.4 Culture is a wave of momentum

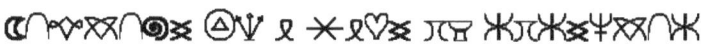

⟎⌒⟍⚹⟍◉⚹ ◉⟅ ⟆ ⚶⟆⟍⚹ ⟍⟊ ⚶⟍⟎⚹⟊⚹⟍⟍

Staff culture, group identity and social norms can lead to lemmings like self-destructive behavior or to successful knowledge workers. It's about their engagement and work satisfaction that fuels culture. Culture is a wave of momentum; it can be positive or negative.

Figure E.1 Execution

⚹⚹⟎⟍⚹◉⟊⟆

Moving from decisions, plans and then execution, probably not. It is so hard, lack of support, inertia, obstacles, indecisions, a culture of mediocrity, fear of change, lack of commitment. Lack of execution is the cumulative effect from all of the above. It requires a holistic approach of having all the ducks in a row.

Figure E.2 Indecision

◉⟊⬦⚹⟎◉⟍◉⟊⟆

Decision analysis, perfect is the enemy of good. We reward indecision by criticizing mistaken decisions. One cannot really lead without making decisions and accepting that you may be wrong.

Figure E.3 Stimulus and Response

⟍⚹◉⚶⌒⟍⟍⟍ ⟆⟊⬦ ◉⚹⟍⟆⟍⟊⟍⚹

⚹⚹⚹⚹ ⟍⟆⟆⟍⚹ ⚶⚹⚹⚹⚹⟊ ⟍⚹◉⚶⌒⟍⟍⟍ ⟆⟊⬦ ◉⚹⟍⟆⟍⟊⟍⚹ .⚹⟍ ⚶⚹

⟆⚶⟍⚹ ⚹⟍ ⚶⟆⟊⟆⟍⚹ ◉⚹⟍⟆⟍⟊⟍⟍⚹⟍⚹⟍⟍ ◉⟍ ⚹⟍ ⬦⚹⟎⚹⬦⚹ ⟍⟆⟊ ⟆

Figure E.4 Faith

Concern that a decision will fail, not because it is a wrong decision, but that it will not be supported through implementation and execution. Leadership must have faith in translation, commitment and accountability in their organization. If they do not, who are they leading?

Figure F.1 Limits and evolved thinking

Figure F.2 Lifeboats

Just like our first metaphor, this is about denial. To quote Jurgen Warmbrunn, *"The problem with most people is that they don't believe something can happen until it already has. It is not stupidity or weakness; it is just human nature."*

Index

3 line experiment, 155
3M, 88
5 Whys- Failures in LEAN, 28

A

A Einstein, 144
A3, 116-117, 141, 163, 183, 189, 193
A New Definition of Waste, Political Conflict, 89
A System Approach, 4, 11, 13, 25-26, 74, 90
A Team Approach and a "Questioning Culture", 140
ABC, 78
Abelson, 171
ability, 17, 28, 47, 61-62, 65-66, 68, 70, 75, 84, 86, 107,
131-132, 134, 144, 149, 154, 156, 158, 162, 176, 191,
197
Abraham, 62
ACA, 6, 21-22, 33, 177-178
accountability, 6, 12, 16, 26, 39, 65, 67, 69, 74, 81, 89,
108, 111, 135, 142, 151-152, 157-158, 160, 202
achievement, 13, 89, 108, 111, 151
ACO, 22
Actions, 89
actualizing, 97
Adams, 42, 51, 96, 130, 169
Adapt or Die, 24, 32
adaptation, 13, 23, 47, 87
Addison, 96, 169
Addressing Social Principles as   Part of
Cultural   Change, 155
administration, 7, 29, 47, 67-68, 77, 86, 90, 98, 142,
154, 172
administrator, 7, 16, 29, 45, 74, 85-86, 89, 91, 142, 154
Advisory Board, 3, 21, 23, 31, 144, 173
Affordable Care Act, 2, 31, 187
agency, 154-155, 166, 178
agendas, 124, 160
AIDA, 192
alignment, 26, 31, 38-39, 49, 62, 71, 81, 90, 116, 125,
159, 167
AMA, 21, 32, 157
ambiguity, 25, 40, 112, 135, 150
ambivalence, 135, 138
An Engaged Workforce, 131
An Innovation in LEAN; A New Definition of Waste
        "NonFlow" and the "Flow" exercise, 163
An Option to Address the Coming Crisis; LEAN
Healthcare Innovation, 183
Andon Cord, 43
Angeles, 187
Angelou, 196
antibodies, 107, 110
Antonacopoulou, 145, 169
Argyris, 84, 96, 162, 169

Aristotle, 143, 196
Armenakis, 52
Armitage, 138, 169, 172
Arndt, 38, 46-47, 51
Aronsson, 52
artefacts, 57
Asch, 155, 169, 173
Ashforth, 51, 115, 120
Ashgate, 169, 171
ASQ, 42, 51
Astrid, 52
attitude, 19, 40, 74, 111, 114, 147-149, 153, 172, 191-
192
attribution, 172
attribution error, 152
Audrain, 173
Aunon, 32
authoritarian, 16
autocratic, 55, 92, 94
autotelic, 163-164
Avery Hiebert, 55
avoidance, 41, 46, 176
awareness, 85, 87, 116, 138, 153, 163, 192
Axelrod, 156, 169
Aztec, 152

B

Backman, 52
Baker, 52
Balance Budget Act of 1997, 183
Baldwin, 171
Balle, 73, 96, 106-107, 120, 176, 187
Ballmer, 180
Banas, 40, 53
Bandura, 144, 150, 169
Barberich, 23, 32
Barrett, 169
Bartel, 21, 31
Bartlett, 115, 120
Bass, 31-33, 96-99, 170-171, 188
Bator, 169
Baum, 52, 172
Bazerman, 151, 172
Beaulieu, 31
Becker, 31
Beckhard, 69, 96, 137, 169
bedside, 45, 51
Beer, 15, 31, 102, 120
Beh, 52
Belbeze, 19, 31
Berger, 140-141, 169
Berkowitz, 152, 169, 172
Berrett, 99

Beyer, 169
Bigelow, 38, 46-47, 51
Bina, 2
Bina, Shideh Sedgh, 31
Birkinshaw, 114-116, 120
Bishop, 154, 169
BJ, 169
Blackmore, 51
Blackwell, 98, 169-170
Blendon, 16, 31
Bloomsbury, 169
Blue Ocean leadership, 61, 97
Blumenthal, 146, 169
Boddy, 61, 96
Bonnici, 59, 90, 98
Boon, 38, 51
Booz, 187
Borycki, 52
Bossidy, 36, 51, 180, 188
bottleneck, 113
boundaries, 12
bounded, 58, 191
Bowles, 17, 31
bowlines, 196
Bracelet, 190
Brackett, 45, 51
brainstorming, 184
Braunholtz, 52
Brealey, 98
Brerrett, 99
Brikinshaw, 113
Brommels, 52
Brook, 32, 173
Bruce, 36
Buch, 15, 31
Buchanan, 61, 96, 101-102, 120
Bull, 171
Burlington, 169
Bush, 2, 31
Business Management Practices and Staff
Incorporation, 142
Business Models in Healthcare and Organizational
Culture Change, 142
Business Practices
Busum, 32
Butler, 52
Butterworth, 97
Byrne, 34, 99, 173

C
Cady, 69, 96
Callahan, 33
Caloyeras, 32
Cambridge, 121
Camera, 190
Cameron, 160, 169
Campbell, 115, 120
Canada, 134
Canadian, 134, 169

Caplan, 44, 51
cardiomyoplasty, 160
Career development, 37, 61, 129, 157
Carlson, 1
Carnegie, 169
Caroline Conway, 65
Cawsey, 136, 169
CBO, 1, 31
CEO, 65, 71-73, 77, 176, 180, 187-188
ceremony, 80, 104, 111, 139
Change Management, 8, 13-15, 32, 35, 38, 48, 57, 59,
66, 97-99, 102, 121, 145, 148, 170-171
Change necessity, 14
Change or Die, 126, 170
Chapman, 57-58, 96
Charan, 36, 51
Charles Darwin, 101
Chen, 32
Chronic Organizational problems, 124
Chugh, 172
Cialdini, 152, 169-170
CLABSI, 51
Clarity, 67
Claydon, 120
Clemens, 178, 188
Clostridium, 154, 169
Clubb, 82, 86, 96
coaching, 61-62, 65, 96, 109, 117, 152
Coalition, 68, 77-78, 90, 109, 115
Co-customers, 8
Cole, 173
Collin, 24, 31-32, 36, 51, 88, 94, 96, 162, 170
Comer, 51
commitment devices, 151, 172
communication, 3, 8, 10, 13, 22, 28, 37, 39-40, 43, 47,
49, 61-62, 69-70, 76, 78, 89-90, 96, 103-105, 111, 119,
129-130, 134-135, 138, 151-152, 156, 166, 169, 182-
184, 187, 192
Competencies, 73
complex systems, 12, 57, 59
complexity, 13, 23, 25, 45, 58, 60, 64, 70, 90, 98-99,
121, 126, 136, 176-177
compliance, 107
Complicated and Complex Systems, 57, 59
Complicated systems, 12, 59
Conclusions, 25, 47, 94, 148, 184
Condon, 52
Confirming a Decision to Change: Insights and Action
Steps, 181
Congressional Budget Office, 1
Connecticut, 6, 169
Connell, 51
Conner, 60-61, 96, 138, 169
Connie, 19
Conscience, 87, 124
conscientiousness, 86
consciousness, 163
consensus, 6, 65, 152, 186
consequence, 41, 73, 101, 126, 148, 153-154, 158

Continuum of Care, 176, 183, 185
Conundrum, 170
Cooper, 17, 31
Corbett, 173
Cortes, 152
countermeasures, 42
courage, 88, 112-113, 133, 159
Covenantal, 157
Covey, 3-4, 12, 15-16, 20, 31, 36, 51, 61, 67-68, 86, 88, 96, 103, 113, 120, 124-125, 128, 143, 149, 151, 162, 170
Coyle, 96
Coyle-Shapiro, 86
CQI, 24, 47-48
Crabtree, 172
Crain, 187
CRC, 97, 120

Crisis-Why LEAN Healthcare Innovation?, 5
        Why Now?, 1
Crosson, 32
Crowe, 42, 51
Csikszentmihalyi, 163-164
culture, 5, 12, 15-17, 19, 21, 23-25, 27, 31-33, 35-39, 43-44, 46, 48-49, 52-53, 57, 60, 63, 71-72, 79, 83, 97-98, 104, 109-111, 114, 116, 130-131, 134, 136, 140-143, 146, 149-151, 153, 155, 159, 161, 166, 169, 173, 182, 185, 201
Cummings, 115, 120
Cummins, 52-53
Current State, 5, 8, 14, 25, 52, 61, 114, 177, 179
customer, 1-3, 10, 24-25, 27, 37, 45, 48, 75, 109, 111, 127, 180

D

Dahlgaard, 12, 15, 20, 31-32
Damanpour, 160, 170
Darnton, 147, 170
Darwinism, 98
Davies, 40-41, 52
Davis, 158, 170
DDI, 60, 96
DeGuzman, 173
Dellifraine, 44, 51
Deloitte, 123, 137, 148, 154, 170
Demaine, 169
Deming, 12, 18, 32
Demos, 96
Depew, 59, 178, 187
deployment, 42, 68, 81, 104, 131
Dermott, 32
descriptive norms, 152
Deszca, 169
Deutschman, 126, 170
Dewart, 171
DFΔ, 70
Diamante, 96
Dickson, 107
DiClemente, 137-138, 172
dilemmas, 59

dingus, 190
diplomacy, 156
Diversification, 47
divided focus, 108
Dobbie, 52
documentation, 43, 142, 162
Donabedian, 146, 170
Donelan, 16, 31
Donoghue, 52
Doyle, 120
Drucker, 11, 14, 23, 32, 56, 66, 88, 102, 143, 150, 188
Dubbs, 33
Dubner, 151-152, 170-171
Dumont, 177, 187
DuPree, 86, 96, 110, 120, 157, 170

E

EBHSM, 134
EBM, 134-135
Eccles, 116, 120
Edison, 13
education, 22, 28-29, 32, 40, 46, 48, 66, 71, 78, 90, 104, 112-113, 117, 119, 123, 125, 129, 132, 134, 138-139, 146, 148, 155, 159, 161-162, 167, 183
Edwards, 12, 18
EIASM, 96
Eichelberger, 182, 187
Einstein, 144
Eisenberg, 40, 53
Eisenhower, 86, 197
Emergent change, 55, 57
Emotion, 64, 92-94, 126, 145, 147
Emotional intelligence, 19, 29, 85, 91
empathy, 7, 20, 56, 64, 72, 85, 87, 91-94
employee rights, 156
empowered, 17, 107, 128-129
empowering, 65, 113, 166
empowerment, 17, 41-44, 61, 67, 72, 88, 104, 107, 110, 117, 119, 125, 144, 167
EMR, 42, 176-177
enablers, 63
engagement, 8, 16-17, 21, 26, 29, 31, 38, 41, 46, 48, 67-68, 74, 81, 107, 123-124, 127-132, 134, 141, 144, 146-147, 149, 153, 157-159, 163-165, 173, 183-185, 201
England, 16, 171
enrichment, 111
Epilogue, 175-176, 178, 180, 182, 184, 186, 188
equilibrium, 74, 98, 171
Erwin, 51
ESM, 31
Estis, 65
Etz, 172
Eureka, 114
Evans, 52, 177, 187
Evergreen project, 36
evidenced based medicine, 7, 134
execution, 27, 36-37, 41, 51, 55, 59-60, 67, 74, 82, 88-89, 111, 139, 149, 175, 200-202
Execution of Cultural Change Changing Habits and
        "Schelling Points", 151

experimentation, 23-24, 26, 59, 61, 88, 114, 116, 141, 160

F

Fairness doctrine, 155
Fallacy, 191
Farnham, 171
Fastabend, 24, 32
Faulkner, 42, 51
Fazio, 192
Feedback loops, 11, 58, 147
Fehr, 157, 170
Ferrari, 145, 170
Findlay, 51
firefighting, 62, 118
Fischman, 42, 51
fishbone, 139
Fiume, 34, 99, 173
Fliegenschnee, 192
flow, 9-10, 25, 42, 44, 52, 150, 163-165, 167, 170
Foe, 98
Fordis, 170
formula for change, 69, 114
Foundational Support for a Cultural Change Model, 140
fragmentation, 11, 17, 24, 45, 48, 107, 125, 153
Freakonomics, 171
free rider, 157-158, 201
Freeman, 169, 197
Freidberg, 32
Friedberg, 21-22
Froude, 197
Furman, 44, 51

G

Gaby, 96
Gachter, 157, 170
Gallagher, 74, 96
Galliea Hospital, 46
Gallouj, 161-162, 170
Galvin, 173
Gamm, 38, 42-43, 53
Gardner, 23, 32, 125
Gates, 180
Gedankenexperiment, 116
Gemba, 43, 90, 130, 184
Gembutsu, 75
Genchi, 75
General Reviews, 42
George Bernard Shaw, 144
George Santayana, 35
Ghoshal, 115, 120
Gibbons, 146, 170
Gibbs, 115, 120
Giglio, 61, 96
Gill, 91, 96
Gleicher, 69
Glick, 173
Goffee, 55-56, 61, 97
Goldfried, 172
Goldsmith, 31-33, 84, 96-99, 170

Goldstein, 152, 155, 170
Goodrich, 26
Goonan, 52
Gould, 145, 171
governance, 67, 75, 108-109
Gowen, 33, 53
Grimes, 52
Grouard, 98
Grunden, 53, 124, 171
Guetzkow, 169
Guilford, 172
Gustafson, 52

H

Habits, 31, 96, 120, 151, 170
HAC, 2
Hage, 40, 51
Hagood, 124, 171
Halo, 190
Halsted, 160, 169, 171
Hamby, 171
Hamel, 120
Hampton, 169
handwashing, 153-154
Handy, 84, 132-133, 171, 179, 187
Handy Curve, 132-133
Hanrion, 65-66, 97, 108
Hansei, 75
Hara, 51
hardwiring, 42, 53, 99, 135, 173
Harper, 32, 51, 170
Harris, 41, 69, 90, 96-97, 137, 169
Harris Poll, 3
Harrison, 170
Harvard, 33, 52, 96-99, 120-121, 171-172
Hastings, 180
HCAHPS, 60, 96, 176, 183-184
Healthcare Staff Characteristics, 40
Heinemann, 97
helicopter vision, 145
Helmut, 197
Henley, 97
Heraclitus, 85
Herzlinger, 160, 171
Hesselbein, 19, 31-33, 96-99, 170
Heuristics, 191
HHS, 32
Hicks, 16, 32
Higgins, 172
Higgs, 13, 32, 58-61, 85, 91, 97, 137, 171
Hill, 33, 52, 120-121, 173
Hiltzik, 177, 187
Hippocrates, 198
Holden, 52
Holweg, 52
Hopkins, 160, 171
Hospital Acquired Condition, 2
Hu, 152, 172
Hudson, 172

human nature, 20, 86, 202
Hume, 191

I

implementation, 3, 8-9, 11, 14, 20, 23-24, 26, 32, 35, 38-49, 52-53, 57, 60-70, 72, 74-75, 78, 82-84, 90-91, 96, 102-109, 113, 115-118, 124-125, 127, 131-133, 135-136, 139, 141-143, 147, 151, 166, 172, 175, 184, 202
improvement, 2-5, 7, 9-27, 33, 35-39, 42, 44-49, 51-52, 57-61, 64, 66-68, 74-75, 79-80, 84, 87, 89, 91, 99, 103-104, 108, 115-116, 124, 127, 129-130, 132-135, 139-141, 143, 145, 150, 153-154, 157-160, 166, 169, 171-173, 176, 178, 182-184, 197-199
    in Business Basics as They Affect Change, 81
    in the Phases of Transformation, 80
injunctive norms, 152
innovation, 1, 3-5, 7, 9, 11, 13-15, 17-19, 21, 23-27, 29, 31-33, 35-37, 39-41, 43-45, 47, 49, 51, 53, 55-179, 181, 183-185, 187, 189, 191, 193, 195, 197, 199, 201, 203
    innovation in Services, 161, 170
    innovation laboratories, 87
Innovators, 88, 99
interpersonal, 15, 104, 149, 173
interrelationships, 11, 20

J

Jaarsveld, 171
Jackson, 121
Jacobs, 96
Jacobson, 73-74, 97
Jaworski, 59, 97
John Wooden, 8, 61
Johnson, 42, 51
Jones, 5, 8, 10, 25, 27, 34, 55-56, 61, 68, 97, 99, 106-108, 120-121
Jordan, 2, 32
Joyce, 36, 52, 98, 120, 198
Jurgen, 202

K

Kahneman, 181, 187
Kaiser, 2, 32
Kaizen, 141
Kanji, 38-39, 52
Kano Model, 103
Kanter, 23, 32, 89, 97, 125-126, 171
Kao, 17, 24, 32
Kaplan, 34, 99, 173
Karlgaard, 17, 32, 88, 97, 109, 120, 157, 171
Kaura, 187
Keefe, 149
Keenan, 121
Kellner, 59
Kieser, 116, 120
Kilo, 146, 169
Kleiner, 98
Knights, 114, 116, 120
knowledge workers, 9, 14, 22, 56, 64, 91, 142, 166, 172, 201
Knox, 197

Koehler, 99
Koenigsaecker, 74-75, 80-81, 97, 108-109, 120
Koller, 96
Kotter, 64-65, 70, 76-81, 97, 124, 171, 179, 187
Kouzes, 61, 91, 98
Kovner, 38, 52, 134, 141, 171
Kruglanski, 172
Kumar, 15, 32
Kuo, 42, 52
Kushniruk, 52
Kutscher, 178, 187

L

LaHote, 125
Laing, 136
Lally, 149, 171
Lane, 170
Langabeer, 51
Lavis, 134, 141, 171
Leaders versus Managers, 62
leadership, 1, 3, 7-8, 12, 14, 17, 21, 28, 31-33, 36-40, 42, 46-49, 55-58, 60-99, 101, 104-105, 108-114, 117, 119-120, 123, 126, 128, 130-132, 134-137, 141-143, 150, 154, 157-159, 162, 166, 169-171, 175-176, 179, 184, 186, 188, 197, 201-202
Leadership Activities in LEAN
        Leadership Standard Work:, 61
Leadership Balance and Competencies in Change, 73
leadership canvases, 61
Leadership Failure, 47, 55, 57, 65-66, 68, 76, 123
leadership grid, 61
Leadership in Systems Management and Change, 57
Leadership of Knowledge Workers, 56
Leadership Roles and Behaviors, 88
Leadership System Management, 58
Leadership Theory and Style, 55
Leading for Change, 73
LEAN communication System, 73
LEAN data program, 73
LEAN education Program, 132
LEAN evaluation day, 150
LEAN Healthcare Innovation, 4-5, 11, 15, 18, 23, 27, 55-177, 179, 181, 183-185, 187, 189, 191, 193, 195, 197, 199, 201, 203
LEAN Leadership Attributes, 74
Lean Staff Education
      "The Wall", 135-136
      Staff Modeling Failure,   132
      the Scientific Method,   11, 15, 26, 29, 35, 73,   103, 125, 134-135
LEAN Thinking, 5, 34, 99, 121
LEAN time, 66, 90
Learning from CEO Failures,   180
Lecce, 52
Lederman, 169
Lee, 52
Lega, 46, 52
lemmings, 201
Lenehan, 52
Leonard, 15

leverage, 78-79, 118
leveraging, 96
Levesque, 138, 171-172
Levitt, 151-152, 170-171
Lewin, 137, 149-151, 153, 171, 182
Lichtenstein, 60
Lifeboats, 196, 202
Lilford, 35, 52
Lindgren, 52
Liston, 52
Litchenstein, 59, 98
Lloyd, 53
Lombardi, 198
Luckman, 141-142, 171

M

Management of Resources and Priorities, 66
Mancur, 157
Mannion, 40-41, 52
Mantone, 42, 52
Marcus Aurelius, 14
Marsilio, 52
Marx, 10, 32
Mason, 43
mastery modeling, 150
Mattke, 32
Mauborgne, 61, 97
Maya, 196
Mayeno, 138, 171
Mayo, 33, 99
Mazmanina, 170
Mazzocato, 42, 52
McCabe, 114, 116, 120
McCaughey, 51
McDermott, 15
McElroy, 51
mcfadden, 33, 53
McGovern, 173
McGraw, 33, 120, 173
McGregor, 110, 120
Mckinsey, 123, 125, 142-143, 171
McLeod, 171
McNamara, 42, 52
Medicaid, 1, 6, 178, 188
Medicare, 1, 6, 32, 178, 188
Megginson, 101
Melanson, 52
mergers and partnerships, 37, 177
Messes, 58
Meston, 98
Meyer, 177, 187
Milgram, 155, 172
Milkman, 152, 172
Miller, 152-153, 172
Mintzberg, 72, 88, 98, 101-103, 105-106, 109, 118, 120
Mission statement, 7, 67, 95, 104, 124
Mistake of Omission, 179
Moffit, 177, 187
Mol, 120

Moore, 19, 98
morale, 47, 107
MORI, 16, 32
Morrow, 96, 144, 171-172
Muchmore, 177, 187
Mullen, 52, 152, 172
Munch, 125, 172
Murdoch, 72, 98
Myatt, 181

N

Nadina, 179, 182, 188
Nakajima, 146
national Center for healthcare leadership, 134
national health service, 6, 16, 31
Naughton, 51
Nembhard, 51
Newton, 190
NHS, 16, 32-33, 45-46
Nicholas, 98
Nohria, 36-37, 52, 82-84, 98, 102, 110, 116, 120
non-flow, 163
Noose, 190
Norcross, 172
norm activation theory, 153
Norms, 169, 172
Norville Barnes, 145

O

Obamacare, 176-178, 187
Ogbonna, 90, 97
Oldham, 115, 120
Olson, 157, 172
Ono, 68
Oradea, 188
Oreg, 40-41, 52
Organizational and Staff Innovations in LEAN, 160
Organizational change, 4, 23, 38, 40, 51-52, 58, 69, 90, 98-99, 106, 123-126, 128, 130, 132, 134-140, 142-144, 146, 148, 150, 152, 154, 156, 158, 160, 162, 164, 166, 168-172, 174, 176, 179, 188

P

Pacesetter, 93
Pagonis, 72, 98
Palgrave, 31, 98
Palma, 158-159, 172
paradox, 49, 73-74, 84, 163
"paradox of success", 84
Paredes, 52
Parente, 1, 33
Pareto, 111, 117-118
Parry, 169
Pascale, 61, 98
Patel, 53
pathfinding, 112-113
Patterson, 51
Pauly, 173
Pay for performance, 40, 52
PCAST, 13, 33
Pear, 183, 188

Pendlebury, 59, 98
Penney, 197
perfection, 10-11, 25, 32, 44, 75
Perrier, 170
Perry, 33, 84
personal development, 4, 18-22, 26-29, 84, 104, 112-113, 139, 141, 143, 146-147, 151, 154, 166
    Personal Development in Change, 84, 147
    Personal Development of Staff Personal Norms,
        Social Norms   and Social Principles in
        Change, 146
            Reflection, Deliberation, 144
            Using Behavioral Models and Theories of
            Change, 147
personality traits, 40, 148, 164
Peterson, 11, 40, 52
Pettersen, 11, 31, 33
Pettigrew, 59, 98
Pham, 32
phases of organizational change, 135
phases of transformation, 80
Phibbs, 31
Phil Crosby, 17
Philips, 114, 121
physician engagement, 3-4, 14, 31, 46, 67, 74, 156-158, 167
Pirsig, 20
Piston, 190
Pitchforth, 32
Pitino, 197
Plan, Organize, Coordinate, Control, 102
Planning and Assessment, 65
Plato, 196
pluralistic ignorance, 152, 155
Poksinska, 44-45, 52
Political conflict, 89-90
Pollard, 15, 33, 88-89, 98, 197
Popper, 120
Porras, 36, 51
Porsche, 68, 107
Posner, 61, 91, 98
Potts, 171
Potus exercise, 11
Pratt, 112
Pratt Whitney, 68, 108
Principles of LEAN, 8, 17
Prochaska, 137-138, 171-172
procrastination, 145-146
Pugh Decision Analysis of Leadership Styles, 92
Puig, 173

Q
Questioning culture, 116, 140-141, 166
Quigley, 32
R
Radnor, 45-46, 52
Ramlet, 1, 33
RAND, 21, 32
Rapid Cycle, 134

Rau, 2, 32
Reardon, 179, 188
Reed, 180
Rewards, 39, 49, 89, 110-111, 125, 191
Reynolds, 169
Rhoads, 169
Ripple, 126
Rivera, 31
Riverhead, 33
Rivis, 172
RM, 32
RN, 144
Rob Wyse, 69
Roberson, 36, 52, 98, 120
Robert, 20, 24, 98, 176
Robert Frost, 80
Robertson, 171
Rogers, 59, 151-152, 172
Roland, 32
Rollout, 65-66, 132
Rosenbaum, 23, 33
Ross, 98, 152, 172
Roth, 98
Rowe, 72, 98, 188
Rowland, 13, 58-61, 85, 97, 137, 171
Ruchlin, 15, 33
Rundall, 38, 52, 141, 171
Rural America, 178
Russell, 96
Rutala, 51
Ryan, 65
S
Sabini, 155, 172
Sagarin, 169
Sammut, 59, 90, 98
Santos, 52
Saucer, 190
Scharmer, 59, 97
Schein, 15, 57-58, 98
Schelling points, 151
Schlipp, 120
Schmidt, 197
Schneider, 40, 53
Schooff, 19, 33
Schoomaker, 24, 32
Schuster, 31, 51, 96, 120, 170
Schwartz, 153, 172
Scientific method, 11, 15, 26, 29, 35, 73, 103, 125, 134-135
Scott, 130
Second loop, 8, 84
Sedgh, 2
Selznick, 79, 98
Senge, 11-12, 33, 57-58, 61, 90, 98, 102, 121, 125
sensei, 115-116, 139
Serrano, 42, 53
Service culture, 131
Shakespeare, 160
Shannon, 42, 53

Shapiro, 96
Shatto, 178, 188
Shaw, 59, 99, 145, 172
Sheeran, 148, 172
Shein, 33
Shellenbarger, 145, 173
Shelokovsky, 192
shepherd, 81
Sheridan, 3, 127-128, 173
Sherman, 42, 53, 180, 182, 188
Shigeo Shingo, 43
Shoemaker, 2-3, 33
short cuts, 107, 192
Silber, 23, 33
Simpler Consulting, 74
Simpson, 24, 32
Singer, 172
Sirkin, 102, 121
Six Sigma, 32, 42-44, 48, 51-53
Slunecka, 42, 53
Smith, 16, 33, 98, 101, 107, 109-110, 121
Soft Edge, 17, 32, 97, 109, 120, 171
Somerville, 31-33, 96-99, 170
Sookanan, 52
Spalding, 96
Spear, 53
Stacey, 59, 90, 99, 102
standard work, 9, 14, 42, 61, 67, 74, 76, 89, 108, 111, 161, 167
Stata, 113
Stern, 147, 173
Stewart, 169
Stjernberg, 114, 121
Stockholm, 52
strategy, 9, 11, 27, 31, 34, 36-40, 42-43, 52-53, 57, 64, 68, 73, 77, 82, 88, 99, 104, 111, 121, 129, 136, 148, 150, 157, 159, 170, 172, 176, 182
Studer, 42-43, 68, 99, 130-132, 135-136, 173
Subramanian, 32, 187
Suchman, 116, 121
Suls, 170
Sun Tzu, 5, 7, 34
Surowiecki, 155, 158, 173
Sushman, 116
sustain, 36, 66, 140, 152
Sustain: Social Norms, Group Identity and Social Principles, Changing Social Norms: Hand Washing, 153
    Enhancing Self Efficacy Linking to Changing Agency Exercise, 154
Sutras, 163
Swain, 176-177, 182, 188
SWOT, 82
synergy, 17, 68, 151
system dynamics, 60

T
Takt, 150
"Talk", 77

Tanasijevic, 52
Tate, 51
TCAB, 45
teambuilding, 15
teamwork, 65, 77, 142, 151, 159
Tenneco, 180
The Change "Necessity", 14
The Chief Executive Officer, 71
The Patient Centered Health Improvement Approach, 126
"the Wall", 135-136, 156
Theoretical Foundation for Service Innovation and Innovation Education Excellence Through Innovation, 162, 167
    Initiation and the Inversion Exercise, 162
Thompson, 19, 33, 85, 99
Thorpe, 170
Thucydides, 7
Tiegs, 51
Toole, 179, 188
Torrence, 52
Total quality management, 24, 31, 38-39, 52, 121
Toussaint, 15, 19, 33-34, 65-66, 84, 99, 173
Toyota, 4-5, 42, 51, 68, 74-75
Toyota Production System, 4-5, 42, 51
TQM, 24, 31-33, 38-39, 47-48, 52, 96
Traindis, 149
Triandis, 173
Troxel, 173
Troxler, 51
Turner, 177
Tutty, 32
Tversky, 181, 187
Twain, 196
UFO, 140

U
Ulrich, 88-89, 99
ultimate game, 155
unfreeze, 150
unfreezing, 70, 151
Unity Model for Organizational Change, 137
Ulrech, 52

V
VA, 16, 21, 32
Vakola, 52
Valins, 172
value based purchasing, 176, 183, 185
Value Stream Analysis, 9, 183
VBP, 33, 144
Veracruz, 152
Verhoef, 51
Vest, 38, 42-43, 53
Veterans Affairs Health Services, 6
Villa, 52
Virginia Mason medical Center, 43
Virkstis, 144, 173
Vision Killers, 69
visioning, 7-8, 61, 67, 69-72, 78, 90

Visioning in Healthcare for Change, 71
voice of the customer, 8, 25, 44
Volpp, 151, 172-173
Vroom, 186, 188
VSA, 9
VUCA, 6, 25

W

Wallston, 170
Walsh, 180, 188
Wan, 173
Wanberg, 40, 53
Wang, 51
Wardle, 171
Waring, 52
Warmbrunn, 202
Warner, 99
warrior, 7, 55, 75
waste, 9-10, 31, 44, 46, 67, 89, 99, 121, 150, 163-164, 183
Webb, 172
Weber, 51, 55, 60
Weick, 85, 99, 115, 121
Weiner, 173
Weinstein, 161-162, 170
Weintraub, 195
Weiss, 188
Welch, 99, 180, 182, 188
Welsh, 71
Wensley, 59, 90, 98

Wesley, 96, 169
"What Leaders Really Do", 61, 64, 97
"What really works", 36, 52, 98, 120
Wheatley, 23, 33, 59-60, 87, 99
Whichello, 51
Why a LEAN Transformation, 15, 110
Wicked, 58
win-win, 143, 151
Womack, 2, 5, 8, 10-11, 17, 25, 27, 34, 68, 72, 99, 107-108, 121, 140, 160, 162, 173
Woodard, 52
Woodside, 171
work satisfaction, 21, 201

Y

Yauger, 32
Yetton, 186, 188
Yoga, 163
York, 98, 155, 170, 172, 188

Z

Zaleznik, 62-63, 99
Zappa, 144
Zbaracki, 114-116, 121
Zemo, 197
zero defect theory, 43
Zhu, 173
Zinger, 128, 173
Zune, 180

www.ingramcontent.com/pod-product-compliance
Lightning Source LLC
Chambersburg PA
CBHW082309210326
41599CB00029B/5744